LEGAL EFFECTS OF
UNITED NATIONS RESOLUTIONS

Number 6
Columbia University Studies in
International Organization

EDITORS
Leland M. Goodrich
William T. R. Fox

LEGAL EFFECTS OF
UNITED NATIONS RESOLUTIONS

JORGE CASTAÑEDA

Translated by Alba Amoia

Columbia University Press

New York and London   1969

Jorge Castañeda is Chief Director in the Mexican Ministry of Foreign Affairs.

Alba Amoia is Associate Professor of Romance Languages at Hunter College of the City University of New York.

Copyright © 1969 by Columbia University Press
Standard Book Number: 231-03378-4
Library of Congress Catalog Card Number: 75-94629
Printed in the United States of America

COLUMBIA UNIVERSITY
STUDIES IN INTERNATIONAL ORGANIZATION

This series of monographs was initiated to provide for the publication under University auspices of studies in the field of international organization undertaken and carried out, in whole or in part, by members of the Columbia Faculties or with the assistance of funds made available under research programs of the University. Work in this field has been substantially assisted by grants from the Rockefeller and Ford Foundations.

The series is not intended to provide a systematic coverage of the field of international organization nor is it anticipated that volumes will appear with any set regularity. The value of the contribution which the monograph makes to knowledge and understanding of the role of international organization and its functioning in the world in which we live will be the dominant consideration in determining inclusion. The series is published under the joint editorship of Leland M. Goodrich and William T. R. Fox, with Andrew W. Cordier and Louis Henkin acting in an advisory capacity.

The other books in this series are *Controls for Outer Space*, by Phillip C. Jessup and Howard J. Taubenfield, *The United Nations Emergency Force*, by Gabriella Rosner, *UN Administration of Economic and Social Programs*, edited by Gerard J. Mangone, *The UN Secretary-General and the Maintenance of Peace*, by Leon Gordenker, and *The United Nations Economic and Social Council*, by Walter R. Sharp.

PREFACE

Since World War II, international organizations have adopted an ever-increasing number of resolutions in most fields of human endeavor. In spite of the growing importance of these resolutions in international life, there is uncertainty and often disagreement as to their nature and value. This book is an attempt to ascertain the legal effects of United Nations resolutions on the basis of a study of the practice of United Nations organs and the attitudes of member states toward it.

The survey of practice and attitudes showed the complexity of the problem. It is generally accepted that resolutions adopted by the General Assembly, although having political and moral force, are not mandatory. The study revealed, however, that aside from the typical "recommendation," that is, an invitation which does not imply for its recipient the obligation to perform what is requested, the General Assembly adopts other types of resolutions which produce, for a variety of reasons, true juridical effects against which members have no legal recourse. At least six categories of nonrecommendatory resolutions can be identified. A chapter of the book is devoted to each. The specific cause or basis for the legal consequences of the resolutions in each category, as well as their character and scope, is discussed.

The subject of this book was first discussed with Professor Leland M. Goodrich of Columbia University. I am indebted to him for his valuable advice and encouragement. The work could not have been completed without the generous assistance provided by the Rockefeller Foundation. I take this opportunity to express my grateful appreciation to the Foundation, and also to El Colegio de México, which made its research and other facilities available. Finally, I am thankful to Miss Ruth Russell of Columbia University, who was kind enough to read the manuscript and make a number of useful substantive suggestions.

JORGE CASTAÑEDA

CONTENTS

ABBREVIATIONS

ESC	Economic and Social Council
FAO	Food and Agriculture Organization of the United Nations
ICAO	International Civil Aviation Organization
ILO	International Labor Organization
IMF	International Monetary Fund
NATO	North Atlantic Treaty Organization
OAS	Organization of American States
OEEC	Organization for European Economic Cooperation
ONUC	United Nations Operation in the Congo (Opération des Nations Unies au Congo)
UNEF	United Nations Emergency Force
UNESCO	United Nations Educational, Scientific, and Cultural Organization
UNICEF	United Nations Children's Fund
WHO	World Health Organization

Chapter 1

INTRODUCTION

THE GENERAL CONCEPT OF INTERNATIONAL RESOLUTIONS

The activity of international organizations is externalized mainly through resolutions, that is, through formal manifestations of opinion. As well as being expressions of collective judgments, resolutions are the normal vehicles for realizing the objectives of international bodies; they represent the culmination of their deliberative and decision-making process.

In spite of the growing number of resolutions and their ever-increasing importance in international life, little has been accomplished, since the first international bodies were created, in determining their nature and in clarifying their scope and effects. The practice of these bodies is no less incongruous and inconsistent today than a century ago, nor is the terminology more precise and uniform, and disagreements still persist over questions as essential and basic as the compulsory or voluntary character of certain budgetary resolutions.

There does not exist today a general theory of international resolutions, nor is it likely that such a theory could be constructed. Beyond simply describing them as formal expressions of the opinions of international bodies, it would be difficult to enunciate certain characteristic traits which could be integrated into a meaningful and sufficiently precise definition. The content of the concept is too vast: a resolution carries equally the meaning of an order, an invitation, or a variety of hybrid intermediate forms. It may deal with political or with technical matters; it may be legislative in a material sense—that is, it may express legal norms—or it may constitute an individual administrative act; it may be addressed to other organs of the same system, to another international body, to all states in general, to some states, or even to individuals; it may be the product of decision-making machinery based on equal or unequal representation; and it may be adopted according to a system of unanimous or of majority consent. From any angle, the concept of international resolutions is complex.

THE RESOLUTION AS A SOURCE OF INTERNATIONAL LAW

The multiform diversity of resolutions and their unequal juridical value have made it difficult to evaluate their function as a source of international law. It is often observed that resolutions of international bodies do not appear as a separate category among the sources of international law enumerated in Article 38 of the Statute of the International Court of Justice. In addition to the commonly stated reason for this, namely, the reluctance of the drafters of the Statute in 1920 to grant the Court extensive powers of interpretation that would have amounted to a legislative capacity,[1] it seems certain that their lack of uniform juridical value was also a factor in the nonrecognition of resolutions as a source of law, particularly when the Statute was revised in 1945.

In this respect, it must be remembered above all that the most significant resolutions from the point of view of the sources of international law are those that create or express general legal norms, that is, truly legislative resolutions. But the San Francisco

Conference rejected all attempts to grant the General Assembly the power to create international legislation.[2] The drafters of the Statute knew very well that within the system of the new Charter, resolutions of this kind would not be binding.

Moreover, when the League of Nations was created (and the same holds basically true for the conference at San Francisco), there was a tendency to make a clear distinction between the adjudication of disputes based on pre-existing juridical rules, which fell to the International Court of Justice, and the political settlement of controversies, which fell to the General Assembly or to the Security Council. The task of bringing about political settlements was conceived mainly as extrajuridical, and the resolutions in which these settlements were incorporated and expressed could hardly have been considered as external manifestations of juridical norms, that is, as sources of law.

As in other aspects of the activity of the United Nations, the situation has changed in the past twenty years. In spite of the predominantly political conception of the Charter, which ascribed relatively scant importance to the principles of justice and law in the search for peace, and, generally speaking, in the life of the Organization, the United Nations has exercised, with the passage of time, a great influence in the development of international law. It is true that the Organization has not become an effective instrument of international legislation. This function has fallen rather, in part, to certain regional and technical organizations, mainly European, which have attained higher levels of integration. But, whether it be directly through promoting the codification and progressive development of international law, or, indirectly, through the search for new legal bases for its political action,[3] it is certain that the activities of the Organization have had an unexpectedly strong impact not only on the content but also on the very conception and scope of important principles and rules of modern international law.

It could not be denied, for example, that the resolutions,

practices, and mechanisms for the protection of dependent peoples, which have been developed by the United Nations through the years with a progressively diminishing direct basis in the Charter, have had the combined effect of modifying the entire chapter of international law pertaining to territorial sovereignty.[4] A similar observation could be made concerning the law of international economic cooperation. Perhaps we are witnessing at present how the aims and principles governing international economic cooperation, which twenty years ago undoubtedly belonged to the sphere of ethics, are slowly taking on a juridical cast, and may some day give birth to a true "institution" in a legal sense, that is, to a web of legal rights and obligations.[5]

This law-creating function of the United Nations is carried out through the imparting of legal effects to certain resolutions. The problem is extraordinarily complex: the legal considerations that give a resolution the character of something more than a mere invitation or something different from an invitation, vary greatly; at the same time, the legal effects of resolutions cannot be reduced to one or two simple categories. The purpose of this book is precisely to examine these diverse aspects of the problem. For now, it will suffice to recall that the drafters of the Statute (both of the old Permanent Court of International Justice and of the present International Court of Justice) were unwilling to recognize resolutions of international bodies as a source of law on the basis of a theoretical schema that no longer corresponds completely to reality.

Thus, as Clive Parry says, "the essential nature of relations between States, in which there is no sharp division between legal and political obligations, has asserted itself within the United Nations."[6] The fiction that the Court resolves controversies according to law whereas the Assembly and the Council settle political disputes, and therefore, that the resolutions of these organs cannot be sources of law, simply has no validity any longer. Frequently, individual political decisions of the United Nations organs are based on general legal conceptions. Moreover, these conceptions are sometimes invoked, thus implying an innovative and creative interpretation of the law. Even when these resolutions concern political matters, they are often external manifestations of what an organ of the United Nations considers the applicable rule of international law.

Furthermore, the General Assembly has given proof, by the terms used in some of its resolutions, that it considers itself competent to participate in its own right in the direct and formal consecration of rules of international law by means of categorical pronouncements about the juridical character of certain practices or of certain principles, without necessarily incorporating them into treaties. Thus, the Assembly has "confirmed" the principles of the Statute and of the judgment of the Nuremberg Tribunal as an expression of international law (Resolution 95 [I]), and it has adopted through the years several "declarations" and other similar pronouncements of a general nature. The adoption of these declarations does not mean that the Assembly creates the juridical norms incorporated in them nor that such norms, per se, have a binding nature. As will be explained in detail subsequently,[7] the legal value of these pronouncements is not uniform: it depends not only on the organ that approves them and on their form, but also and especially on their content. Even if there is no real creation of norms, there is often legal recognition and confirmation that certain practices or principles are, in the judgment of an organ largely representative of the international community, either customary rules or general principles of international law.

The preceding discussion reveals that some resolutions of international bodies can be manifestations and means of externalization of international legal norms, that is to say, formal sources of international law. This does not mean, however, that resolutions of international organs ought to constitute an autonomous and distinct source (in the singular) in the same way as do treaties, custom, and general principles of law. It is not suggested that Article 38 of the Statute of the Court ought to be modified by the addition of a new clause relating to resolutions of international bodies. The heterogeneous nature of resolutions does not allow this. It is true that treaties, which constitute one autonomous source, also contain dissimilar elements, but, contrary to resolutions, *all treaties have in common the generation of legal obligations.* Nor would the problem be solved by maintaining that only mandatory resolutions, true decisions, constitute a source of law. In the present evolutionary state of this matter it is difficult to determine the extent of the binding force of certain categories of international resolutions.

Moreover, the omission of this source in Article 38 has not prevented the International Court of Justice and other tribunals from recognizing on various occasions that certain resolutions, whether they have strict legislative character or not, are expressions of law and carry with them obligations in the juridical sense. The reason that is usually given—implicitly invoked, in effect, by the Court in its advisory opinion on reparations for losses incurred in the service of the United Nations[8]—is that the application of resolutions amounts to the application of international treaties such as the United Nations Charter, in which the power of the organs to adopt resolutions is established. Thus, it is said, there is no additional need, beyond Article 38 of the Statute, for a specific reference to the decisions of international bodies as a source of international law distinct from treaties.[9]

THE CONCEPT OF RECOMMENDATION

The vastness, complexity, and present fluidity of this topic renders extremely difficult its study and systematization. It is not easy even to delimitate accurately the subject under study; in particular, no clear distinction is usually made between the concepts of "resolution" and "recommendation."

Most of the few authors who have specifically studied international resolutions have tended to focus their attention, as the titles of some of their works reveal, on recommendations, that is, on only one of the several categories of resolutions passed by international bodies.[10] Recommendations are numerous, and from many points of view they are the most important resolutions. However, they far from exhaust the subject.

The object of this study is, precisely, to examine those resolutions that are not recommendations, those that are something more or something other than an *invitation* extended by an international organ implying for its recipient no legal obligation to perform the requested act.

Before describing in greater detail the goal of this research, however, and before indicating the method that will be used, the concept of recommendation must be examined, even if in broad terms. Clarifying this notion from the outset will allow its use throughout the study as a point of comparison and reference, and thus will permit a better understanding of the characteristics of the remaining categories of resolutions.

The first difficulty, responsible for a good part of the confusion that exists, is the lack of uniformity in the understanding of the concept of recommendation. A multiplicity of connotations surrounds this term as it is used in treaties as well as in doctrine and even as it is used in the practice of international organizations.

Virally, for example, includes under "recommendations" the orders that a hierarchically superior organ directs to another organ within the same juridical system.[11] Malintoppi, in turn, criticizes Virally's position, contending that in the case of a recommendation directed by an organ to a subordinate one, the very existence of an obligation does not allow the use of the term "recommendation," but rather requires the use of "directive."[12] Malintoppi bases his conception on "the historically demonstrable fact that today international recommendations never produce as an effect the concrete obligation, in its narrowest meaning, to carry out the content. . . ."[13]

Sloan, even though he recognizes that the Charter's use of the term "recommendation" undoubtedly reflects the wish of the San Francisco Conference to prevent the Assembly from becoming a supranational organ with power to promulgate international legislation, believes that there is no authorized interpretation originating in the Conference concerning the exact scope and meaning of the term.[14] Therefore, he thinks it necessary to examine the meaning of the term "recommendation" according to general international law, prior to the establishment of the United Nations; he reaches the conclusion that ". . . there was no simple meaning of the term 'recommendation' that was accepted in international practice. It is true that prevailing practice has employed the word in a non-imperative sense. However, there is sufficient contrary usage to cast a reasonable doubt on the assumption that a 'recommendation' under Articles 10 to 14 of the Charter can obviously have no legal effect."[15] Moreover, according to Sloan, the Charter itself does not use the terms "recommendation" and "decision" in a sufficiently consistent way to allow the conclusion that recommendation always means a non-mandatory determination. With regard to the practice of United Nations organs, the meaning of the term is even less uniform: the General Assembly sometimes uses it to transmit orders to its subordinate organs.

Theoretically, each meaning is as legitimate as the others, and from a certain point of view the problem is one of semantics. But if the useful task of systematization is to be performed, it seems advisable to adopt the meaning that might be called *normal,* to accept as valid only the meaning that has prevailed historically —that is, to describe as recommendations only the acts that the great majority of their authors have characterized as such.[16]

From this point of view, there is no doubt that the prevailing meaning is that of "invitation;" hence recommendations are only the resolutions adopted with no intention of binding their addressees. It would be necessary to exclude from the concept of recommendation, consequently, decisions that carry the legal obligation to execute their content—whether on the basis of a provision of the constitutive instrument or of the structural hierarchical relationship that exists between the author of the decision and the addressee—as well as resolutions in which the international body does not request anything of anyone, but rather intends to carry out other types of activities.[17]

According to Malintoppi, a recommendation is the manifestation of a wish that the addressee follow certain conduct, positive or negative, that can be carried out either in the international or in the domestic domain. Contrary to other expressions of desire that are also externalized in the international sphere, a recommendation is the manifestation of a wish that is juridically relevant, since it has been formulated within the frame of a legal rule. It is not exactly a wish in the phenomenological sense, but rather an objective display of particular intensity, better described, perhaps, by the Italian term *sollecitazione*.[18]

Recommendations are relatively few in the internal sphere of a state because they are not juridical instruments congruous to the state structure. Because of the frequency of hierarchical relationships within the state and the existence of a power superior to that of the members of the national society able to take decisions without asking for their individual consent, the state disposes of other instruments that are more effective for the juridical discipline of the community; consequently, the normal instrument that expresses the relationship between the state and the recipients of juridical norms is the "order." Owing to the embryonic structure of international society, based on the sovereign equality of states and still requiring in most cases the voluntary collaboration of members for the fulfillment of international obligations, it is logical and natural that the usual and typical instrument be the recommendation, a manifestation of the wish of the majority that does not necessarily bind the minority.

Furthermore, the recommendation is the appropriate and

characteristic vehicle of cooperation within traditional international organizations, such as public international unions; it corresponds exactly to the nature and needs of this type of organization. The recommendations of the organs specify and actualize for the members the obligations enunciated in the constitutive treaty, but without trespassing on the vast domain of autonomy preserved by the members of these organizations; at the same time, they represent a tolerable form of pressure on the members for the achievement of the union's aims.

The recommendation is not equally adequate, however, for the needs of certain more recent and evolved organizations that reflect a greater degree of regional or functional integration. The intensive cooperation required for the realization of the communal ends in certain types of organizations demands juridical instruments more effective than recommendations. Thus, the charter of the European Coal and Steel Community (ECSC) foresees the existence of resolutions formally called recommendations (Article 14) which "shall be binding with respect to the objectives which they specify but shall leave to those to whom they are directed the choice of appropriate means for attaining these objectives." In accordance with the constitutive treaty, these recommendations are distinct from decisions, which are mandatory in all respects.[19]

Aside from these hybrid forms of resolutions, some treaties provide that recommendations be accompanied by ancillary mandatory elements designed to augment their effectiveness. The constitutions of FAO, WHO, ILO, and UNESCO establish the obligation to submit certain recommendations adopted by the respective Organizations to the competent national organs (usually the Congress), with a view to their fulfillment. The obligation does not consist in effectively carrying out the provisions of the recommendation, but only in submitting it to the national organs. Moreover, the above-mentioned constitutions require the members to inform the Organization of the extent of their fulfill-

ment of the recommendations. In the case of ILO, the constitution goes further. According to Article 30, if a member does not
fulfill certain obligations imposed by Article 19 (especially the
one requiring submission of recommendations to the appropriate
internal organs), any other member may ask the Council to make
an investigation, and eventually, if this organ finds proof of default, it may submit the case to the Conference, with all the political consequences that that entails. This could be considered an
indirect form of sanction.

It is generally admitted that recommendations lack sanction
in the juridical sense. Their value (or strength, as is usually said)
is political and moral.[20] The distinction, however, is neither obvious nor clear. In the abstract, it is possible to distinguish between,
on the one hand, a sanction in the technical sense, directed toward
the observance of true pre-existent juridical obligations, and on
the other, a "pressure" aimed at the realization of nonmandatory
conduct that is considered desirable and recommended by an international body. But the means of pressure employed by international bodies to achieve the execution of a typically political,
nonmandatory recommendation, are the same as those used to
impose the compliance of juridical obligations. In practice, it is
difficult to know where the dividing line is.

As will be seen later,[21] the enforcement measures of the
United Nations do not have the punitive character of sanctions;
they are not an inevitable accompaniment of the Organization's
reaction against a violation of the Charter by a member. Inversely,
identical enforcement measures can constitutionally be applied to
achieve the primary *political* objective of the Organization, the
maintenance of peace, even if it does not entail a "punishment"
against the antijuridical attitude of a member.

As rightly observed by Tammes, mandatory decisions as
well as recommendations frequently carry their own sanction in
the mere strength of the language they use, or in designations
such as "Uniting for Peace," etc.[22] The objective sought by the

United Nations in adopting certain language, in reiterating previous resolutions, or in exercising political pressure on a member, is fundamentally the same as when it uses sanctions: to mobilize public opinion with the objective of eliciting a certain conduct.

Malintoppi has formulated a suggestive thesis to provide sanction for recommendations with a juridical framework. He reasons thus:

In every international organization there is a general rule according to which member states are bound to cooperate in achieving its purposes. The basic obligation of the members is to act in such a way that the charter's goals may be fulfilled. There is a strict correlation between this obligation and the purposes of the organization. The organ's adoption of a recommendation represents an expression of a general social feeling. It is a manifestation of the manner in which the purposes of the treaty must be fulfilled in the eyes of the organization. The member who does not observe it is opposing not only a social consensus but also the juridical system that is the normative superstructure of that social environment. The pressure that a recommendation brings to bear on its addressees means this: faced with conduct contrary to the recommendation, and to the extent to which it is contrary, the social group can act, in its turn, against the asocial conduct of whomsoever does not carry out the recommendation, directing its reprobation against the author of the conduct. This is the *social sanction* of recommendations. The essential element in this ingenious theoretical construction is not so much the nonfulfillment of the recommendation in itself as the reaction of the group against the divergent attitude of the delinquent recipient.[23]

Except for some incidental and brief explanations,[24] this is, up to the present, the most serious and complete attempt to provide a foundation for the possible *juridical* effects of recommendations. Perhaps because of the very scope of this thesis, some limitations to it should be proposed.

It can easily be agreed that the members of an international organization have a basic obligation to contribute to the realization of the purposes postulated by a constitutive treaty; they have all accepted these goals. The difficulty is that the treaty does not juridically compel the members to agree that the means used by the organization to attain them be necessarily the most adequate. In other words, the treaty gives members a margin for judgment concerning the best way to realize its institutional ends, at least when the organization makes a recommendation. When the treaty does not allow this margin for judgment, it provides other technical means to achieve its goals which, unlike recommendations, have a mandatory character.

A second problem arises from the multiplicity of purposes, which sometimes conflict. This tends to happen particularly in the Security Council, where the primary aim of maintaining the peace sometimes clashes with other aims. When the Council makes a recommendation, it means that the Charter has bestowed upon the members the power to evaluate different aims and to choose among them. The veto is a special and extreme manifestation of this power granted specifically to the five permanent members.

The thesis of the violation of the basic obligation becomes more persuasive when it refers to technical organizations and technical matters, as in the case of nonobservance of recommendations concerning, for example, aerial navigation or epidemic control. It is easier to accept the thesis that the delinquent state does not contribute to the community's aims when these aims are of a technical nature and are, therefore, more demonstrable. The aims of the United Nations are more general and vague; there is a larger tolerable margin for individual judgment, and a greater possibility of honest differences of opinion concerning the best way to further the aims of the Organization.[25]

NONRECOMMENDATORY RESOLUTIONS

It was stated above that the United Nations adopts numerous and diverse resolutions which are not recommendations. It is now necessary to confirm this and to ascertain the basis of the Organization's competence to do so.

The problem is not only one of semantics. It involves an investigation as to whether the organs of the United Nations, and especially the General Assembly, may constitutionally adopt resolutions that do not correspond to the concept of recommendation that has been advanced. An affirmative answer is evident for certain interorganic resolutions such as those directed by a hierarchically superior organ to inferior ones, or when the Charter expressly bestows powers of decision on the Assembly, as in the cases of the "appointment" of the Secretary-General (Article 97), the "expulsion" of members (Article 6), the "approval" of the budget (Article 17), etc. The problem lies in the intersubjective resolutions, since in regulating the relationship between the Organization and the States, the Charter refers only to the power to make recommendations.

It is useful to recall here, as an introductory consideration, Sloan's research on the juridical connotation of the term "recommendation" and the conclusion he reaches that this term does not have a uniform meaning according to the text of the Charter, to the general international law which was in force when the Charter was drafted, or to the practice of United Nations organs.[26] From such a conclusion one cannot deduce directly the power of the Assembly to adopt nonrecommendatory resolutions, but it does prove at least that the use of the term "recommendation" by the Charter in defining the Assembly's competence (Articles 10–13) is not, in itself, a legal obstacle preventing it from adopting resolutions different from a recommendation. To reach positive conclusions, however, it will be necessary to take into account considerations other than the Charter's terminology.

The essential factor that must be studied in order to know whether the Assembly can also perform nonrecommendatory functions, is the actual practice of this organ. To determine the competence of an organ such as the Assembly, whose powers are formulated in such a general way, is not very different, in reality, from inquiring how that organ has interpreted its own competence, that is, to examine its practice. It is not denied, of course, that it is possible to determine *in abstracto* the competence of an organ by referring exclusively to the pertinent constitutional provisions. Neither is it intended to question the validity of the important Kelsenian distinction between *sein* and *sollen*, between the domain of what *is* and the domain of what *ought to be*. Theoretically, the competence of an organ is what it is, as a result of the applicable legal rule, and independently of its practice. An organ's assumption of powers that constitutionally do not belong to it is a violation of existing law and not an act that creates new law.

Within the international legal order, however, the validity of these theoretical conceptions must be qualified by taking into account certain realities and limitations of that order. Contrary to what occurs within the state, in the international order there is no organ whose specific function is to determine the constitutionality of the acts of the authorities that apply legal norms. *In fact, as well as in law, each international organ (not subordinate to another) determines the constitutionality of its own acts.* This factor, plus the extreme vagueness with which the powers of a political organ such as the Assembly are enunciated, easily explain why the very practice of the organ becomes, with the passage of time, the decisive factor in determining the legal scope of its own functions.

If the Charter says nothing about whether certain resolutions are only recommendatory and if the conclusion that they are does not result ineluctably from an objective fact—as for instance, from the structural relation that may exist between two organs of a system—the mere assessment by the organ that drafts or applies the resolution that it is mandatory, can, in effect, constitute the decisive element for this resolution to have, or to acquire, a mandatory nature. That is why the practice of the organs, as well as the reaction of the states to whom they are addressed, assume particular relevance as factors in evaluating the juridical significance of resolutions.[27]

This does not mean that the problem of the juridical validity of a norm is not different, in theory, from the problem of its efficacy, of its actual observance. In international law, however, the survival of institutions such as the maritime blockade, the legal validity of which depends in some cases on its effectiveness, and, above all, the enormous importance of the customary creation of norms and even their gradual derogation owing to desuetude, prove that *the validity of norms, in international law, is not independent of their actual observance.* This could not be otherwise since, in the international legal order, states are at one and the same time authors and recipients of the very norms they create.[28]

RESEARCH METHOD

For these reasons, it was thought best to base this research on the study of the practice of United Nations organs and, when necessary, on the attitude of member states with regard to this practice. The basic working materials were the resolutions of United Nations organs, especially those of the General Assembly. A methodical and analytical survey was made of the resolutions adopted up to the present, first separating those that did not correspond to the theoretical scheme of recommendation explained above. Next an effort was made to systematize and classify them according to the diverse juridical *cause* or *reason* for which those resolutions were thought to be different from typical recommendations. Thus, certain groups or types of resolutions were identified which, observation shows, produce, for a variety of reasons and circumstances, concrete juridical effects of very different kind and degree that sometimes may be characterized as mandatory.

The question of the juridical effects produced by a resolution is, of course, the very heart of this study. However, the juridical effects of resolutions and, in general, their legal scope, are not the criteria adopted for their classification. They constitute, rather, the *conclusions* of the present research, contrary to other studies in which the starting point is precisely the use of *a priori* categories concerning the production of juridical effects: resolutions that have direct effects, resolutions that have indirect effects, and resolutions that can never have any effect at all. Naturally, the reason a resolution has a certain effect and, in general, its legal nature, cannot be separated from the study of the juridical effects it produces. But, as has been indicated, the conclusions one may reach concerning the production of juridical effects will be, above all, the result of direct and objective observation of the practice of the Organization.

In the same manner, the factors that the present work identifies as causes of the binding force of certain resolutions do not correspond to dogmatic *a priori* conceptions. The classification adopted here is rather the result of a methodical survey of the resolutions of the General Assembly.

PRINCIPAL TYPES OF NONRECOMMENDATORY RESOLUTIONS

The first category of resolutions studied is that of "internal" resolutions. These resolutions are extremely important because, among other things, they are so numerous. They concern the structure and operation of the Organization considered per se and not in relation to the result of its activities. Examples of these resolutions are those requesting the members to contribute to the expenses of the Organization, those creating organs, or those dealing with the admission of new members. This category is the subject matter of Chapter 2.

All the other resolutions are the result, the consequence, the *product* of United Nations action. Because of this, they may be characterized as "external." They are not concerned with the intrinsic operation of the United Nations; rather they guide the action of the Organization directly toward the fulfillment of its general aims, such as the maintenance of peace, the well-being of dependent peoples, etc.[29]

External resolutions are quite varied. Each of the principal groups is studied in a separate chapter, except that of typical recommendations whose essential characteristics have been outlined above, since, as has been said, the specific purpose of this work is not the study of recommendations, but of resolutions of non-recommendatory nature.

The first group comprises, in addition to the compulsory decisions of the Security Council, certain resolutions of the General Assembly, few in number but very important, related to the maintenance of peace. Their legal effects, which from a certain angle can be viewed as obligatory, do not derive directly from the Charter but from the practice of the Organization, or rather, from a customary development not foreseen by the framers of the Charter. This group is the subject of Chapter 3.

In other cases, the Assembly makes "determinations" concerning facts or legal situations from which derive, under certain circumstances and as a result of the interplay of the organs and decision-making processes of the United Nations, juridical consequences that members cannot legally oppose. Here, the Assembly does not demand of anyone a definite course of action, positive or negative, either imperatively or by invitation. It is not a question then, of decisions or of recommendations, but of acts of a different kind. The object of these resolutions is to utter a pronouncement of a particular nature, or, as has been said above, to take a formal stand regarding a fact or a legal situation. This type of resolution is studied in Chapter 4.

Sometimes, the binding force of certain General Assembly resolutions rests on an exceptional legal foundation, outside the Charter, such as a treaty. These resolutions are examined in Chapter 5. In other cases, the binding nature of certain resolutions— like those relating to peace, not numerous but very significant— has its origin in the fact that they are the expression and the reflection of an *agreement*, usually tacit, among all or part of the members of an organ. These resolutions have a certain external similarity to, and essentially the same legal basis as, "executive agreements," except that they have a multilateral character. They are treated in Chapter 6.

Finally, the purpose of certain resolutions is to "declare" in more or less solemn terms the value of certain principles. Some of them can be considered mandatory to the extent that their primary object is to confirm the existence of customary rules or to express general principles of law. These resolutions are the subject of Chapter 7.

As is to be expected, the problem of the complex phenomenology of effects cannot be reduced to inquiring whether the addressee is under the obligation to perform a requested act. A frequent error is the assumption that all resolutions are either decisions or recommendations. As we have seen, resolutions sometimes may not directly request anything of anyone. But they can nevertheless produce *legal* effects that may or may not be obligatory, although not in the usual sense of the word.[30]

This enumeration of causes or reasons from which the binding force of certain resolutions exceptionally derives is neither exhaustive nor sufficiently precise to permit a categorization or "typology" of resolutions. Moreover, the heterogeneity of the reasons for which the resolutions examined here may have a diversity of effects, together with the frequent innovations and the

inordinate pragmatism of United Nations organs, renders systematization extraordinarily difficult. Sometimes, the attitude of
an organ, which seemed to reveal the legal value it attributed to
one of its own resolutions, is contradicted by a subsequent position of the same organ or of another. Atypical situations are very
frequent. At the same time, many resolutions can fit into various
groups, that is, they can be mandatory for more than one reason
at a time. Because of all these circumstances, the classification of
resolutions used here is intended to serve only as an orientation
for the necessary subdivision of the work into chapters, without
aspiring to suggest a scientific criterion for classification.

USE OF THE TERM "OBLIGATORY FORCE"

The terms "obligatory force" and "production of legal effects"
require certain clarifications. The concept "obligatory legal effects," with reference to resolutions of contemporary international bodies, is not univocal. In its widest sense, within the
politico-juridical context in which it is used, it means any altering of a pre-existing legal situation. But this alteration does not
consist only in the creation, modification, or extinction of rights
and obligations of the member states. It can also mean, for example, an enlargement in the legal competence of an organ, as will
be seen in examining the legal consequences of the customary
rule developed on the basis of the "Uniting for Peace" Resolution. This latter meaning is equally adequate and pertinent: on
the one hand, the modification of an organ's original competence
has inevitable consequences, both political and juridical, in the
situation of members; on the other, the nonconforming state lacks
all legal recourse effectively to oppose such modification.

Moreover, given the complex character of many resolutions,
their "binding force" may assume an indirect aspect. A resolution can contain recommendations directed to the members, and
at the same time impose clear and direct obligations on an organ,

such as the Secretary-General. But the fulfillment of the tasks assigned to the Secretary-General may entail mandatory consequences for the members, such as those of a budgetary nature. Finally, the binding force of a resolution may mean not only the *creation* of obligations, but also, as will be seen in discussing the Uniting for Peace Resolution, the *suspension* of a legal obligation.

Also, when postulating the binding character of a resolution, one can refer to something other than a concrete and direct juridical duty (commission or omission) imposed on the recipient. Sometimes, as has been suggested, United Nations organs make definitive determinations as to the existence of a fact or even of a concrete juridical situation, against which there is no recourse and from which can flow legal consequences that the members cannot oppose in a legally significant way, that is, in a way that would authorize the interpretation that they maintain the freedom of judgment they usually enjoy when pondering whether or not to accept an ordinary recommendation. In these cases, it can be said that such a determination is mandatory in the sense that it has full and unopposable legal validity. Here, the term "binding force" denotes a concept very similar to that of "legal truth," when the latter refers to a binding determination made by a tribunal in the sense, for instance, that a person is the heir of another. Such determinations of tribunals can also very well be characterized as mandatory although they do not of themselves constitute or impose an order to carry out a certain action.

Throughout the following chapters, therefore, the terms "binding force," "legal validity," or "obligatory effects," as the case may be, are employed not in the limited sense of creation, modification, or extinction of the rights and obligations of the addressees of resolutions, but rather in the wider sense of modification of the pre-existent legal situation, including all the specific interpretations that can reasonably result from the changing circumstances under which resolutions may be applied.

Chapter 2

RESOLUTIONS PERTAINING TO THE STRUCTURE AND OPERATION OF THE UNITED NATIONS

THE INTERNAL LAW OF THE UNITED NATIONS

Every corporative institution tends to generate its own law. Based on its Charter, the United Nations has created, since its establishment, through statutes or custom, a great number of legal rules concerning its internal structure and operation. These rules, externalized mainly through resolutions, constitute the internal law of the United Nations.

Even though the concept of an internal law of international bodies has been accepted for a long time (the Administrative Tribunal of the League of Nations had recognized the existence of "an internal law" of the organization since 1929), there is no uniformity in the doctrinal opinions regarding the nature of this law. For some, these rules are part of general international law and are fundamentally of a conventional origin.[1] For others, on the contrary, the internal law of international bodies constitutes, by virtue of its sources, its recipients, and its content, an autonomous legal order different from both international law and state law.[2] According to more recent thought, the internal law of international bodies belongs within a wider conception of international law, which would take into particular consideration the position of the individual in modern international society and would also encompass such branches as penal international law, administrative international law, etc. Verdross, for example, although he refers to a "new group" of rules that he calls the "internal law of an international body," composed of "rules of private law, penal law, administrative law, and procedural law established by a *community of states* for those *individuals* who are *directly* subject to them," maintains that such a body of rules, *jointly* with others that regulate the relationship among states, "constitute the juridical order of the international community . . . ," and therefore it is necessary "to distinguish, *within* a wider concept of public international law, these two groups of rules."[3] The acceptance of one or another of the above-mentioned theses will not greatly influence the conclusions that will be arrived at here concerning the legal value of internal resolutions. For the purposes of this study, it will suffice to point out that internal resolutions have created, and are at the same time an external expression of, a relatively coherent and identifiable body of legal rules.

Generally, not much stress has been laid on this, owing in part, perhaps, to the fact that the framers of the United Nations Charter grouped their provisions around the concept of principal organs, without distinguishing between rules concerning the constitutional structure of the United Nations Organization and those concerning its external functions.[4] It is significant, for example, that in the well-known work of Goodrich and Hambro entitled *Charter of the United Nations*, the notion of an internal law of the Organization does not explicitly appear.

Resolutions relating to internal law are very numerous. Almost four-fifths of the resolutions adopted up to the present by the United Nations are of this type. Their nature and importance vary considerably and may concern the most diverse matters. The majority of these resolutions are administrative, but some are legislative, and others even have a jurisdictional character.

They may deal with matters of such political weight as the admission of members, or with questions of little consequence such as the schedules of sessions. Many resolutions embody, separately or jointly, true juridical norms, whereas others, on the contrary, are a manifestation of an individual juridical act, such as those declaring the Secretary-General elected or a new member admitted to the Organization. Owing to the increasing number and growing complexity of the Organization's activities, the range of its internal law could, in time, become much wider and include new questions. An example would be the body of law, to a certain extent *sui generis*, that would have to be created if the United Nations were to assume directly the trusteeship of a territory, as contemplated in Article 81 of the Charter, although this does not seem probable at present.

The principal internal functions of the Organization are the following: the admission of new members, the suspension of rights and privileges of members against whom a preventive or coercive action is being taken by the Security Council, the expulsion of members, the consideration and approval of the budget, the adoption and application of statutes and regulations, the creation of subsidiary organs, the election of states or persons, as the case may be, to the principal and subsidiary organs, the coordination of its activities with those of the specialized agencies, the regulation of the activities and situation of the Secretariat staff, and the election of the Secretary-General.

All these functions, and others that complement them, pertain to the internal structure and functioning of the United Nations. Many of the resolutions on these matters are interorganic, that is, they are directed to different organizations or to other organs in the same system, although a great number of them are addressed to member states.

The technical instrument normally used by the Organization for its internal structure and operation is the mandatory resolution, the "decision." The very nature of internal tasks requires it. The functioning of the Organization—or even the functioning of a simple temporary diplomatic conference—would be inconceivable if it depended on the voluntary cooperation of the members for the efficacy of its action in the internal sphere. Therefore, as will be noted throughout the present chapter, the Charter expressly established the mandatory character of the majority of resolutions that pertain to the internal activity of the Organization. However, among the great variety of activities therein comprised, there are exceptions. A rather obvious one concerns the eventuality that a hierarchically superior organ may think it sufficient to make nonmandatory recommendations when assigning certain tasks to a subordinate one.

Although the technical distinction between internal and external activities could not have been sufficiently appreciated until the former attained a considerable degree of development in permanent international bodies, internal decisions appeared relatively early, almost as a spontaneous outgrowth. The first Pan-American Conferences adopted all kinds of decisions that transcended the brief duration of the Conference; they even created permanent organs by simple resolution, without the help of treaties, in spite of the fact that it was to take half a century more for their participants to create an organization.[5]

This useful practice developed without difficulty owing to the sense of permanency lent by the foreseeable regularity of the meetings. The Conferences were wont to employ a terminology characteristic of mandatory decisions, even when they concerned political matters that now would be considered typical of the external activity of an international organization, long before a formal union of States was created.[6] Of course, the resolutions adopted by the American Republics could not in most cases, in spite of appearances, legally have any other meaning than that of recommendation because of the absence of permanent organic ties, except when they clearly reflected a unanimous agreement among the members (see Chapter VI); but the terminology employed reveals the vigor of the institutionalizing tendency that was present in those periodic conferences.

The principle that resolutions of an internal nature should have a mandatory effect prevailed in the League of Nations. However, the system of unanimous voting had unexpected consequences. Tammes cites the case of a clearly internal question (the selection of the nonpermanent members of the Security Council on a regional basis) that was not resolved through a mandatory resolution as would have been normal, but rather through a recommendation, owing to the difficulty of obtaining a unanimous vote.[7]

The Charter of the United Nations does not distinguish between internal and external activities of the Organization, whether they concern the applicable voting majority or the legal scope of resolutions, undoubtedly because the provisions of the Charter are systematized around the notion of principal organs. The enumeration of "important" questions contained in Article 18, for which a two-thirds majority is required, comprises, without distinction, internal questions such as those concerning finances and elections, and external ones such as the maintenance of peace and security.

The legal scope of internal resolutions is sometimes explicitly set forth in the Charter, as in the case of the admission of new members, which takes place by decision of the Assembly (Article 4), or in the case of the "approval" of the budget (Article 17); and, on occasion, it derives from the structural link between the organ that makes the resolution and the addressee, or from other factors.

As will be seen when each of these questions is examined, it is not possible to postulate the existence of a uniform system with respect to the legal validity of internal resolutions, although the mandatory decision, in general, prevails in this sphere.

ADMISSION, SUSPENSION, AND EXPULSION OF MEMBERS; APPOINTMENT OF THE SECRETARY-GENERAL

The admission of members (Article 4 of the Charter), the suspension of their rights and privileges (Article 5), and their expulsion (Article 6), as well as the appointment of the Secretary-General (Article 97) are carried out through the "combined action"—not simply coincidental action—of two organs: an initial positive recommendation from the Security Council and a subsequent decision of the General Assembly in the same sense as the recommendation of the Council.[8]

The terminology of the Charter in reference to these four questions, together with the practice of the United Nations, clearly demonstrate the nature and extent of the Assembly resolutions: they are mandatory decisions. The result (admission, suspension, expulsion, or appointment) is consummated by the action of the Assembly, but this action, in itself, is juridically ineffective to achieve the result. The Council's recommendation must be previous and positive: the International Court of Justice rejected the possibility of ascribing juridical efficacy (in the matter of admission) to the lack of a recommendation by the Council interpreted as the equivalent of an "unfavorable recommendation";[9] moreover, as the Court said:

The word "recommendation" and the word "upon" preceding it (in French *sur*) imply the idea that the recommendation is the foundation of the decision to admit, and that the latter rests upon the recommendation. Both these acts are indispensable to form the judgment of the Organization. . . . the General Assembly can only decide to admit upon the recommendation of the Security Council. . . . [their] *combined* action is required before admission can be effected. . . . the recommendation of the Security Council is the condition precedent to the decision of the Assembly by which the admission is effected.[10]

It could well be sustained, with the backing of the Court's

very words, that the procedure of admission (as well as that of suspension of rights, expulsion, or appointment of the Secretary-General) constitutes a *complex juridical act*, composed of two constitutive elements, necessarily successive, concurrent in their content, and combined, in the sense that the first is a prerequisite necessary for the actuation of the second.[11]

The Charter characterizes as a recommendation the act of the Security Council, but in view of its peculiar function within the complex operation of the process of admission (or of expulsion, suspension, or appointment of the Secretary-General), technically it might better be considered a *proposal* in the same sense in which this concept is used in Administrative Law. In effect, given its purely contributive function, and since it is combined with another act of a different organ in forming the will of the Organization, the act of the Council does not have the autonomous profile that is characteristic of the recommendation;[12] this situation, on the other hand, is typical of proposals. But if the recommendation of the Security Council is examined, no longer from the point of view of its function as a constitutive element of a complex act, but only from the point of view of its content, it is unquestionable that it constitutes the manifestation of a wish of an organ (the Security Council) directed to an addressee (the General Assembly) so that the latter will perform a certain action (decide on the admission of the applying member)—a wish that the addressee may legally heed or ignore; in other words, it contains elements identical to those of a typical recommendation.

If the analysis concerning the juridical nature of these Security Council resolutions is carried further, it will be noticed that even if they are examined only from the point of view of their content, they imply something more than a recommendation. A resolution contains, besides the manifestation of a wish, the expression of a judgment. The evaluation made by the Council of the merits of the candidate to enter the Organization is not simply the antecedent motivation of the expression of a wish, that is, of the recommendation directed to the Assembly; it also constitutes in itself a political pronouncement of the Council that the candidate is a peace-loving state, that it accepts the obligations imposed by the Charter, and that it is able to fulfill them and is willing to do so.[13] These pronouncements or determinations of the United Nations organs, as we shall see later, may also have juridical significance and relevance in certain circumstances.[14]

In the cases that are now being examined, however, owing to the prohibition implicit in the sequence of combined acts set forth in the Charter for the admission, suspension, or expulsion of members and for the appointment of the Secretary-General, the Security Council's pronouncement does not have, in itself, efficacy or even juridical relevance if it is not integrated, together with a subsequent and concurrent pronouncement of the Assembly, in a decision of that body.

By virtue of the agreements between the United Nations and some specialized agencies, the admission of members to the agencies is carried out through a combined process similar to the one described above, but between the two organizations. According to Article II of the agreement between ICAO and the United Nations, applications for admission submitted to ICAO ". . . shall be immediately transmitted by the Secretariat of the Organization to the General Assembly of the United Nations. The General Assembly may recommend the rejection of such application, and any such recommendation *shall be accepted* by the Organization."[15] For reasons similar to those indicated above concerning admission into the United Nations, the "transmission" of a candidacy from ICAO to the United Nations Assembly has the nature of a proposal (indeed, the agreement does not say that the ICAO "shall recommend" the admission but rather that it shall transmit the request). On the other hand, in spite of the terms used by the agreement, the United Nations Assembly does not "recommend" the rejection, but rather it "decides" it, inasmuch as it "shall be accepted" by ICAO.[16]

In the same way, applications for membership in UNESCO submitted by nonmember states of the United Nations were, during the early years, transmitted to the Economic and Social Council, which could recommend rejection, and UNESCO was compelled to accept its recommendation.[17]

THE INTERNAL LEGISLATIVE FUNCTION
General Observations

The term "legislative" is used, from the point of view of substance and not of form, to designate a function realized through the creation of general legal categories and not through individual decisions. This function of the United Nations is not based on one general provision of the Charter, but rather on diverse provisions.[18] The categories of subjects that belong to this function are few but important: the regime for the creation of subsidiary organs, the power of organs to adopt their own rules of procedure, and the staff rules and regulations.[19] The basic financial function, consisting in the approval of the budget and the apportionment of expenses among the members, provided for in Article 17, does not really belong to this category since such acts are not legislative but administrative; however, this function has given rise to and served as a basis for, among others, the important Financial Regulations of the United Nations approved by the General Assembly in Resolution 456 (V), of which it is an annex.

The organs of the United Nations have had to regulate by way of statutes a greater number of internal questions than the few to which the Charter explicitly refers in its scant pertinent provisions. In order to give legal validity to those activities, an indirect legal basis in some article of the Charter has been sought whenever possible. In the majority of cases, however, it has been necessary to have recourse to the doctrine of the implied powers of the Organization, as will be seen later on. In this eventuality, the problem of determining the legal scope of the resolutions in question naturally presents greater complications.

The Power of Organs to Adopt Their Own Rules of Procedure

One of the most significant legislative resolutions is that which embodies the Rules of Procedure of the General Assembly (Resolution 173 [II]), based directly on Article 21 of the Charter. Here is a typical case of self-limitation by the Assembly, in the sense that this collective organ decided, through a legal expression of its own will, to submit its deliberations to a general normative order. The provisions of the Rules of Procedure are, therefore, mandatory, as long as they are not modified or abrogated, for the Assembly itself, for the member states, for the non-member states who exceptionally participate in the Assembly's deliberations, and for the Secretary-General in the numerous functions that are attributed to him in the Rules.

In the proceedings of the Assembly, the concept that "the Assembly is sovereign" or that "the Assembly is the master of its own procedures" is frequently invoked as a reason to apply a special procedure different from the general ones provided for in the Rules or not to apply one of them. In practice, the Assembly and its commissions often deviate from the Rules of Procedure.

The practice of the Assembly and the explanation that is invoked to justify it can make one lose sight of the true juridical scope of these rules. As long as they are not modified through the procedure established in Article 164, the provisions are mandatory for the Assembly. In spite of the fact that this organ is "sovereign," it may bind itself for the future. If the Assembly is legally able, as recognized by the International Court of Justice, "to create a competent subordinate organ (the Administrative Tribunal) in order to make decisions which bind the creator organ," it can with even greater justification take decisions that bind itself.[20]

The reason why the Assembly engages, without too many scruples, in the nonobservance of its own rules, is probably the following: since, according to Article 164, a simple majority suffices to modify the Rules of Procedure permanently, it is considered that this same majority may, with all the more reason, suspend temporarily the application of one or several of its provisions. Applying the juridical aphorism that "celui qui peut le plus peut le moins," and thus utilizing a more expedient means, the Assembly obtains the same practical result, bypassing the additional requirement mentioned in Article 164 that the modification of the Rules be made "after a committee has reported on the proposed amendment."

Although this practice may have been useful on occasion, there is no doubt that it is illegal and that it offers certain disadvantages. The formulation of a prior report by a commission and its subsequent discussion by the Assembly partially guarantee that the decision will be inspired mainly by considerations of general and permanent value. In any case, this practice does not legally modify the mandatory nature of the Rules of Procedure for the Assembly itself or with even greater justification, for its other addressees, the Secretary-General and the states.

The rules of procedure of other principal organs expressly provided for in the Charter (Security Council, Article 30; Economic and Social Council, Article 72; Trusteeship Council, Article 90), do not offer different problems with respect to the legal scope of the resolutions that embody them: they too are equally mandatory.

The Doctrine of the Implied Powers of the Organization According to the International Court of Justice

Concerning internal resolutions that incorporate legal rules not directly based on the Charter, it is necessary in the majority of cases to have recourse to the doctrine of the implied powers of the Organization developed by the International Court of Justice in order to establish their legality, and, when appropriate, to justify their mandatory character.

The famous advisory opinion of the Court, relating to the death of Count Bernadotte, is too well known to recall in detail.[21] It will be sufficient to refer to the essential elements of the doctrine of implied powers. The General Assembly asked the Court if the Organization had the power to present an international claim against a state for losses suffered by an agent of the United Nations in the exercise of his functions. The Court considered that the initial question to be decided—whether the Organization is or is not "an entity capable of availing itself of obligations incumbent upon its Members"—was not resolved by the words of the Charter. It was necessary to recognize, however, that in order to attain its goals, it is indispensable that the Organization enjoy an international personality. The exercise of the functions of the Organization and the enjoyment of its rights "can only be explained on the basis of the possession of a large measure of international personality and the capacity to operate upon an international plane. . . . It must be acknowledged that its Members, by entrusting certain functions to it, with the attendant duties and responsibilities, have clothed it with the competence required to enable those functions to be effectively discharged." But the recognition of its international personality does not mean that its rights and obligations are the same as those of the state. "Whereas a State possesses the totality of international rights and duties recognized by international law, the rights and duties of an entity such as the Organization must depend upon its purposes and functions as specified or implied in its constituent documents and developed in practice." As a result, "the Organization must be deemed to have those powers which, though not expressly provided in the Charter, are conferred upon it by necessary implication as being essential to the performance of its duties."

The doctrine of implied powers means, then, that the Organization has the legal competence to carry out certain activities neither expressly provided for in the Charter nor prohibited by it, when these are indispensable for the fulfillment of its purposes and functions, and to the extent to which this may be necessary. According to the Court, it is not necessary that certain purposes and functions be explicitly enumerated in the Charter in order to give rise to a correlative power; it is sufficient that such purposes or functions be *implied* in the Charter. Moreover, the terms used by the Court mean that the quality and degree of these implied powers also depend on the measure and condition in which the purposes and functions that form their basis are "developed in the practice (of the Organization)." It is easy to see the far-reaching character of this thesis of the Court: the very activity of the Organization is recognized as a contributive factor, legally pertinent, for the increase or diminution of the range of powers of the organs of the United Nations.[22]

On the other hand, however, the Court was careful to point out that each implicit power is limited by the degree to which it is necessary to exercise it in order to fulfill an aim or function. Thus, for example, the Court explained that the Organization may exercise "to a certain extent" protection of its agents that is characterized as "functional," protection whose scope is different —less vast in most cases—than the one exercised by the state over its diplomatic agents.

Resolutions Whose Validity Rests on the Doctrine of the Implied Powers of the Organization

The above-mentioned Advisory Opinion refers to the legal capacity of the Organization to present an international claim; that is, it concerns one aspect of the relationship between the Organization and the states. The Court further developed the same thesis of implied powers in connection with the internal law of the Organization in the case of the United Nations Administrative Tribunal.[23] Between these two advisory opinions, the doctrine of implied powers covers almost the entire field of United Nations action. As long as the two limitations pointed out above are respected—first, that the Charter does not prohibit the attribution of a power to an organ, either directly, or indirectly, by attributing a power to one organ and thus excluding another; and second, that the degree to which this implicit power is exercised is commensurate with the necessity of achieving the purpose or function on which it is based—the Court's thesis may serve as a foundation to justify the legality of numerous resolutions that are not directly based on the Charter, and, on occasion, to explain their mandatory character. Owing to the wide range of action to which this doctrine is applicable, it can mean a considerable advance in the theory and practice of international organizations and can contribute even to the creation of new international rules.

Besides the specific matters referred to in the two opinions of the Court, the theory of implied powers may serve as one foundation, among others, for certain juridically significant resolutions:

Resolution 92 (I), concerning the seal and emblem of the United Nations, enabled the Assembly to "resolve" that a certain design should be the emblem of the Organization and be used as a seal. To avoid the improper use of the emblem, the same resolution recommended that the member states adopt legislative or other pertinent measures. The promulgation of legislative measures by the member states, as such, is not mandatory, but the adoption of the emblem by the Assembly is legally "imposed" on the member states. Since the emblem (as well as the flag), is an attribute of the juridical personality of the Organization, the latter has the legal power to demand that a member's conduct in a given case conform with the aim of the resolution, requiring of him, for instance, that he prevent the improper use of the flag or the emblem.

Similar observations can be made with respect to *Resolution*

167 (II) concerning the United Nations flag and *Resolution 168 (II)* concerning United Nations Day. The statute concerning the use of the flag, as well as the rules referring to its size and proportions formulated by the Secretary-General according to instruction from the General Assembly, are also mandatory for the member states.[24]

Resolution 483 (V), concerning the creation of a distinctive insignia for the United Nations troops that participated in the Korean War, has some similarity with the two previous ones. The markedly political content of the Resolution and the fact that its adoption was opposed by a group of states do not have any juridical relevance as to its legal scope. In adopting it, the Assembly recalled its Resolution 167 (II) concerning the flag, and the Security Council resolution of July 7, 1950, authorizing the Unified Command in Korea to use the United Nations flag, as a foundation for "resolving" that the Secretary-General should formulate rules for the granting of the insignia. The effect of the resolution could not, obviously, be extended to compel the members who opposed it to recognize the insignia in their territories; but the resolution had legal effects for all the members, including those who voted against it, in the sense that their opposition could not prevent its creation and recognition as the "official" insignia of the United Nations and not merely of a group of states. Moreover, in this case as in many others involving Assembly resolutions, the mandatory effect was manifested through its financial implications. Through the inclusion in the budget of the expenses they entail, all the members are legally constrained to contribute to the fulfillment of internal resolutions that some oppose from a political point of view.

Other resolutions that are not directly based on the Charter, and whose scope—greater than that of an ordinary recommendation—can be explained through the doctrine of implied powers are the following: *Resolution 79 (I)*, concerning the transfer of the assets from the League of Nations to the United Nations, by which the Assembly approved an agreement between the two organs; *Resolution 84 (I)*, approving the agreement between the United Nations and the Carnegie Foundation concerning the use of the Hague Peace Palace, and *Resolution 586 (VI)*, approving a supplementary agreement on the same subject; *Resolution 90 (I)*, by which the Assembly, *inter alia*, approved an agreement between the International Court of Justice and the Dutch government concerning privileges and immunities of the judges of the International Court of Justice, of the Secretary, etc.; *Resolution 98 (I)*, approving the agreement between the Swiss government and the United Nations concerning privileges and immunities of the United Nations and concerning the headquarters at Geneva; *Resolution 169 (II)*, approving the June 26, 1947 Agreement between the United Nations and the United States concerning headquarters and authorizing the Secretary-General to put the agreement into force and "to perform on behalf of the United Nations such acts or functions as may be required by that Agreement;" and *Resolution 481 (V)*, complementary to the preceding one, by which the Assembly asked the Secretary-General to submit for its approval a draft regulation (which the United Nations has the right to draw up in accordance with Article 3, section 8 of the Agreement, for application inside the headquarters, and designed to establish in it, in all respects, the necessary conditions for the full exercise of its functions), but authorizing the Secretary-General to put it into effect in case of urgency, and subsequently inform the Assembly.

The Financial Regulations of the United Nations contain numerous provisions that affect member states. *Resolution 456 (V)*, by which the General Assembly "approved" the Regulations superseding the previous ones, and to which the Financial Regulations are an annex, is a typical legislative resolution. However, it is not directly based on the Charter, since Article 17 grants to the Assembly the power only to examine and approve the budget and to determine the proportion in which members shall contribute to the expenses of the Organization. The provisions of the Financial Regulations cover a wider range and can only be legally justified when considered as the expression of the implied powers of the Assembly, which are necessary to fulfill the basic financial function attributed to it by the Charter.

The Function of the International Court of Justice in the Development of International Law

Some of the resolutions examined above were adopted prior to the advisory opinions of the Court that developed the thesis of the latent powers of the Organization. The legal validity of such resolutions could at the time have seemed disputable since, on the one hand, they clearly had the intention of creating mandatory legal effects over the organs and the members—that is, they were resolutions that by their nature constituted something more than recommendations—without, on the other hand, having a specific foundation in the Charter. Kelsen, for example, referring to five of them (those relative to the emblem, the flag, United Nations Day, the agreement with the Carnegie Foundation, and the transfer of the assets of the League), emphasizes the absence of a Charter provision authorizing them, and without affirming it explicitly, he seems to give the impression that in his judgment they are illegal.[25]

Even before the Court's opinions were handed down, the legality of such resolutions could perhaps have been upheld for several good reasons. From a certain point of view, the Court did not really create new law. Through an interpretation of the Charter inspired by the changing needs and conditions of the Organization, and using legal arguments long known in American constitutional law,[26] the Court perceived and recognized, beyond the mere letter, the existence of virtual powers that had to be activated to serve the Organization.

The above-mentioned advisory opinions of the Court and their consequences for the interpretation of the Charter illustrate the important function that the Court can have in the development of international law.

In the transitional phase that sometimes precedes the creation of international, and especially customary law, in which there is already an awareness that changing needs and situations call for new solutions; in which potential powers strive, so to speak, to become actual; in which the practice of the organs shows a certain tendency but is not yet uniform; in which the radical opposition of a group of states changes first into tolerance and later into an acceptance of a new tendency that gradually gains more and more adherents; in sum, in that period that could be called prejuridical, a pronouncement, a determination of the Court can be decisive, whether because it acts as a catalyst that hastens the birth of new law, or because it provides authorized criteria for determining whether or not a full-fledged legal rule already exists.

It is true that in theory one can distinguish between the creation of law through a decisionary act of a legislative organ—or even of a judicial organ that may in exceptional cases act as a legislator, such as the judge in Switzerland[27]—and the ordinary *application* of pre-existent norms. In international practice, however, this theoretical schema is not so clearly delineated. Concerning international norms—abstract notions whose existence does not admit either tangible or instrumental verification or rigorous mathematical demonstration—the conclusion of a tribunal, in the sense, for instance, that such a rule can be inferred as a general principle of law or that it was potentially present in a more basic norm, must be the result of a logico-juridical evaluation that in marginal cases will be very subjective and disputable. *Customary rules and general principles of law are not vested with any formal and exterior sign that authentically prove their existence.* In many cases, the distinction between *creation* of new law and *recognition* of pre-existent law, as essentially distinct acts, loses much of its meaning and importance.

But when this logico-juridical judgment concerning the previous existence or nonexistence of a norm—which in itself may be quite subjective—is carried out by the highest authority competent to "declare" the law, such a judgment acquires a certain formal objectivity that does not tolerate any significant or effective individual dissidence. The mechanics of decision-making in modern international institutions are affected by the absence of a certain organ—an international legislature—and the presence of another—the Court—which is bound to give a juridical solution to every case submitted to it whether or not there is directly applicable law; because of this, the dissidence of an individual state would lack efficacy and even juridical relevance if it opposed a pronouncement of the Court as to whether a certain principle or practice did or did not constitute a legal rule in force.

RESOLUTIONS CONCERNING THE FINANCING OF THE UNITED NATIONS

Other internal resolutions of the highest importance are those that approve the budget and apportion the expenses of the Organization among the members according to a scale of assessments. Article 17 of the Charter provides that the Assembly shall "approve" the budget (paragraph 1) and that the "expenses of the Organization shall be borne by the Members" (paragraph 2). From the outset, there was never any doubt that such resolutions were of an obligatory nature. Thus, Goodrich and Hambro point out that Article 17(2) "gives the General Assembly the power to 'apportion' the expenses of the United Nations among its Members, and obliges the latter to bear those expenses."[28]

The application of budgetary resolutions gives rise to various problems. First, it is necessary to define the meaning of "expenses of the Organization" in the context of Article 17, which is tantamount to defining the limits of the Assembly's power to determine what expenses must be borne by the members. Another aspect of the same question is whether only the expenses of the "regular" or "administrative" budget (as opposed to "operational" budget) may be compulsorily apportioned.

Second, and as a corollary to the preceding question, it should be asked whether the members are obliged to bear, under any circumstances, *all* the expenses of the Organization. This is closely related to the problem of the relationship between the substantive resolution that gives rise to financial implications, and the consequential financial resolution itself; or, in other words, the relationship between the obligation to bear an expense, and the cause of that expense. More particularly, in order to be able to apportion an expense obligatorily, is it a relevant factor or not that the substantive resolution may have been adopted illegally (by exceeding the limits of the Organization itself, or by exceeding the powers of the organ that adopted it, or by a serious aberrance from established practice)? In this connection, it must also be determined whether a political, nonobligatory resolution (supposing it was legally adopted) may serve as the legal basis for a binding financial resolution.

All these problems were considered and fully discussed with respect to the financing of so-called peace-keeping operations. The specific question of whether the expenses authorized by various Assembly resolutions for United Nations operations in the Middle East and in the Congo were or were not "expenses of the Organization" within the meaning of Article 17 was submitted to the International Court of Justice. In one of its most important advisory opinions, the Court gave an affirmative answer.[29]

Certain aspects of these problems, especially those pertaining to the Assembly's power to act for the maintenance of peace, will be examined below in another context.[30] At this juncture, we shall examine only the definition of "expenses of the Organization" and, correlatively, whether the Assembly's determination of expenses always gives rise to an obligation by the members to pay them in the proportion it has determined.

The Court interpreted the text of Article 17 first in its ordinary and natural sense, arriving at the conclusion that the term "budget" in paragraph 1 does not pertain exclusively to the administrative budget. After noting that the distinction between administrative budget and operational budget had not escaped the framers of the Charter, inasmuch as they made the distinction when referring to the budgets of the specialized agencies (paragraph 3 of Article 17), the Court argued as follows:

If it had been intended that paragraph 1 (of Article 17) should be limited to the administrative budget of the United Nations organization itself, the word "administrative" would have been inserted in paragraph 3. Moreover, had it been contemplated that the Organization would also have had another budget, different from the one which was to be approved by the General Assembly, the Charter would have included some references to such other budget and to the organ which was to approve it.[31]

Furthermore, the Court pointed out that the Financial Regulations of the United Nations, unanimously approved in 1950, had not made the distinction either, and that the practice of the Organization has been entirely in conformity with the natural sense of the terms of the Charter.[32] With specific regard to the UNEF and ONUC expenses, the Court recognized that the Assembly had been treating them, year after year, as expenses of the Organization within the meaning of Article 17 of the Charter.[33]

In establishing the Assembly's authority to apportion the expenses of United Nations operations in the Middle East and in the Congo, from a positive point of view, the Court relied upon both the rule of interpretation known as the "rule of effectiveness" and on the doctrine of "implied powers" of the Organization, which it had previously invoked.[34] The Court began its reasoning by declaring as a general proposition that "the 'expenses' of any organization are the amounts paid out to defray the costs of carrying out its purposes, in this case, the political, economic, social, humanitarian, and other purposes of the United Nations." As the next step, the Court examined "whether the resolutions authorizing the operations here in question were intended to carry out the purposes of the United Nations and whether the expenditures were incurred in furthering these operations."[35] Observing that the answer to these questions was in the affirmative, the Court concluded that such expenses were "expenses of the Organization" within the meaning of Article 17 of the Charter.

In order to reach this conclusion, the Court had to pronounce itself implicitly on a difficult question, which it did not examine directly, and which is the very core of the entire problem: the supporting basis of the financial resolutions that apportion obligatorily the UNEF and ONUC expenses consists of political, nonobligatory resolutions, that is, mere recommendations.[36] It seems contradictory that a substantive nonbinding resolution can give rise to a binding financial consequence. If the Charter bestowed upon the members the right to reject certain resolutions on the political level, which is the most important one, why would the right to reject a dependent, financial implication of those same resolutions be denied the members?

Both Judge Winiarski and Judge Koretsky gave convincing arguments regarding this matter in their dissenting opinions. Judge Winiarski stated:

It is difficult to see by what process of reasoning recommendations could be held to be binding on States which have not accepted them. It is difficult to see how it can be conceived that a recommendation is partially binding, and that on what is perhaps the most vital point, the financial contribution levied by the General Assembly under the conditions of paragraph 2 of Article 17. It is no less difficult to see at what point in time the transformation of a non-binding recommendation into a partially binding recommendation is supposed to take place, at what point in time a legal obligation is supposed to come into being for a Member State which has not accepted it.[37]

Judge Koretsky, in turn, pointed out:

The General Assembly may only *recommend* measures. Expenses which might arise from such recommendations should not lead to an obligatory apportionment of them among all Members of the United Nations. That would mean to convert a non-mandatory recommendation of the General Assembly into a mandatory decision; this would be to proceed against the Charter, against logic, and even against common sense.[38]

On the other hand, there is no doubt that the clear intention of Article 17 is to underline the obligation of members to bear the expenses of the Organization; and the Charter did not distinguish between the different types of resolutions on which these expenses were based. As Judge Fitzmaurice stressed in an individual opinion, the *travaux préparatoires* at San Francisco clearly demonstrate the intention of Article 17.[39] It is possible to maintain that the specific purpose of the Assembly resolutions based on Article 17 is to provide the content of this provision of the Charter. The Charter simply sets forth the obligation of members to bear the expenses of the Organization, but does not indicate—nor, indeed, could it have done so—what those expenses are, leaving it to the Assembly to fill in this "blank" legal rule, to *determine* those expenses in a binding form.[40] Technically, this would appear to be the correct solution. *From a juridico-formal point of view, the Assembly's apportionment of expenses is binding, independently of whether the resolution that gives rise to the expenses is imperative or voluntary.*

Another quite different problem, which has no juridical solution, is whether the Assembly *legally must determine* that expenses arising from recommendations are to be borne obligatorily by all the members. It is obvious that a positive unconditional answer to this question could have immeasurable consequences.

The logical and inevitable results of the Court's thesis is that any expense that a majority decides to include in the budget, thereby rendering it an "expense of the Organization," must automatically be apportioned in a binding way among all the members. The condition indicated by the Court, namely that the expenses be directed to the furthering of the political, economic, social, humanitarian, and other purposes of the United Nations lacks practical value in view of the wide scope of such purposes. It suffices to read Articles 1, 13, and 55 of the Charter to realize that the aims of the United Nations embrace almost all fields of international activity.

Judge Fitzmaurice, who voted with the majority, nevertheless pointed out that the Court's view, which he characterized in this respect as "too extreme," opened up disquieting perspectives. In order to limit its effects, he distinguished between the different functions of the Organization as well as between certain "expenditures" that might not be "expenses" of the Organization. For him, not every amount paid out by the Organization had to be obligatorily apportioned under all circumstances.

According to Judge Fitzmaurice, "the 'action' to be taken under certain resolutions consists *solely* of provision for making a payment or financial contribution (e.g. for some purpose of aid or relief), so that the making of this payment or contribution is not merely a means to an end—viz. enabling the resolution to be carried out—but the end itself, and the sole object of the resolution. . . ."[41] In the case of these resolutions—as distinct from the other, ordinary ones—member states would not be obliged, in conformity with Article 17, to bear the expense in question.

This distinction does not seem to correspond either to reality or to a generally accepted theoretical conception. No payment or financial contribution can be considered as an "end itself" and as "the sole object" of a resolution. These expenses are not brought into existence *in vacuo*. If, for example, the United Nations voted for a financial contribution to assist a country in case of a natural disaster, such a contribution can and must be interpreted, not as an end in itself, but as a means of furthering a typical purpose of the Organization, that of international cooperation in the social, humanitarian, and economic fields. This observation is not intended to suggest that the expense referred to in the above example must be apportioned obligatorily. But it does stress that there exist equally valid reasons for considering as binding or nonbinding, both a payment intended for aid or assistance, or any expense that arises from an ordinary nonimperative resolution.

Judge Fitzmaurice makes a second distinction to prove the same point. He states: "There are broadly two main classes of functions which the Organization performs under the Charter—those which *it has a duty to carry out,* and those which are more or less *permissive* in character. Peace-keeping, dispute-settling and, indeed, most of the political activities of the Organization would come under the former head; many of what might be called its social and economic activities might come under the latter." (A little further on he calls the latter activities "non-essential.") The expenses incurred for the first category of activities are true "expenses of the Organization" and must be apportioned obligatorily. On the other hand, the expenses that the second category gives rise to are not obligatory for the states that have voted against them.[42]

This distinction does not seem to be based either in the Charter or in international practice. The United Nations has the same "duty to carry out" its political functions as it does the economic and social functions assigned to it by the Charter. And the latitude of the Organization to act or not to act in the field of economic development or technical assistance, for example, is no greater nor lesser than its discretion in this respect in the political field, including the maintenance of peace.[43] It is difficult to perceive the essential distinction between the two types of tasks that would give a binding character to the expenses entailed by one, and a voluntary character to those entailed by the other.

Even if it were possible to accept as a general proposition that the political functions of the Organization are more important than those of an economic and social nature, it would not follow that the United Nations has a (legal) "duty" to carry out the first while the second have only a "permissive" character. Consequently, there seems to be no basis for the correlative distinction between "essential" activities—the political ones—that give rise to obligatorily apportioned expenses, and the "non-essential" ones—of an economic and social nature—that do not have that effect. It could even be questioned whether such a distinction is not contrary to the philosophy that inspired the Charter and to the innumerable resolutions adopted in the postwar period that underlined the indissoluble link between economic and social conditions and peace.[44]

It is not easy to reach a definitive conclusion that would interweave the various facets of the problem. As was said above, the correct solution from a juridico-formal point of view might be the obligatory apportionment of expenses created by resolutions that tend to further the aims of the United Nations, even though they may not be imperative. But this is only one of the aspects of this question and does not afford more than a partial answer.

It is clear that from one point of view, the Court's opinion "signifies a tentative step toward the principle of international taxation of States by the world community. More broadly, it lends support to the principle of majority rule in international relations."[45]

Obviously this is desirable in itself. Moreover, if such a thesis succeeded in becoming consolidated, it would become a legal reality. But it may be asked, precisely, in view of the incomplete and clearly insufficient real support that this position has received in the General Assembly, whether we are truly witnessing the consecration of the Court's thesis as an indubitable legal rule.

From the very beginning of this study, it has been emphasized that there is a need to distinguish between the legal validity of, and the effective compliance with, resolutions.[46] But it has also been maintained—and this is a leitmotiv of the work—that the practice of organs very frequently has a decisive impact in determining whether certain theses may have or acquire the character of international rules. Such could be the situation in regard to the thesis that expenses originating from recommendations must be apportioned obligatorily.

It is true that a strong majority in the Assembly endorsed the Advisory Opinion of the Court; but it is equally true that the advocates of this thesis had to resign themselves to accepting noncompliance with it, thus renouncing the application of the sanction in Article 19 (loss of vote) relating to UNEF and ONUC expenses, because a sufficient number of important countries were not willing to follow it. In the face of the impasse thus created, and in view of the preliminary results of the work undertaken by the Special Committee for Peace-Keeping Operations (the Committee of 33) established to study the problem in all its aspects, one can justly ask whether the Assembly still supports, in fact, the thesis of mandatory apportionment of expenses originating in recommendations.

It is too soon to predict the ultimate fate of this principle. In the long run, the tendency that will prevail—be it that of financing peace-keeping operations through voluntary contributions or the obligatory assessment of all the members or a combination of the two—will necessarily depend on changes in the delicate underlying political balance that are reflected in the distribution of powers between the Security Council and the General Assembly. These changes will probably not come about through an explicit accord or in a clear-cut way, but rather as the gradual result of a practice whose course it is impossible to predict.

REGISTRATION AND PUBLICATION OF TREATIES

The regulation adopted by the General Assembly for the registration and publication of treaties (Resolutions 97 [I], 364 B [IV], and 482 [V]) offers a special difficulty. It has already been said that one of the two conditions to the doctrine of implied powers was that the Charter should not prohibit the attribution of a power to a certain organ, either explicitly or by granting it exclusively to another organ. According to Article 102 of the Charter, the registration and publication of treaties are the responsibility of the Secretary-General; therefore it could be said that the Assembly lacks the power to adopt general rules, that is, to adopt a legislative act in a material sense, in this matter. Kelsen doubts the constitutionality of such regulations[47] precisely because, according to the Charter, only the Secretary-General has the power to adopt rules on this subject. Moreover, Kelsen maintains that Resolution 97 (I) "goes far beyond the provisions of Article 102," among other reasons, because it compels the Secretary-General to register treaties other than those that are subject to registration according to Article 102: treaties entered into by the United Nations and the specialized agencies, or by members before the Charter came into force, or by nonmember states.

This matter is clearly the responsibility of the Secretary-General; since, moreover, the very general provisions of Article 102 are obviously insufficient in practice, it would have been more in compliance with the Charter that the Secretary-General should have formulated the necessary regulation for the registry and publication of treaties. From this point of view, the legality of the Assembly's regulation is doubtful, since it could not be considered the exercise of an implied power based on a function conferred by the Charter upon the Assembly.

Concerning the scope of the functions this regulation bestows on the Secretary-General, and which, according to Kelsen, goes beyond Article 102 of the Charter, his objection is less solid. The purpose of Article 102 was to avoid secret diplomacy in accordance with the precedent established by the Covenant of the League. This Article established, undoubtedly as a minimum, the obligation of members to submit the international agreements they entered into after the Charter came into force for registry with and publication by the Secretariat. The fact that other treaties, mentioned above, are similarly registered and published cannot be construed, however, as contrary to Article 102, but rather as completely in conformity with its aim, if their authors voluntarily submitted them to the Secretary-General for these purposes.

The juridically significant difference between the two situations is the following: as recognized by the General Assembly in its Resolution 172 (II) and 254 B (III), Article 102 imposes on the members a categorical juridical obligation to register the treaties that they enter into. The nature of the obligation does not change because the sanction set forth in paragraph 2 of the same Article (that is, a member cannot invoke a nonregistered treaty before an organ of the United Nations) has a relative and limited character. The debates that preceded the adoption of these resolutions show this clearly.[48] But nonmember states cannot be subject, for obvious reasons, to the same obligation; if, however, they voluntarily submit the treaties they enter into to the Secretary-General, nothing in Article 102 would seem to prohibit imposing on him the obligation to register and publish them. Similar arguments justify other provisions of the same regulation, which require the Secretary-General to register *ex officio* and to publish the treaties considered in Article 4 of the regulation (for example, those in which the United Nations is a party or depository) and to file (rather than register) and publish other treaties mentioned in Article 10.

STAFF REGULATIONS OF THE UNITED NATIONS

The Staff Regulations of the United Nations "approved" by Resolution 590 (VI) of the General Assembly are based directly on the Charter: Article 101 explicitly states that the staff "shall be appointed by the Secretary-General under regulations established by the General Assembly." The term "appointed" is used here by the Charter in its widest interpretation: the rules established by the Assembly not only regulate the very modalities of the appointment, but also the working conditions in general, since these conditions form the content of the agreement between the Administration and the personnel, that is, of the appointment.[49]

The Staff Regulations, according to the terms of its preamble, "represent the broad principles of personnel policy," but it is the Secretary-General "as the Administrative Officer [who] shall provide and enforce such Staff Rules consistent with these principles as he considers necessary." This is a case of a delegated regulatory power enjoyed by the Secretary-General by virtue of a decision of the Assembly.

The provisions of the Staff Rules and Staff Regulations and of the Administrative Manual of the Secretariat are mandatory for the Administration and for staff members (as recognized by Decision No. 15 of the Administrative Tribunal).[50] Some of these regulations have a political content and may indirectly affect the position of member states. This is the case, for example, of the provisions in the former regulation that prohibited the hiring of persons who had had connections with Fascism or Nazism, or those that required that the personnel of the United Nations Korean Reconstruction Agency be in agreement with the basic United Nations objectives in Korea.[51] These requirements modify the members' normal expectation that their nations be appointed, under equal conditions of "efficiency, competence, and integrity" (Article 101 of the Charter), with due regard *only* to equitable geographical distribution, and no additional political qualifications. Such provisions can be considered, however, as an expression of the regulatory power granted to the Secretary-General by the Assembly to interpret the requirements indicated in the Charter for the hiring of personnel. The Secretary-General's interpretation of the Charter through his regulatory powers—his implicit decision, for example, that integrity was incompatible with Nazism—produces for the member states effects that do not admit any legally significant opposition.

A more patent case of binding effects for member states and even for the Assembly itself, is that of the financial implications resulting from the application of staff regulations by the Secretary-General. Certainly, member states exercise some control over the action of the Secretary-General in personnel matters when they examine and eventually approve or modify the respective chapters of the Organization's budget. But this does not affect the argument that the application by the Secretary-General of his own rules regarding staff can have compulsory budgetary implications. In the Advisory Opinion concerning the effects of the judgments of the Administrative Tribunal, the International Court of Justice found that the power of the Assembly to examine and approve the budget, according to Article 17 of the Charter, "does not mean that [it] has an absolute power to approve or disapprove the expenditure proposed to it; for some part of that expenditure arises out of obligations already incurred by the Organization, and to this extent the General Assembly has no alternative but to honour these engagements."[52]

RESOLUTIONS THAT CREATE SUBSIDIARY ORGANS

The Charter explicitly authorized three of the principal organs (the General Assembly, in Article 22; the Security Council, in Article 29; and the Economic and Social Council, in Article 68) to establish the subsidiary organs they deem necessary for the performance of their functions. On the basis of these provisions, numerous and diverse organs have been created. In his statement before the International Court of Justice in the case concerning the Administrative Tribunal, the representative of the Secretary-General commented on the diverse nature, composition, and functions of the subsidiary organs created up to 1954, which then numbered over one hundred.[53]

Some of these organs are permanent, others are temporary; most are composed of states, some of individual experts, and others even of representatives of international bodies, such as the Administrative Committee on Coordination constituted by the heads of the Secretariats of the United Nations and the Special-ized Agencies; some act under precise instructions from the parent body, others enjoy a reasonable degree of autonomy; many undertake studies, others perform more concrete political tasks, and the important functional commissions operate on a more or less permanent basis for the purpose of administering general programs, usually of rehabilitation or aid, such as the UN Korean Reconstruction Agency or UNICEF. At least one of them, the Administrative Tribunal (besides the Libya Tribunal, which no longer exists), performs a truly judicial function, although it is a subsidiary organ of the Assembly owing to the manner in which it was established.[54]

The creation of subsidiary organs is complemented on occasion by the adoption of a statute, especially when the terms of reference of the new organ are wide and its activity important and permanent. The General Assembly, for example, established the International Law Commission through a legislative resolution that regulated its composition, working methods, and other details, and at the same time formulated certain general directives concerning the codification and progressive development of international law.[55]

INSTITUTIONAL RESOLUTIONS

Some resolutions have a special legislative character: their essential purpose is not the formulation of a statute for a new organ, but rather the programming and implementation of important activities whose realization requires, among other things, the establishment of one or more organs. This is the case of two of the most significant resolutions adopted by the United Nations: No. 222 (IX) of the Economic and Social Council (confirmed by Resolution 304 [IV] of the General Assembly) whose "guiding principles" constitute the basis for multilateral technical assistance, and No. 1240 (XIII), which created the Special Fund, conceived as "a constructive advance in United Nations assistance to the less developed countries . . . ," that would make easier "new capital investments of all types by creating conditions which would make such investments either feasible or more effective."

The principles contained in both these resolutions form the constitutive charter of multilateral technical assistance. The special meaning of these resolutions from the point of view presented here, is that they are not mere expressions of the power to create organs and to bestow a statute upon them, but are also legislative resolutions of a special kind: they are perhaps the only cases up to now in the United Nations of true institutional resolutions, in the sense given to this concept by the famous French doctrine of the "institution" that has had so much influence on the evolution of modern public law.[56]

The guiding principles of these resolutions form an organic whole of rules, which express, establish, and organize, on the international level, the fundamental idea on which technical assistance rests: the idea that prosperity is indivisible. Through the years there have appeared important "expressions of consensus" about and in favor of this idea, although the process is far from being concluded. At the same time, as is characteristic of the birth of an institution, organs have been created and procedures established to direct and regulate the action of states in the service of this "idea." In spite of its present limitations, technical assistance is becoming, within the frame of the United Nations system, an authentic "institution."

The institutional character of the above resolutions makes the problem of their legal scope more complex. They are legislative resolutions in the sense that they establish general rules and guiding principles, but at the same time they create organs and regulate the activities of the members and of the Secretariat, thus producing an intimate connection between different elements rotating around a central objective, as is characteristic of legal

institutions. Moreover, the mandatory apportionment of administrative expenses among the members is an integral part of the
whole system, although the applicable provisions do not appear
in the resolutions themselves. This set of articulated rules produces legal effects on members from which they cannot legally
exempt themselves. In practice the resolutions embodying these
rules create legal effects similar to those that would be produced
if the entire system of technical assistance had been organized
by a treaty.

The essential element of this institution still has, however, a
voluntary character: the funds for the operation of the Expanded
Program of Technical Assistance and of the Special Fund (unlike administrative expenses) are raised through voluntary contributions of member and nonmember States.

POLITICAL AND LEGAL PROBLEMS RESULTING
FROM THE CREATION OF SUBSIDIARY ORGANS

The establishment of organs by resolution involves certain problems concerning both the legal competence of the main organ to
bestow certain functions upon the subsidiary organ and the purpose of its creation.

Article 5 (2) of the Covenant of the League made the establishment of committees of inquiry a matter of procedure requiring only a simple majority for approval. But it was soon realized
that the creation of an organ of investigation could be something more than a means to clarify facts, and "might actually
amount to a mode of dealing with the matter by extending inci-
dentally the institutional machinery of the organization."[57] For
example, when the Council of the League was seized of the Sino-
Japanese controversy in September 1931, it refrained in the end
from creating a commission of inquiry without the approval of
Japan.

The United Nations Security Council, following the directives of the four sponsoring powers at the San Francisco Conference on voting procedure in the Security Council (especially the thesis of the "chain of events," beginning with the Council's decision to carry out an investigation which might culminate, in its final phase, in the adoption of enforcement measures), has refrained until now, except for the case of Laos in 1959, from creating organs without the unanimous consent of the five permanent members.[58]

The General Assembly does not apply, in accordance with the Charter, different majorities according to the substantive or procedural nature of the question. In conformity with Article 18, the creation of new organs is normally decided by a simple majority, unless the Assembly wishes to employ the exceptional procedure indicated in paragraph 3 of that article.

The main debates concerning the legal power to create organs have taken place in the Assembly. When the possibility of establishing an international criminal court was discussed, it was held that the Assembly had no power to do so by means of a resolution because, among other reasons, the Charter does not confer any jurisdictional functions on that organ. This reason in itself is not necessarily a decisive obstacle to the creation of an organ by the Assembly that in its turn would exercise jurisdictional activities, as recognized by the International Court of Justice in the case of the Administrative Tribunal. But, on the other hand, it would have been necessary to find some power conferred on the Assembly by the Charter that would be the foundation for the jurisdictional activity of the proposed criminal court, just as the Assembly is invested with the power to regulate the activities of the staff by Article 101 of the Charter. To this effect, the general power of the Assembly to preserve international peace and security was invoked.[59]

Here, however, the link between the general power of the Assembly and the specific function of the subordinate organ seems to be very tenuous. The best method for creating the criminal court would surely have been by means of a treaty. However, had the Assembly really wished to establish an international criminal court, it would have perhaps considered that the foundation invoked by some (the general power to preserve peace and security) was not too indirect and therefore sufficient. Surely, reasons of substance, more than lack of legal competence, prevented the Assembly from creating the court.

The first condition for establishing a subordinate organ would seem to be, therefore, not that the function conferred upon subsidiary organ may be legally and directly exercised by the main organ, but that the main organ possess a power that can be fulfilled through the activity entrusted to the subsidiary organ.

The second condition is that only part of the power and some of the matters that fall within the competence of the main organ, but not all, should be transmitted to the subsidiary body. This condition was debated in relation to the creation of the Interim Committee. The Soviet Union questioned its legality, advancing the argument that it was not a subsidiary organ of the Assembly, but actually the Assembly itself, since it had the same composition and its competence, *ratione materiae*, was practically identical. Although it is true that the matters that could be treated by both these bodies were substantially the same, their respective powers were different. The Interim Committee could not make recommendations to states or to the Security Council; it could only "study" and "report" its conclusions to the General Assembly.[60]

In the case of the Interim Committee, and also in that of the Assembly's establishment of the Collective Measures Committee through the "Uniting for Peace" Resolution (337 [V]), the Soviet Union and other states also objected to the *purpose* in creating the subsidiary organ. They claimed that an attempt was being made to invest the Assembly indirectly, through its subsidiary organs, with functions that belonged exclusively to the Security Council.

In other cases, the objection that an organ is incompetent to establish a subsidiary body has been more radical: it has been argued, for example, that the subject matter and function to be assigned to a new organ are not within the competence of the United Nations but belong exclusively to a member state. In the Assembly debates (2nd Session) on the creation of an *ad hoc* committee to examine the information transmitted by virtue of Article 73(e) of the Charter, and in the debates that took place in 1949 in order to give a permanent character to such an organ (now called the Committee on Information from Non-Self-Governing Territories), the state administering non-self-governing territories opposed first the establishment of the committee, and later its permanent character. They argued that the entire Chapter XI of the Charter had a declaratory and nonmandatory character and that therefore "the administering authorities had not accepted international accountability; that nothing in Article 73(e) permitted the discussion of the information, and, therefore, no committee was necessary [to examine it]."[61] In the end, the Assembly accepted the opposite interpretation and created the subsidiary organ.[62]

Resolutions that create subsidiary organs have mandatory legal effects for all the member states, including those who oppose their establishment on constitutional grounds. The objecting state lacks legal recourse to prevent the creation of the organ, the calling of its meetings, and the integration of its activities in the decision-making mechanism of the Organization, with all the legal and even budgetary consequences this implies. The resolutions of the subsidiary organ will have the legal effects intended by the act of its establishment, in spite of the fact that objecting states may refrain from participating in its meetings.

In practice, however, the vigorous and especially the prolonged opposition of a politically important group of states may prevent the new organ from acting effectively and even from holding sessions as intended. The initial studies of the Interim

Committee—some of which were of considerable theoretical interest—did not have a political impact proportionate to their quality, and the Committee did not meet again, owing to the opposition of the Eastern European states. Another subsidiary organ, which had an even more precarious life although its creation did not provoke any opposition and its function seemed important, was the Peace Observation Commission created by Resolution 377 (V) of the General Assembly.

Objections to the composition of subsidiary organs are not constitutionally as serious, but they have proved to be politically effective. Article 22 of the Charter does not contain any criteria for the composition of subsidiary organs of the Assembly. Equitable geographical distribution, sometimes difficult to apply, is the principle usually employed. But it cannot be used in all cases. Sometimes the object and function of the organ being created may require a membership based on other criteria, and geographical distribution would then have only a marginal or complementary role. Two examples that best illustrate this situation are those of disarmament and the peaceful use of outer space.

For obvious reasons, disarmament plans cannot be imposed by a majority decision. Given their nature, they have to be the object of negotiations leading to an agreement, and at the present time this means, in effect, an agreement between the two great military blocs. This circumstance, irrelevant to other questions subject to multilateral consideration, has to some extent inevitably influenced the composition of the successive bodies dedicated to disarmament. In the beginning, the membership of United Nations disarmament committees reflected above all the principle of geographical distribution. With time, however, the function of such bodies prevailed over other considerations, so that the negotiating organ subsequently was given a balanced composition: five members of NATO and five members of the Warsaw Treaty group. The membership of the present Eighteen Nation Disarmament Committee, created by Resolution 1722 (XVI), reflects in addition the idea that the participation of a certain number of nonaligned countries could stimulate agreements between the two main parties by offering suggestions and exercising a conciliatory function. The eight nations so characterized were elected only after previous agreement between the United States and the Soviet Union, on the basis of partly political and partly geographical considerations.

The question of the peaceful use of outer space presents similar although not identical aspects. The organ created by the General Assembly was to elaborate programs of international cooperation, especially in the technical field, which require an agreement between the only two powers that up to now have explored outer space. But at the same time, the organ was designed to study the legal problems resulting from the exploration of space in order eventually to establish a general normative order in the interest of all humanity. Both aims had to be reflected concurrently in the membership of the organ. The *ad hoc* committee created by the General Assembly in 1958 (Resolution 1348 [XIII]) included three states of the Socialist bloc out of a total of eighteen. These states considered that such a proportion was insufficient and did not participate in the work of the committee. In 1959, the General Assembly created a new committee (Resolution 1472 [XIV]) whose membership had been previously negotiated, and the Socialist states have since been represented by seven members out of a total of twenty-four. (The Soviet group in the United Nations numbered nine states at that time.)

RESOLUTIONS ADOPTED BY INTERNATIONAL CONFERENCES UNDER THE AUSPICES OF THE UNITED NATIONS

The calling of international conferences has, in the internal order of the convening body, consequences similar to those of the creation of subsidiary organs. Conferences under the auspices of the United Nations have always been called by a decision of the Assembly, although it may only recommend to states that they participate, and their convening produces binding administrative and budgetary effects, even for those states that decline the invitation to participate in them.

In the case of international conferences concerning matters within the competence of the Economic and Social Council, the legal capacity of the Assembly to decide their convening, with the accompanying legal implications, is based directly on Article 62(4) of the Charter. With respect to conferences regarding the progressive development of international law and its codification (such as the important Conferences on the Law of the Sea held in Geneva in 1958 and 1960), the task of convening them must be considered an implied power of the Assembly for the purpose of fulfilling the function assigned to it by the Charter in Article 13(1a).

The fact that an international conference is called by the United Nations and is held under its auspices may in itself have a certain relevance in establishing the legal value of the nonconventional results of the conference, such as the resolutions, *voeux*, and declarations that the conference usually adopts. Obviously, the legal value of these acts depends first on their content and on the greater or lesser impact they may have on the subsequent behavior of states. However, the fact that they are adopted "under the auspices" of the United Nations may represent an additional weighty element and may be a contributory factor in evaluating their legal scope, especially when the nature of the act itself is uncertain. Owing to the universality of the United Nations, and to the fact that practically all states—with the significant exception of China and a few others—are invited to participate in the plenipotentiary conferences it convenes, and because important resolutions are adopted by a two-thirds majority, it can certainly be said that the resolutions and declarations they adopt reflect the will of the organized international community. When these conferences adopt not a typical recommendation but a declaration, a general political or legal pronouncement, or a determination, it may be said that their legal value and their scope are the same as if they had been adopted by the General Assembly itself.[63]

RESOLUTIONS DIRECTED TO INDEPENDENT BODIES

Interorganic resolutions vary in their legal scope according to the hierarchical relationship existing between the organ that adopts them and the organ to which they are directed. These relationships may be of equality, of superordination, or of subordination. The relationship of equality may be found within a single international organization, as for example, between the General Assembly and the Security Council of the United Nations, or between independent international organizations.

Within the United Nations, only the Security Council, the General Assembly, and the International Court of Justice may be considered organs independent of each other. The Economic and Social Council (ESC) and the Trusteeship Council, although the Charter calls them principal organs, and although they enjoy a certain degree of autonomy (especially the ESC) are subordinate to the General Assembly. The Secretary-General is subject to the authority of the General Assembly and the Councils.[64]

Resolutions directed by the Assembly to the Council and vice versa can only be nonmandatory recommendations, given the independence and equality of the two bodies. When the Charter grants to both a power of codecision (as in the admission and expulsion of members, suspension of rights, and appointment of the Secretary-General), resolutions directed by the Council to the Assembly have the character of proposals, as explained above. According to the Charter, the initiative in these matters rests with the Security Council alone. In the case of UNESCO, the power of initiative also rests with the Executive Council alone in matters of admission (Article 2[2] and Article 5[6]), in spite of the fact that this organ is subordinate to the General Conference. Moreover, the equal status of the General Assembly and the Security Council in the United Nations does not exist in the case of the specialized agencies which, following the pattern of ILO, have a more hierarchical structure.

The relationships between the United Nations and the specialized agencies may give rise to a variety of situations. Since the specialized agencies were created by treaty, and therefore constitute entities independent of the United Nations, their relationship with that Organization is expressed mainly through recommendations. However, owing to the necessity of adequately coordinating their activities, an entire system of auxiliary measures and instruments has been established in order to enhance the efficacy of those recommendations. These measures are provided for in the agreements entered into by each of the specialized agencies with the United Nations in conformity with Article 63 of the Charter. In spite of certain differences reflecting peculiar requirements of some specialized agencies, the provisions that regulate the relationships between the agencies and the United Nations constitute a sufficiently uniform and institutional arrangement to be properly called a "system."

The main common provisions regulating these relationships, as set forth in the respective agreements, are the following:

The agreements envisage only the case of recommendations directed by the United Nations to the specialized agencies, but not vice versa, the sole exceptions being the agreements with the World Bank and the Monetary Fund. Article 4 of both agreements provides that the United Nations and the other organization may address recommendations to each other. All the specialized agencies have the right to request the inclusion of items in the agenda of the various organs of the United Nations, and vice versa. In both instances the inclusion is mandatory, except in the cases of the World Bank and the Monetary Fund, for which the agreements state only that the respective organs must give due attention to requests for inclusion of items in the agenda (Article 3 of both agreements). All the specialized agencies must submit the recommendations of the United Nations to their competent organs in the shortest possible time, and the Universal Postal Union and the World Meteorological Organization must submit them directly to their members. Moreover, the specialized agencies are required to consult the United Nations on the implementation of the recommendations it addresses to them. Finally, the specialized agencies must inform the United Nations of the measures taken to comply with its recommendations, except in the cases of the Bank and the Fund. In the case of the Bank, the recommendations of the United Nations must not deal with specific requests for loans or with the conditions or circumstances of financing such operations.[65]

RESOLUTIONS BETWEEN HIERARCHICALLY LINKED ORGANS

Resolutions directed by a juridically subordinate organ to a superior one do not have, by their very nature, any binding effect. Generally, they are true recommendations, but in certain cases, when the initiative of the inferior organ is legally necessary for the superior body to take a decision, such resolutions have, rather, the nature of a proposal. The only decisions of a subordinate organ that are binding on the parent body are the judgments of the Administrative Tribunal, for reasons already stated.

Conversely, a resolution addressed by a superior organ to an inferior one is, in principle, a binding decision. However, the terminology used by the organs of the United Nations is haphazard and lacks precision: sometimes terms such as "invites," "asks," "instructs," and occasionally "recommends," are used for true orders addressed by some organs to others. The terms used, in themselves, do not affect the legal nature of the resolution, but they usually express shades or degrees of imperativeness or urgency, as well as the freedom of action allowed to the inferior body. The degree of imperativeness of the order may vary considerably: it is sometimes sufficient for the superior organ merely to invite the inferior one to take into account its opinion. Moreover, nothing prevents a superior organ from carrying its self-limitation to the extreme by entrusting to the inferior body the final decision, without its being subject to revision from above.

The frequent lack of precision in the instructions addressed to inferior organs is generally due to the natural difficulty of formulating precise directives within collective bodies. In certain significant and important cases, however, this lack of precision has a political explanation.

Perhaps the most revealing example of this was seen in the United Nations Congo operation. As will be noted later, the Security Council and the General Assembly elaborated gradually, as the situation evolved, a series of relatively general directives addressed especially to the Secretary-General, which defined the goals of the United Nations and guided its military, political, and civil action in the Congo. The approval of such directives by the Security Council was possible because the basic interests of the principal groups of states coincided, at least in one essential respect: they wanted to avoid a civil war in the Congo and, if that proved impossible, at least to prevent the situation from becoming the source of an international conflict. The very fact that an international action was carried out under United Nations auspices was both a consequence and a reflection of this basic implicit agreement.

But at the same time, the lack of precision and insufficiently specific nature of the Security Council's directives reflected in turn a lack of agreement among the principal groups of states as to the conditions, modalities, and terms under which this international action should be undertaken. None of the basic positions was backed by a sufficient political force to prevail over the others; but since each of the principal groups could prevent in turn the triumph of the opposite camp, it was impossible to reach agreement except on very general directives. And thus, the necessarily discretionary implementation of those directives was entrusted to the Secretary-General who, at that time, enjoyed the trust of all the member states.

The interpretation and implementation of decisions addressed to an inferior organ sometimes presents special difficulties when the organ is a collective body. The Assembly, as well as other bodies, frequently follows the practice of adopting a position of principle or a general directive, either on political matters or in the social or economic fields, and, on the basis of such a position or directive, enjoins an inferior organ, be it permanent or *ad hoc*, to carry out a study or to draft a proposal or report to be submitted to the main organ. In principle, except where the terms employed in the resolution reveal a different intention, the instructions given by the superior body are binding. But if the inferior organ is a collective one, the possibility of its implementing such a resolution depends greatly on the will of its individual members.

It is not a question here of the superior organ's inability to impose its decision coercively for lack of legal means to do so. We are not now considering whether the Charter provides effective machinery and procedures for implementing decisions by United Nations bodies directed to their subsidiary organs. The question is whether a clear legal obligation incumbent upon a subsidiary collective organ entails for its members an implicit obligation to act individually, within it, in a manner consistent with the instructions that the organ has received. The situation becomes extreme when the main element of the mandate is a political position approved by a majority in the main organ but opposed by some members who are also represented in the subsidiary body. This situation occurs frequently in practically all United Nations organs.

A case well suited to illustrate the problem, although not one of capital importance, is that of the definition of aggression. The General Assembly recognized in clear terms (Resolution 599 [VI]) that it was "possible and desirable" to define aggression. After some unfruitful attempts, it appointed a Special Committee (Resolution 895 [IX]) with the precise mandate, not of studying the advisability of defining aggression, but of formulating a "draft definition" for submission to the Assembly. The various resolutions of the Assembly on this matter were approved by relatively small majorities. The membership of the Special Committee, in accordance with customary practice, reflected an equitable geographical distribution, and for this reason it included a great number of states that had asserted in the Assembly that it was inopportune and even ill-advised to formulate a definition of aggression. As expected, in spite of the pronouncement of the Assembly, these states maintained their initial position in the Special Committee, so that this body was unable to formulate the definition the Assembly had ordered.

The question of the degree of individual obligation that fell on the members was not explicitly discussed in the Committee. Several representatives expressed the view that the "orders" of the Assembly should be carried out, but none of them maintained that the purely negative attitude of other members, who criticized the definitions proposed without offering any alternatives, violated a legal obligation.[66]

Although there is no doubt that the instructions given by a superior organ have, in principle, an imperative character, the obligation that falls on the subsidiary collective body does not give rise to a legal obligation for its members to maintain, within that body, a position in conformity with it. Members individually preserve their freedom of judgment. The relationship of subordination is established only between the organs. The only practical solution is for the superior organ to dissolve the subsidiary body, when possible, and create another one whose composition is compatible with the tasks assigned to it.

"SERVICES" RENDERED BY MEMBERS OF THE ORGANIZATION TO CARRY OUT ITS FUNCTIONS

Among resolutions concerning the structure and functioning of the United Nations, there exists a group of interorganic resolutions that has its origin in the double role states may have in fulfilling the Organization's aims. States may act, under certain circumstances, as if they were organs carrying out functions of the Organization. Tammes distinguishes between the "Member's contribution to the Organization *for* the performance of its functions, from the Member's complying with a resolution which is the *result* of the performance of the Organization's functions."[67]

Undoubtedly, it is possible to distinguish between the position of the member state as an international *agent*, as an instrument that performs the Organization's purposes and, on the other hand, its position as a sovereign state to whom are addressed the resolutions adopted by the Organization. Within the contemporary conception of the international organization, based on the sovereignty of its members, the well-known thesis of Georges Scelle on the *"dédoublement fonctionnel"* of the state still has considerable application.[68]

The character of "services" to the Organization, which may be attributed to the activities requested by certain resolutions, has a certain relevance to the evaluation of their legal scope. It would seem justified, as will be seen later,[69] to interpret the obligations of an administering state over a trust territory in a stricter way when there is uncertainty as to their scope, in view of the fact that such a state acts in that instance as an organ of the international trusteeship system, operating under the authority and supervision of the United Nations.

Sometimes, however, the distinction between the two notions becomes blurred or its application impossible. Thus, measures not involving the use of armed force, such as the interruption of economic relations or of communications, the severance of diplomatic relations, etc., which the Security Council is authorized to decree by Article 41 to give effect to its decisions, assume a dual nature. On the one hand, these measures are "services" or contributions that the Council requests of the members; the members act as instruments of the Organization for the performance of a function, that is, the implementation of collective security. At the same time, such measures have a clear political significance and are the expression of the external functions of the Organization. They typically represent the enforcement action of the Organization, especially when seen from the viewpoint of the state against which they are directed. In this case, the distinction between the two notions lacks any sense or relevance.

Chapter 3

CERTAIN RESOLUTIONS CONCERNING INTERNATIONAL PEACE AND SECURITY

GENERAL OBSERVATIONS

Chapter 2 considered those resolutions that directly concern the internal life of the Organization, those related to its structure and operation, to its functioning as such. The following chapters will examine resolutions that may be considered the result or product of United Nations activities, and which for that reason have been characterized as "external."

In general, the resolutions examined here are addressed to states, not to request from them anything related to the functioning of the Organization, such as payment of a financial contribution or participation in an electoral process, but rather to call upon them to act so as to achieve the general aims of the United Nations (for example, maintenance of international peace and security through the adoption of collective measures or the peaceful settlement of disputes).

In theory, although with numerous exceptions, each group of resolutions corresponds to a different legal regime. As seen in the last chapter, a resolution pertaining to the internal activities of the Organization is generally binding. Conversely, resolutions dealing with the external activity of the Organization do not legally require their recipients to comply with their content, that is, they are recommendations. As pointed out in the introduction, the main reason is that the external activity of the Organization is generally concerned with matters in which international solidarity is not yet sufficiently strong to allow, as a general rule, the assumption of true international obligations. Therefore, the typical legal instrument at the disposal of the international community for achieving the necessary cooperation in the sphere of external activities is the recommendation, a type of resolution whereby an international organ *invites* an addressee to follow certain conduct.

However, as also indicated, recommendations are not the only resolutions in the external sphere. Within this large sector, there are certain groups of resolutions—to each of which a chapter is devoted—that produce binding legal effects. This chapter examines a group directly related to the maintenance of international peace and security, comprising decisions of the Security Council as well as certain resolutions of the General Assembly whose binding force originates in the practice of this body.

FOUNDATIONS AND SCOPE OF
SECURITY COUNCIL DECISIONS

The clearest and most important case of binding United Nations resolutions is that of the decisions adopted by the Security Council. According to Article 25 of the Charter, the members agree to "accept and carry out" these decisions. Their binding force is patent because it derives directly from the Charter; they are especially important because they represent the supreme instance of the Organization's authority and, from the constitutional point of view, are the axis around which revolves the mechanics of collective security.

The first problem in regard to these decisions lies in determining their nature. It has been maintained that the Council may adopt *decisions* binding the members solely within the framework of Chapters VI, VII, and VIII of the Charter.[1] Moreover, it is also claimed that the decisions of the Council, in conformity with Chapter VII, may refer only to enforcement measures for maintaining or restoring peace, but that the provisions of that Chapter do not authorize the Council to impose decisions concerning the substance of the dispute. The practice of the Council has been to accept the opposite thesis, that is, to recognize and assume its authority to take action with binding effects on the members, in conformity with Article 25, even outside the framework of Chapters VI, VII, and VIII.[2] One general argument—although not a decisive one—in favor of this practice is the fact that Article 25 does not make a distinction among the types of decisions that the members "agreed" to accept and carry out. According to an old legal aphorism, "where the legislator does not distinguish, the interpreter must not not distinguish."

In the case of the Free Territory of Trieste, the Council interpreted implicitly the meaning of Article 24 of the Charter whose text gave rise to the difficulty. This Article, after establishing that the members confer on the Council the "primary responsibility" for maintaining peace (paragraph 1), and after recognizing that this organ acts on their behalf in carrying out its duties, states that "the specific powers granted to the Security Council for the discharge of these duties are laid down in Chapters VI, VII, VIII, and XII" (paragraph 2). The decision adopted in the case of Trieste,[3] clearly signified the Council's recognition of its own authority to take binding decisions based on the *general* power conferred upon it by paragraph 1 (power that has been characterized as a "residual competence"), and not necessarily on the specific powers mentioned in paragraph 2.

The decisions of the Security Council in the cases of Iran[4] and Indonesia[5] also contributed to strengthen the same tendency; moreover, the case of Indonesia underlined the capacity of the Council to take decisions and not merely to make recommendations on the substance of a dispute. The questions regarding the Greek border dispute (1947) and the passage of ships through the Suez Canal (March 1954) were less conclusive because the negative votes of a permanent member prevented the adoption of a decision, but debates in each case showed the consistency and force of the arguments advanced in favor of the general competence of the Council.[6]

In the Palestine case, the Security Council rejected a proposal (263rd Meeting) to "accept, subject to the authority of the Security Council under the Charter, the requests addressed by the General Assembly to it in paragraphs (a), (b), and (c) of Section A of the General Assembly Resolution of November 29, 1947." This resolution comprised the Plan of Partition with Economic Union of Palestine, nothing less than the outline for the creation and temporary administration of two new states, all of which was obviously not included in the specific powers of the Council listed in paragraph 2 of Article 24 (nor within the normal powers of the Assembly, since, as will be seen later,[7] some provisions of the Plan implied something more than mere recommendations). The Council's refusal to enforce the Assembly plan was probably due to political considerations of substance and did not necessarily imply its assertion of a constitutional incapacity to act in that case outside the framework of the powers defined in Chapter VII. This is confirmed by the fact that in the resolution finally adopted (S/691), the Council asked the members to consult among themselves and to make recommendations enabling it to give instructions to the Palestine Commission, "with a view of implementing the resolution [of November 29, 1947] of the General Assembly."

United Nations action in the Congo, based on four resolutions of the Security Council and an equal number of General Assembly resolutions, also confirms the recognition by the Council of its authority to act according to a broad conception of its competence. The eight resolutions may, in retrospect, be considered an organic aggregate of interwoven decisions that complement and reinforce each other; in all the resolutions, with the obvious exception of the first (S/4387), the adopting organ undertook to confirm the earlier ones. Certainly, some international aspects of the resolutions—such as the order ("calls upon") to withdraw the Belgian troops, the urgent "request" to all states to abstain from any action that could undermine the territorial integrity and independence of the Congo—and others, fall within the general framework of Chapter VII of the Charter. Resolution S/4426 of August 9, 1960 expressly invoked, moreover, Article 49 (of Chapter VII) in "request[ing]" all states to "accept and carry out" the decisions of the Security Council and to lend mutual aid in the implementation of the measures decreed by the Council.[8]

However, other important aspects of the operation cannot be considered covered by the specific powers conferred on the Council by Chapter VII, or even by Chapter VI of the Charter, since there did not really exist an "international controversy." Moreover, these aspects essentially were concerned with domestic affairs of the Congo—for example, the emphatic request by the Council ("urges") to convoke Parliament and to reorganize the armed forces of the Republic of the Congo (S/4741 of February 21, 1961). The decisions of the Council in these instances can be based on its general competence, in conformity with Article 24 (1), and with Article 25 (which also was expressly invoked in Resolution S/4426 of August 9, 1960).

There is in such situations, however, a close link between domestic matters and international peace, which allows questions such as the convening of Parliament and the maintenance of internal order to be related to Chapter VII of the Charter. This connection is explicitly set forth in Resolution S/4405 of July 22, 1960, as follows: "Considering that the complete restoration of law and order in the Republic of the Congo would effectively contribute to the maintenance of international peace and security. . . ."[9]

Finally, Council resolutions on the situation in South Africa are likewise pertinent in this respect. Although Resolution S/4300 of April 1, 1960 also established clearly (1st operative paragraph) the connection between the prevailing internal situation and the danger to international peace, the emphatic decision urgently requesting South Africa to "abandon its policy of apartheid and racial discrimination" is legally based on the general powers of the Security Council, in conformity with paragraph 1 of Articles 24 and 25, and is not based concretely on the specific powers defined in Chapters VI and VII of the Charter.[10]

CONCLUSIONS DERIVED FROM THE PRACTICE OF THE SECURITY COUNCIL

From the cases examined, two conclusions can be drawn:

Even if the Council has not invoked Article 25 (except in the case of the Congo Resolution S/4426 mentioned above), several of its resolutions may be interpreted as a recognition of its own legal capacity to take binding decisions based on the general powers specified in that Article when such action could not have been related to Chapters VI, VII, VIII, or XII of the Charter, and even when the connection between the question decided and the maintenance of peace was extremely slight, as in the case of Trieste.[11]

When the connection between the subject of the resolution and the maintenance of international peace and security permits, juridically, the placing of the decision within the framework of Chapter VII (even without any direct reference to it in the text of the resolution), the Council has recognized its own competence to act for the general purpose of maintaining or restoring peace through decisions it deemed binding, even outside the concrete procedures specified in Chapter VII, such as those provided for in Articles 41, 42, 43, 46, and 47.[12]

NATURE OF SECURITY COUNCIL RECOMMENDATIONS RELATIVE TO THE MAINTENANCE OF INTERNATIONAL PEACE AND SECURITY
Theoretical Analysis

Thus far, this chapter has examined Decisions of the Security Council, that is, resolutions based on authority conferred by the Charter with the purpose of binding the members. But the Charter itself expressly provides that the Council may also act through recommendations, within the context of both Chapter VI (Articles 33, 36, 37, and 38), and Chapter VII (especially Article 39). It has been argued that resolutions by which the Council recommends measures to maintain or restore international peace and security, under Article 39, have a truly binding nature, and thus cannot be considered as recommendations in a substantive sense. Based on his famous conception of law as a coercive order, Kelsen maintains that: "In order to establish a legal obligation, a sanction must be attached to the contrary behaviour. And if a sanction is attached to a certain behaviour, the contrary behaviour is the content of an obligation. . . ." Thus, an order by the Security Council will constitute a legal obligation if the opposite conduct, noncompliance with the Council's order, is under a sanction provided for by the Charter. "Under Article 39," adds Kelsen, "the Security Council may consider noncompliance with its recommendation . . . to be a threat to the peace and take enforcement action. If such enforcement action is interpreted to be a sanction, then it must be assumed that the Members are under the obligation to comply with a 'recommendation' (of the Council)."[13]

Kelsen admits (as he does frequently throughout his work) that his interpretation is questionable and that it does not exclude others. In fact, he himself qualifies that interpretation when he rests it on the hypothetical premise that the enforcement action of the Security Council be considered a "sanction" in the legal sense. When Kelsen later examines[14] whether the enforcement measures the Security Council may take in conformity with Article 39 constitute either sanctions in the legal sense—that is, a reaction against the violation of a legal obligation established by the Charter—or purely political measures that the Council may apply at its discretion to maintain or restore peace, he admits the possibility of both theses and sets forth in detail the arguments in favor of each. However, he concludes that to consider enforcement measures taken by the Council as discretional political measures, and not as sanctions, is more in conformity with the general tendency that prevailed in drafting the Charter—the predominance of the political over the legal approach.

The Charter, contrary to the Covenant of the League of Nations (Article 16), does not establish any automatic collective action of the members, even against a recognized aggressor. The action of the Security Council is not punitive: the Council may choose not to take action against the Charter violator if, in its discretion, it feels that universal peace is thereby better preserved; or, on the other hand, the Council may take action not based on the illegal character of a state's conduct. As Kelsen states elsewhere,[15] "The purpose of the enforcement action under Article 39 is not to maintain or restore the law, but to maintain or restore peace, which is not necessarily identical with the law."[16]

Consequently, if conduct in violation of a recommendation of the Council (that is, noncompliance with its recommendation) is not subject to a sanction in the legal sense, it cannot be maintained that the recommended behavior constitutes the contents of a legal obligation.

Moreover, as Malintoppi correctly stresses, even admitting the hypothesis that enforcement measures may be interpreted as sanctions, this would not be proof of the binding force of the recommendation. The connection between the initial recommendation not complied with and eventual enforcement measures is too slight and indirect. The "enforcement action eventually ordered by the Council because of the noncompliance with one of its recommendations does not depend on the fact, considered in itself, of the incompatibility between the requested conduct and that actually pursued by the addressee of the recommendation. It depends rather on the fact, substantially different from the former, that such incompatibility of conduct has given rise to a situation which threatens the peace."[17] What produces the enforcement action is the *objective* situation of a threat to the peace created *inter alia* by noncompliance with a recommendation; although the unobserved recommendation is certainly an important element in a complex situation, it cannot be evaluated in isolation and, above all, it cannot give rise, of itself, to a legal obligation.

Conclusions Derived from the Practice of the Security Council

It is difficult to establish whether a Security Council recommendation is binding. The binding force of such a recommendation was upheld by Great Britain before the International Court of Justice in the Corfu Channel case without conclusive results, since the Court did not rule specifically on this point.[18] In addition, a complete study of the practice of the Security Council does not demonstrate convincingly that this organ considered any of its recommendations as binding.

On one occasion, however, the Council did base a recommendation for military measures (resolution of June 27, 1950) on the fact, among others, that the North Korean authorities had not complied with the "call" made to them in a previous resolution (of June 25) to cease hostilities and to withdraw north of the 38th parallel. In view of what was said above on the nature of enforcement action and on the objective and complex character of a situation determining the adoption of enforcement measures, it could not be concluded that the initial resolution of the Council was binding just because a subsequent resolution was based on it.[19]

Other Possible Effects of Security Council Recommendations

Once it is accepted as a general proposition that the Council can make true recommendations concerning the maintenance or the restoration of peace, in accordance with Article 39, there remains a related question, deriving both from the text of the Charter provisions and from the practice of the organs: can some recommendations on this subject have binding effects, and if so, can these effects have a legal basis different from that examined above?

It is possible that some Council recommendations may have as a legal effect the *suspension* of the general obligation to refrain from the threat or use of force (in accordance with Article 2 [4]), when such conduct is *recommended* by the United Nations. The same situation also may be viewed from the opposite angle: the effects of a recommendation addressed to a state which, according to a Council determination, has violated the obligation of Article 2(4), and which is requested, by means of a recommendation, to restore the *status quo ante*. These two problems will be considered below, when the scope and legal effects of certain recommendations related to the maintenance of peace are examined in general. An effort will be made then to clarify the difference between such recommendations depending on whether they emanate from the Security Council or the General Assembly.

COMPETENCE OF THE SECURITY COUNCIL TO RECOMMEND ENFORCEMENT MEASURES

A related question, which has also been a matter of controversy, is whether the adoption of enforcement measures by the Security

Council can be constitutionally *recommended,* or only ordered. Doubt stems both from the text of Article 39 of the Charter and from the probable intention of its drafters, as well as from the structural requirements of the Organization. In this case, as in many others, the generality and the frequent vagueness and contradictions of the Charter permit two or more interpretations. This has allowed the different organs, without encountering insurmountable obstacles, to choose the interpretation that seemed most in conformity with the needs of the Organization at a given moment.

Kelsen discussed this problem in examining the Council Resolution on Korea of June 26, 1950:

Article 39, it is true, authorises the Security Council, after it has determined the existence of a threat to, or breach of, the peace, to "make recommendations" without restricting the content of these recommendations. But it is doubtful whether a recommendation of an enforcement action corresponds to the intention of those who framed the Charter. Article 39 distinguishes between " 'recommendations' and 'measures' . . . taken in accordance with Articles 41 and 42," which Articles provide enforcement measures involving or not involving the use of armed force. Making recommendations and taking enforcement measures are, within the meaning of Article 39, two different functions of the Security Council. If the Security Council, after having determined under Article 39 the existence of a threat to, or breach of, the peace, is of the opinion that enforcement measures are necessary to maintain or restore international peace, the Council must take these measures itself by acting under Article 41 or 42, that is to say, by ordering Members. . . . That means that enforcement measures under Article 39 can only be ordered by the Security Council, but not recommended.

However, the same author later adds that "it must be admitted that the wording of Article 39 does not exclude an interpretation according to which the Security Council may, under this Article, recommend to Members to use force and especially to use armed force."[20]

The action of the Security Council in the case of Korea,

particularly through the resolution of June 27, 1950, proved that the Council considered that it possessed constitutional competence to *recommend* the use of armed force, after having determined the existence of a breach of the peace. Since there has not been, up to the present, another instance of the Council recommending the use of armed force as an enforcement measure—that is, against a state (or *de facto* government) characterized as an aggressor or as responsible for a threat to or breach of the peace— the Council's interpretation, implicit in the Korea action, must be considered as its official interpretation on this issue.

THE UNITING FOR PEACE RESOLUTION
General Observations

The most important, but not unique, element in the strengthening of the United Nations collective security system was Resolution 377 (V) of the General Assembly, called "Uniting for Peace."

The opinion to be sustained here is that this Resolution could not of itself produce the legal consequence of altering the Charter system of collective security, but that it served as a point of departure, constituting the nucleus of a practice shaped during subsequent years through conscious and repeated acquiescence, tacit or stated, of all groups of members; and that by virtue of this practice, the prevailing legal situation concerning the United Nations collective security system differs, to an appreciable degree and in various respects, from the original system of the Charter.

According to the essential provision of the Uniting for Peace Resolution, the General Assembly

resolves that if the Security Council, because of lack of unanimity of the permanent members, fails to exercise its primary responsibility for the maintenance of international peace and security in any case where there appears to be a threat to the peace, breach of the peace, or act of aggression, the General Assembly shall consider the matter immediately with a view to making appropriate recommendations to Members for collective measures, including, in the case of a breach of the peace or act of aggression, the use of armed force when necessary, to maintain or restore international peace and security.

Among the various arguments in favor of the constitutionality of this resolution, the following has particular relevance:

First, Article 24 confers upon the Security Council the "primary" responsibility for the maintenance of international peace and security. This implies, logically and juridicially, that the Charter envisages a secondary responsibility, which can only devolve on the Assembly and which comes into play when the Council does not fulfill its role. Second, the functions vested in the Assembly, as provided by Article 10 read together with paragraph 4 of Article 11, are sufficiently broad to justify the competence of the Assembly to deal with matters of peace and security and to make appropriate recommendations concerning them. Third, the bestowal of primary—but not exclusive—responsibility on the Council rested on the assumption that it would be able to act effectively to maintain or restore peace; but when, in practice, an objective situation arose in the form of the Council's inability (owing to the veto) to fulfill its institutional functions, the secondary responsibility of the Assembly had to come into play to avoid the paralysis of the Organization.

Analysis of the Uniting for Peace
Resolution in the Light of Charter Provisions

This resolution can be examined, as will be done later, in the light of subsequent reactions of the members and of the practice of United Nations organs; but in order to evaluate the legal significance of the reaction, as well as the scope of the practice, it will also be necessary to make a judgment on the initial legality or illegality of the resolution; and this judgment must be made with exclusive reference to the only elements that could have been taken into account at the time of its adoption, the provisions of the Charter.

From this perspective, the legal arguments in favor of the constitutionality of the Resolution seem rather unsatisfactory, even granting that the vagueness and occasional ambiguity of the key provisions of the Charter in this field and the contradictory character of some of them, lend themselves, at least literally, to opposing interpretations.

Such is the case of the meaning attributed by those upholding the constitutionality of the Resolution to the term "primary" in Article 24 (and, by implication, to the term "secondary" used to denote the responsibility of the Assembly). Although such an interpretation is not contrary to the literal text of Article 24, an overall analysis of the entire system of distribution of powers between the two organs would lead rather to the conclusion that the responsibility of the Council is primary precisely because it alone has the power to take enforcement action; and that the reason the Charter did not use the term "exclusively" instead, was that it conferred other functions on the Assembly, different from enforcement action, but also pertaining to the maintenance of international peace and security.

It is also true that Articles 10 and 11(2) contain opposing provisions (as well as paragraphs 2 and 4 of Article 11, *inter se*), and that by a strictly literal interpretation it can be maintained that any of the two provisions (in each pair) abrogates or restricts the scope of the other. But there is no doubt that paragraph 2 of Article 11 is, from a logical and juridical point of view, of a more particular character; in other words, it is an exception to the general rule contained in Article 10. According to an old canon of interpretation, the particular rule, the exception, prevails over the general rule: *"lex specialis derogat generali."*[21]

Of course, this objection is not merely legalistic chicanery nor does it involve only the problem of which rule should prevail over the other. The whole Charter conception of collective security is legally based on the interplay of Articles 10 and 11 (2).

Similar observations can be made in connection with another essential question: the interpretation that, according to the Charter, should be given to the term "action" in the context of Article 11(2). It may be argued that the restrictive interpretation given to it by the drafters and those who were in favor of the Uniting for Peace Resolution—that "action" means only enforcement action that the Security Council may take under Chapter VII (Articles 39, 41, 42, and 43)—is not incompatible with the strict wording of Article 11(2). But as Kelsen says, "If such a specific and far-reaching restriction of the meaning of the term 'action' had been intended, the framers of the Charter would have probably expressed their intention in another way, and would not have chosen the simple word 'action.'"[22] According to the same author, however, the meaning of the term "action" that most likely corresponds to the intention of the framers of the Charter is the following: "enforcement action, i.e., any use of force, especially any use of armed force."[23]

Finally, for the Assembly to recommend the adoption of collective measures necessarily requires a prior "determination" that "a threat to the peace, a breach of the peace, or an act of aggression" has occurred. Article 39 confers that power exclusively on the Security Council, and no other provision bestows it on the Assembly. Here, too, the contention that the letter of Article 39 does not explicitly *forbid* the Assembly to exercise the function of "determining," is a purely verbal argument. This is not a case where the Charter is silent and which could therefore be resolved as though a lacuna existed. From a legal point of view, the specific and singular attribution of a function to one of the two organs means its denial to the other: *"expressio unius, exclusio alterius."* The prohibition *is* in the Charter.[24]

The most persuasive argument in favor of the resolution in question was undoubtedly the following: owing to the repeated use of the veto, there developed an objective situation in which the Council's institutional function of maintaining the peace remained unfulfilled. This argument, however, is more political than juridical.

The Charter envisaged the possibility that a veto might prevent the Council from taking action, despite the wish of the majority; thus, when nonaction is the result of the Council's deliberations, it must be considered as precisely the *institutional* solution provided for by the Charter. One cannot legally speak of nonfulfillment of functions when the Council acts within the provisions of the Charter. Nonaction because of the veto is one of the normal ways provided by the Charter for the Council to perform its institutional function. The reason is that for the framers of the Charter, nonaction might sometimes be the best way of safeguarding universal peace. Juridically, and even politically, abstaining from action is not necessarily synonymous with not preserving the peace. The entire system of the Charter was based on the foreknowledge and acceptance of this possibility. Reaching a negative conclusion because of a veto is not juridically equivalent, for example, to the Council's inability to meet, although their practical results might be the same. In the latter case, there is no decision of any kind, and one may speak of the Council's objective and institutional default. But if this organ, after deliberation, arrives at a negative conclusion owing either to the veto or to the lack of the necessary majority, the nonaction of the Council must be considered the legally proper solution for carrying out the aim of the Charter—maintenance of the peace.

In conclusion, from a strictly legal point of view, and with exclusive reference to the Charter provisions—the only existent standard for evaluating constitutionality at the time of the resolution's adoption—the Uniting for Peace Resolution must be considered contrary to the Charter. Only through an ultraliteral interpretation of each of the applicable provisions, isolating them artificially from their natural legal context and admitting as "possible" those interpretations that seem less plausible and less faithful to the intention of the framers of the Charter, might one accept the argument that these provisions were not violated.

Nor can it be maintained that the defenselessness of a victim of aggression resulting from the Council's inaction because of a veto is sufficient and decisive reason to silence any legal scruple and to admit the juridical validity of the Resolution. As rightly affirmed by René de Lacharrière in one of the most original and provocative studies on this topic, the proper legal remedy provided for by the Charter, when there is disagreement among the Great Powers, is collective self-defense. According to this author, under contemporary conditions, collective self-defense is more effective than the orthodox form of enforcement action available to the United Nations when the Great Powers do not agree on its use, as was shown by the action in Korea.[25]

The real justification of the Uniting for Peace Resolution is political, in the sense that political necessity should be a reason to modify the existing law, rather than to attempt to establish its legality *within* the juridical system in force at the time of its adoption. Only through universal or quasi-universal acceptance of the initially illegal basis of a resolution could a juridical norm be established over the course of time.

Analysis of the Uniting for Peace Resolution from the Political Point of View

On strictly political grounds, it may be said that the Uniting for Peace Resolution gave rise to a beneficent and desirable evolution of the collective security system of the Organization. First, Assembly action permits the more effective mobilization of public opinion in favor of the victim of an aggression. Second, a broadly representative organ (as Laski observed with respect to Parliament), is an irreplaceable forum for the discussion of general principles; and perhaps, it may be added, it permits more stress on considerations of permanent value. Because of the deliberative nature of the Assembly and its representative character, its resolutions facilitate the formation of a collective conscience and, eventually, the crystallization of currents and tendencies that, with time, may become new juridical norms.

Another important consequence of the new role of the Assembly is the greater democratization of the United Nations, as pointed out by a noted Latin-American jurist,[26] which has permitted more effective action on the part of the smaller and medium-sized powers in the defense of peace. Moreover, when the action of the Assembly proves to be ineffective, as in the case of Hungary, it at least makes clear who bears the legal and moral responsibility for conflicts.

The system established by the Uniting for Peace Resolution presents, however, certain risks. In any case, its application must be subject to serious political and legal limitations, whose observance is essential if the disadvantages of this new instrument are not to cancel out the advantages.

First, the Assembly is not the best forum for negotiations, for taking into account simultaneously the points of view of both sides and coming to mutually acceptable agreements. The very character of a deliberative body of such broad composition predisposes the majority to turn away from conciliatory efforts and to adopt measures that sometimes do not take minority interests sufficiently into account. This attitude, frequently adopted, can only lead to viable solutions if the majority disposes of the necessary means for politically and militarily enforcing such measures. But obviously, it is not adequate when a serious confrontation between the two great blocs arises, nor when the permanent solution of a matter requires mutual agreement. These limitations were not always observed in the case of Korea, with the negative consequences underlined in Lacharrière's article in *Politique Étrangère*. The peace-keeping function of the Organization was not enhanced by the Assembly's intervention, which was far from successful. The arrangements to end the armed conflict, whose terms reflected the military balance of the contestants, were not wrought or even vigorously debated by the Assembly; rather, they were in the end the result of a direct accord among the Great Powers principally concerned. From this essential point of view, such arrangements were also subject to the principle of unanimity, just as if they had been negotiated in the Security Council.

In conflicts in which the two blocs are radically opposed and which affect the vital interests of the main Great Powers, the new system can operate only under severe restrictions that limit its effectiveness. However, in a certain type of threshold situation, the system established by the Uniting for Peace Resolution may have a useful and important role: sometimes the Great Powers may veto in the Council certain resolutions they feel affect their interests, although perhaps not vitally; but faced with the mobilization of forces generated in the Assembly, they may finally accept a solution desired by the majority and thus permit the Organization to take effective action. This occurred in the Suez crisis and in certain aspects of the Congo operation.

APPLICATIONS OF THE UNITING FOR PEACE RESOLUTION

General Observations

The Uniting for Peace Resolution was not an operative resolution, since it did not determine the existence of a threat to or breach of the peace or an act of aggression; nor did it recommend to the members the adoption of collective or other measures relating to a specific situation.[27] In essence, the General Assembly resolved that, if the Security Council did not fulfill its responsibility in future cases of a threat to or breach of the peace or an act of aggression, the Assembly itself would examine the matter with a view to making appropriate recommendations.

From a technical point of view, it is difficult to determine the legal meaning and value of a pronouncement by which the Assembly *resolves* that in the future it will act in a certain way, since such a pronouncement obviously does not deprive the Assembly of its freedom to act differently. But aside from this incidental question, the Resolution may be considered, in essence, as the Assembly's interpretation of its legal capacity to act in the future according to the conditions set forth in the Resolution. In other words, the Assembly gave itself in the Uniting for Peace Resolution a legal framework for future action. In view of its nature, the Resolution could not by itself have generated changes in the Charter's system of collective security. The changes subsequently brought about were the consequence of the various specific actions carried out by the Organization on the basis of the Resolution.

The Case of Korea

The Uniting for Peace Resolution was first applied in General Assembly Resolution 498(V) of February 1, 1951. After noting that the situation foreseen in the Uniting for Peace Resolution had arisen (lack of unanimity of the permanent members of the Security Council), it determined (the Resolution used the term "finds") that the Central Government of the People's Republic of China had committed aggression in Korea; it requested that Chinese forces and nationals cease hostilities against the forces of the United Nations and that they withdraw from Korea; and it asked all states and authorities to continue lending every assistance "to the United Nations action in Korea." Since the request was made on the basis of a determination that China had committed aggression, Resolution 498(V) can be interpreted as a recommendation for the adoption of enforcement measures, in this case the use of armed force, against the Chinese forces present in Korea.

Another General Assembly Resolution of May 18, 1951 (500 [V]) recommended to all states that they establish an embargo on the export of weapons and strategic materials to the Chinese People's Republic and to North Korea. This Resolution was a logical sequel to the action previously taken.

These two resolutions alone do not explain the nature and meaning of the United Nations' collective action in Korea. As will now be seen, the different elements of the Organization's action were fused into an aggregate composed of the three initial resolutions of the Security Council, the important General Assembly Resolution 376 (V) of October 7, 1950, which preceded the Uniting for Peace Resolution, and the two Assembly Resolutions just mentioned. The report of the Collective Measures Committee (created by the Uniting for Peace Resolution), presented to the following regular session of the General Assembly (6th Session, 1951), also helps in evaluating the scope of the United Nations action.

The Security Council resolution of June 25, 1950 determined that the armed attack against the Republic of Korea constituted a breach of the peace, and requested the cessation of hostilities and the withdrawal of North Korean troops to the 38th parallel. The resolution of June 27 recommended to members that they help the Republic of Korea to repel the armed attack and to restore international peace and security "in the area"; that of July 7 created a Unified Command for the military forces, requested the United States to appoint a commander for the forces, and authorized the Unified Command to use the flag of the United Nations at its discretion. After the objective of repelling the armed attack to the 38th parallel was achieved several months later, the opportunity arose to continue military operations north of that parallel with the object of destroying the

North Korean forces as combat units, and of militarily occupying North Korea. As it did not seem possible to obtain the approval of the Security Council on this action (owing to the return of the Soviet representative to the Council), the Assembly provided the necessary authorization through Resolution 376 (V) of October 7, 1950, which recommended that "all appropriate steps be taken to ensure conditions of stability throughout Korea." This provision of the Assembly Resolution constitutes an essential complement to the Council Resolution of June 27, which had established the objective of United Nations action as being "to repel the armed attack and to restore international peace and security in the area." Since the Council had not specified what should be understood by "area," the Assembly interpreted it to mean "all of Korea." The Assembly thus defined an essential element of the politico-military objective of the United Nations action, and in that sense, its resolution became integrated into that of the Council.

The six resolutions on Korea thus constitute an aggregate in that their provisions mutually complement, sustain, and articulate each other. From the overall analysis of these resolutions, several conclusions can be drawn concerning the role assumed by the Organization and the scope and value it claimed for its resolutions. For the time being, these conclusions will be examined independently of their legal effects since those effects depend partly on the reaction and attitudes of states vis-à-vis such resolutions— a matter that will be considered separately below. These conclusions are the following:

1. The United Nations clearly assumed that it was acting within Chapter VII of the Charter, that is, that it was taking enforcement measures. In effect, both the Council and the Assembly made the basis of their respective actions the determination regarding the existence of a breach of the peace or an act of aggression; in the case of the Council, this determination was made

in accordance with Article 39, the foundation for the enforcement measures authorized by Chapter VII. Several members supporting the three Council resolutions believed that they represented an intervention under Chapter VII, and especially under Article 39, even though that provision had not been explicitly invoked.[28] Moreover, the Council had recommended that members providing military forces should put them at the disposal of the Unified Command, which directed the military operations, used the United Nations flag, periodically informed the Organization about the progress of operations, and finally negotiated the armistice in the name of the United Nations. All these activities seem incompatible with the conception of the Korean action as collective self-defense. Furthermore, the military operations were not limited to repelling armed attack, which is the characteristic objective of self-defense. The Assembly authorized carrying them beyond the point of repelling attack to militarily occupying additional territory.[29] Finally, the Assembly recommended an embargo on the export of weapons and strategic materials to China and North Korea, which constitutes, at the least, an enforcement measure and, at the most, a sanction in the legal sense.

In spite of their coercive character, all these measures were asked for through recommendations, except, significantly, the request to cease hostilities and to withdraw troops, in which the imperative term "calls upon" was used.

2. Both organs recommended the adoption of collective enforcement measures but they did not organize, nor did they carry out, the military action in the manner specifically provided for in Articles 42 and 43 of the Charter. The Resolutions clearly showed that, not only was it possible for the two organs to take a different type of enforcement action (as opposed to that stipulated in Articles 42 and 43), but also that they deliberately organized the execution of enforcement measures according to a different pattern, in view of the practical impossibility of acting

in the manner provided for in the Charter.[30] In the beginning, a certain degree of improvisation was inevitable; but as the action in Korea developed, new methods of action and new procedures were deliberately put into effect by the Security Council and complemented in part by the Assembly. In a short time, they came to be considered by a great majority of members as an unavoidable and adequate substitute for the procedures of Articles 42 and 43, and even as a system with a certain claim to permanent validity, or at least as a model for future action.

The conclusions of the Collective Measures Committee, created by the Uniting for Peace Resolution to study methods that could be employed to strengthen international peace and security, are illustrative in this respect. In its first report to the Assembly, the Committee recommended the following: if the United Nations decided on the adoption of collective measures in the future, there should be created, until the Military Staff Committee provided for in Article 47 was able to fulfill its functions, an agency responsible for the direction and conduct of military operations; it should have power to coordinate the efforts of individual states and to organize the forces and facilities offered, in order to initiate effective military operations against the aggressor with a minimum delay. The report also proposed that a state or a group of states be authorized to act on behalf of the Organization, as an Executive Military Authority.[31] In general terms, according to Goodrich and Simons, the Collective Measures Committee incorporated in its recommendations the fundamentals of the Korean experience.[32]

The Assembly did not explicitly approve the conclusions of the Committee; it merely took note of them (Resolution 503 [VI], section A). However, the very formulation of the report and the debates that resulted from it in the Assembly strengthened the impression that, in the opinion of a considerable majority of Members, the Organization could carry out collective measures of a coercive nature, including the use of force, according to procedures and formulas totally dissimilar from those provided for in Articles 42, 43, and 47 of the Charter.

Moreover, as already indicated, the Uniting for Peace Resolution itself recommended that members maintain troops ready to serve as United Nations units, not only on the recommendation of the Council but also on that of the Assembly, that is, outside the arrangements of Articles 42 and 43. Although only a few states implemented this recommendation, its adoption proves that in the view of the Assembly, collective security could be built upon principles and procedures different from those anticipated in the Charter.

The Cases of Hungary and Suez

Subsequent applications of the Uniting for Peace Resolution were the result of the Soviet armed intervention in Hungary and of the invasion of Egypt by Israeli, French, and British troops. In both cases, the situation foreseen in the Resolution (veto in the Security Council) arose, and the General Assembly met in separate emergency sessions called concurrently during the first ten days of November 1956. The Assembly continued to be seized of both these matters throughout its 11th Regular Session.

In the case of Hungary, the Assembly repeatedly condemned the Soviet military intervention in strong terms, explicitly invoking on one occasion the obligation of Article 2(4) of the Charter (Resolution 1127 [XI]), and urged repeatedly that the Soviet Union withdraw "all of its forces without delay" from Hungarian territory. Some of these resolutions on Hungary were significant in establishing the competence of the Assembly to act in matters concerning the maintenance of peace; but since it did not recommend that members contribute armed forces for collective action, and took no enforcement action whatsoever, the resolutions adopted had no relevance as contributive factors in building the new system of collective security.

In the case of the invasion of Egypt, although the Assembly did not make an explicit determination that a threat to or breach of the peace or an act of aggression had occurred, it did "[take] note that . . . the armed forces of Israel have penetrated deeply into Egyptian territory . . . and that the armed forces of France and . . . Great Britain . . . are conducting military operations against Egyptian territory" (Resolution 997 [ES-I]). In this and in subsequent resolutions, the Assembly urged the parties "as a matter of greatest urgency" to cease hostilities; and it repeatedly urged France, Great Britain, and Israel to withdraw their forces, behind the armistice lines in the case of the last and from "Egyptian territory" in the case of the first two (Resolution 1002 [ES-I]). Moreover, the Assembly established a United Nations Command for an Emergency Force, whose purpose was to "secure and supervise the cessation of hostilities." Subsequently, the Assembly directed that the Force be stationed on "the Egyptian-Israeli demarcation line" established by the Armistice . . . with a view to assist in achieving situations conducive to the maintenance of peaceful conditions in the area" (Resolution 1125 [XI]).

From the texts of the Resolutions and from the circumstances under which they were adopted, it is clear that the objective sought through the creation of the Emergency Force was not essentially military in character, but political.[33] The action taken by the Assembly was not an enforcement action in the sense that military measures were taken against a state, nor was it directed toward the coercive execution of its initial resolution of November 2, 1956 (997 [ES-I]).

In the case of Bizerte, the same situation provided for in the Uniting for Peace Resolution again arose and the General Assembly met in emergency session; but it contented itself with reaffirming the content of a resolution vetoed in the Security

Council (of July 22, 1961), urging a cease-fire and the withdrawal of armed forces to their original positions, and requesting immediate negotiations between Tunis and France.

The Congo Operation

The Organization took a series of strong measures with regard to the Congo that are directly related to the topic under study. The principal action of the Organization was taken by the Security Council, which defined the aims of United Nations intervention and initiated the operation through the authorization and instructions it gave the Secretary-General. The General Assembly, meeting on one occasion in an emergency session because of veto in the Security Council, adopted Resolution 1474, Rev. I (ES-IV) of September 21, 1960. In its regular session, the Assembly adopted several other resolutions on the substance of the case, in addition to those dealing with the financing of the operation. The Assembly's aim was to reaffirm with its authority essential Council resolutions, and on occasion, to complement the Council's action.

The Security Council also authorized the creation of a United Nations Force (ONUC), whose mandate, owing to successive and complementary authorizations, became considerably broader than that of the Emergency Force in Egypt. In the terms of the important resolution of February 21, 1961, the Security Council "request[ed] that the United Nations take immediately all appropriate measures to prevent the occurrence of civil war in the Congo, including . . . the use of force, if necessary, in the last resort."[34] The Council resolution of November 24, 1961 authorized the "Secretary-General to take vigorous action, including the use of requisite measures of force if necessary, for the immediate apprehension, detention pending legal action and/or deportation of all foreign military and paramilitary personnel and political advisers not under the United Nations Command, and mercenaries. . . ."

These forms of using force did not constitute, as recognized by the International Court of Justice, "enforcement measures" against a state under Chapter VII of the Charter; nor were the armed forces used in the Congo authorized to take military measures against any state. But their function was obviously more than that of a body of observers, a force stationed along an armistice line, or police maintaining law and order. The Force was authorized to take military action, that is, to engage in combat and to occupy parts of the country militarily, if the Secretary-General deemed it necessary (as indeed occurred) in order to achieve two of the specific aims assigned to it: to avoid a civil war and to solve permanently the problem of unauthorized foreign military personnel and mercenaries.

The United Nations operation in the Congo constitutes one more link in the practice of the Organization that reinforces the Assembly's authority to act to maintain peace. But it does not additionally strengthen the Council's authority to decide on the use of armed force as an enforcement measure against a state through procedures other than those specifically mentioned in Articles 42 and 43. The legal significance of the Congo action is therefore very different from that of the action in Korea.

Yet, the legal basis for the use of force in the Congo offers special problems. Recognizing that it did not have a coercive character far from exhausts the matter. There is no doubt that, at least after February 21, 1961, the Force was authorized to take real military action on behalf of the United Nations; on the other hand, neither is there doubt that the only use of armed force on behalf of the United Nations provided for in the Charter is that of enforcement action under Chapter VII. Although it is true that the military operations in the Congo were not directed against a state, they were directed against important groups of foreigners identified by the Council's Resolution (foreign military or paramilitary personnel or mercenaries not under the United Nations Command) or against the rival factions that could prevent attainment of the goal of avoiding civil war, some of which were politically organized and exercised *de facto* control over entire parts of the country. The powers enjoyed by the Force were considered sufficient for it to take military initiatives resulting, *in extremis,* in the destruction as combat units of the forces opposed to the two aims specified by the Council. In practice, the point is easily reached where it is very difficult to distinguish, as in the Congo, a large-scale police action from a military action with limited objectives.

The most important element in evaluating the legal meaning of the operation in the Congo is the essential aim, the basic objective sought through military action. This objective was fundamentally and immediately internal, although in a long-range perspective, it could be considered international: to avoid a large-scale civil war that might overflow its national boundaries and become an international conflict. In order to attain this objective, it was necessary to eliminate foreign elements and prevent an armed struggle among rival factions, by military action if necessary. The nature of this military action was, therefore, conditioned by the established objectives.

As already stated, this objective was directly domestic and indirectly international: to prevent enlargement of the civil war *in order to* preserve international peace. In the view of the International Court of Justice, the question was "to assure the peaceful solution of the [Congo's domestic] situation"; but, at the same time, the Security Council recognized that "the complete restoration of law and order in the Republic of the Congo would effectively contribute to the maintenance of international peace and security." Furthermore, the primary aim of United Nations intervention was "the maintenance of the territorial integrity and the political independence of the Republic of the Congo."

Considering the complex character of the objective of the Congo military action, with its clearly international aspects, the legal basis of the limited use of armed force can be found in the specific powers granted to the Security Council by Chapter VII, and, more concretely, in Article 40, since the adoption of the measures in question was intended mainly to avoid any aggravation of the situation.[35] On the other hand, other related measures of an internal nature, such as the convening of Parliament and the reorganization of the Congolese army, as indicated, can be derived from the general powers of the Council under Article 24 (1) and Article 25.

In conclusion, the United Nations operation in the Congo, although not coercive, was a case of the use of armed force on behalf of the United Nations, undertaken outside the only procedures and mechanisms contemplated in the Charter for the use of force by the Organization. The aim pursued by the United Nations in creating the Force was so close to the Organization's general aim of maintaining international peace and security, that this form of using armed force can be considered an additional instrument of collective security, or better still, a *sui generis* procedure of collective security required by the needs of an unprecedented situation, and which undoubtedly was not foreseen by the framers of the Charter.[36]

Comparison of the Egyptian and Congo Interventions

The juridical significance of the United Nations action in Egypt is similar, or better, parallel, to that in the Congo. In Egypt, too, the Organization created a collective military force and authorized its use, which ultimately means an authorization to use armed force in the name of the United Nations, even if its intention is noncoercive. The differences between the mandates of the two Forces reflect the diversity of the immediate political problems that their use was purported to solve. But the essential element common to both actions—which characterizes them as steps in a single evolutionary process—is that the Organization authorized the use of armed force in its name, for noncoercive purposes, *as a decisive contribution to the maintenance of international peace and security*. Their distinguishing element was the organ that authorized the action: in Egypt, it was the Assembly, and in the Congo, the Council; but there was no essential difference in the content of the two actions from the point of view of their juridical significance.

ACQUIESCENCE BY GROUPS OF MEMBER STATES IN THE APPLICATIONS OF THE UNITING FOR PEACE RESOLUTION

The Uniting for Peace Resolution was passed in the Assembly by a strong majority, in the face of opposition by the five states that at the time formed the Socialist bloc. Resolution 376 (V) (adopted before the Uniting for Peace Resolution), implicitly authorizing the military occupation of North Korea by United Nations troops, had been adopted under similar circumstances. Resolution 498 (V) of February 1, 1951 (based explicitly on the Uniting for Peace Resolution), by which the Assembly declared the People's Republic of China to be an aggressor in Korea, was passed with the sole opposition of the five states of the Soviet bloc, as was Resolution 500 (V), which established an embargo on the export of armaments and strategic materials to China and North Korea, and which may be considered a corollary of Resolution 498 (V).

In the case of Egypt, the attitude of the Soviet Union and the other Socialist countries was more complex and difficult to evaluate, and sometimes appeared contradictory.

When the combined veto of Great Britain and France successively prevented the adoption of an American and then of a Soviet proposal in the Security Council, Yugoslavia proposed the convening of an emergency session of the General Assembly on the basis of the Uniting for Peace Resolution. In spite of its prior repeated opposition to that Resolution, the Soviet Union voted in favor of this clear, direct, and concrete application of it.[37]

It is not easy to derive from this vote, in itself, a clear legal consequence. The Danish government maintained before the International Court of Justice that the Soviet Union, by its acquiescence in the Security Council's resolution to refer the matter to the Assembly on the basis of the Uniting for Peace Resolution, was legally estopped from denying the legality of the Emergency Force in Egypt.[38] The Soviet government retorted that its delegation had been in favor solely of the Assembly's making "suitable recommendations," which could not include the use of force, since that was exclusively the responsibility of the Security Council.[39]

During the debate in the Assembly, representatives of the Socialist countries repeatedly maintained that "the creation of the Emergency Force was a violation of the Charter" since the Security Council alone could, on the basis of Chapter VII, create an international armed force.[40] But in spite of this stand, those countries did not vote against the various resolutions pertaining to the Force. They voted in favor of Resolution 997 (ES-I), which called for a cease-fire; they abstained on Resolution 998 (SE-I), which called on the Secretary-General to submit to the Assembly within 48 hours a plan for the creation of the Force; they also abstained on Resolution 1000 (ES-I), which established the Emergency Force, and on Resolution 1001 (ES-I), which approved the guiding principles for its organization and functioning. The Soviet representative stated that the only reason for his abstention, instead of a negative vote, was that Egypt, the victim of the aggression, had accepted the presence of the Force on her territory.

Moreover—and this confirms the fact that such abstentions cannot be interpreted as insurmountable opposition to the legality of the Emergency Force—some Socialist countries offered armed contingents to serve in the Force,[41] and even asked to be represented in the Advisory Committee created by Resolution 1001 (ES-I) to assist the Secretary-General in certain aspects of its planning and operation.[42]

The categorical statements of the Soviet delegates represent, undoubtedly, an important general stand on the question of the legality or illegality of international forces created outside the provisions of Articles 42, 43, 46, and 47 of the Charter. But they do not suffice to invalidate the legal significance of the votes—which are the specific means provided by the Charter for states to express their consent legally—and of other actions of a contrary character. The combined effect of the Soviet Union's vote in favor of referring the case from the Security Council to the Assembly, on the basis of the Uniting for Peace Resolution, and the Socialist states' not voting against the creation of the Force, and their offering contingents to serve in it, could justify the view that their attitude, interpreted as a whole, reveals—and legally means—at least their clear tolerance of the Assembly's creation and use of such an armed force, with no enforcement purposes, by other means than those specified in Chapter VII.

Concerning the Security Council's recommendations for the use of armed force against governments guilty of a breach of the peace or an act of aggression, but outside the framework of Articles 42, 43, 46, and 47, the Soviet Union and other Socialist states invoked the illegality of the resolutions adopted in the case of Korea, citing both procedural reasons (the illegal representation of China and the absence of a permanent member) and substantive ones (the Korean conflict was a civil war). The legal incapacity of the Security Council to use armed force other than that provided for in Articles 42, 43, etc., did not receive the same emphasis, because the other Soviet objections were logically of a preliminary nature. But in any case, the Soviet representatives always insisted that "the USSR does not recognize the United Nations Unified Command nor its so-called special reports."[43]

The Central Government of the People's Republic of China, on the other hand, dealt officially with the authority appointed by the Security Council, the Unified Command, recognizing it as such; it established contacts with representatives appointed by the General Assembly to negotiate the end of the conflict; it sent representatives to the Security Council; it addressed several complaints to the United Nations about the violation of its territory; and, finally, it signed the armistice with the Unified Command as representative of the United Nations.[44]

Despite its refusal to recognize the Unified Command, the Soviet Union approved, through a favorable vote in the General Assembly, the armistice reached by the United Nations, North Korea, and the Chinese Volunteers.[45]

This acceptance of the role of the United Nations as a belligerent in Korea necessarily implies, in the last instance, the recognition of the competence of the organs that assigned that role, and of the legal capacity of the authorities created by such organs to act on behalf of the United Nations by directing military operations and by negotiating to bring them to an end. In other words, *it implies tolerance of the use of force by the United Nations outside the provisions of Chapter VII of the Charter.*

Finally, the Security Council's decisions providing for the use of force in the Congo, although differing essentially in purpose from those concerning Korea, were actually accepted by all the United Nations members, either directly, in the Council, or indirectly, through the emphatic support of the General Assembly.

THE CREATION OF CUSTOMARY LAW WITHIN
THE PARTICULAR NORMATIVE ORDER OF THE
UNITED NATIONS; MEANING AND SCOPE
OF THE MEMBERS' ACQUIESCENCE

What are the meaning and scope of the members' acquiescence, in successive instances, which complemented one another and directly or indirectly resulted in the modification of certain essential rules of the Charter's system of collective security?[46]

It is evident, on the basis of what has been stated, that the action of the organs in some of the cases referred to above, could not *ab initio* have been based directly on the Charter. Therefore, the possibility that the potential rule implicit in the new practice of the organs, which differs from the original charter rule, may become a new legal norm, valid for the future, depends on proving that this new practice is likely to change the original rules of the system. Regarding the provisions of a multilateral treaty, this transformation may take place only if it is shown that the parties to the treaty have given their consent, express or tacit, to the modification in question.

The Charter provides, as do other multilateral treaties, certain special procedures for the formal modification of its provisions (Articles 108 and 109). But it is not unusual within normative systems of a constitutional nature, especially those as comprehensive and general as the Charter, that new norms are created, parallel to or outside the formal reform procedure, that reflect the will of members to adapt gradually the original system to changing circumstances and needs. These new norms are manifested or externalized through the practice of the organs, especially in unprecedented situations, by extensive interpretation of the original norms. To the extent that it can be shown that the heterodox practice of the organs faithfully reflects the will of the members, there is no essential legal obstacle preventing the reform of the original normative system outside the ordinary formal procedures provided for its modification.[47]

Of course, the most important problems lie in defining what should be understood by the "will of the members" within the concrete politico-juridical frame in which this concept is used; in evaluating, quantitatively as well as qualitatively, the manifestations of the will of the members, in view of the essential aims and principles sought by the normative system in question; and, finally, in determining the legal appropriateness of the modes of expressing the members' will to bring about changes in the pre-existent juridical situation.

The phenomenon that prima facie would seem applicable to this situation is the creation of new rules through custom. It is not infrequent that new customary rules originate spontaneously within a given normative system and that they eventually annul or modify pre-existent conventional rules. However, in studying whether this phenomenon can serve to explain the transformations in the United Nations system of collective security, the following initial consideration should be kept in mind:

The creation of customary international law is a phenomenon that has taken place within a milieu that might be characterized as natural and proper. This is the general legal order of unorganized international society, a decentralized and scarcely institutionalized system, lacking organs specifically entrusted with the creation of law. These characteristics of international society give full meaning to the two conditions traditionally required by general international law for the creation of customary rules: the generalized repetition of acts and the *opinio juris vel necessitatis.*

In examining the applicability of this creative process within a particular legal order (the law of the United Nations) that is relatively institutionalized and operates through the action of organs with pre-established competence, and in which the consent of the members is clearly and deliberately expressed in specific predetermined ways, it is logical to conclude that the conditions for the birth of customary rules must be different in scope and must be interpreted, not in their traditional form, but in a way consistent with the characteristics of this order.

Thus, when the objective element of custom (the practice of states) is externalized through the concrete attitudes of states vis-à-vis the resolutions of organs, whose meaning, implications, and consequences have been discussed and considered before their adoption, it is natural that the repetition of a great number of acts should not be required in order to consider that a "practice" has begun.[48]

The subjective element—the conviction that those repeated acts are, according to international law, obligatory or right—acquires a special meaning when the legal order within which a custom is taking shape establishes certain precise and predetermined forms for the expression of the will of states: primarily, the vote, and secondarily, the publicly expressed reasons for it. In this legal order a peculiar situation exists: an act (whose repetition might generate a custom), carried out without the conviction of its legality, is inconceivable. It would be absurd to accept as a normal working hypothesis that states can vote in favor of actions they consider antijuridical. Furthermore, with all due reservations, one could reasonably venture the suggestion that the vote cast by a state in favor of a proposed resolution is necessarily based on a *juris et de jure* assumption, that is, on a legal fiction that does not admit contrary proof: the conviction of the legality of the resolution in favor of which the vote has been cast. Within the particular legal order of the United Nations, the existence of the subjective element of a custom does not practically require further proof than an established pattern of votes.

With the terms of the problem thus outlined, the thesis could be advanced, albeit with a certain margin of doubt, that the practice of the organs has created—and from another angle, that it reflects and expresses—one or more customary rules (whose precise contents will be studied later on) concerning the United Nations system of collective security, which diverge from the original rules of the Charter. In any case, there is no doubt that all the groups of states and practically all countries, individually considered, who were members when these developments came into being, accepted expressly or tacitly the diverse aspects of these new rules.

The acquiescence of the various members was given in connection with the Security Council's initial action or the Assembly's confirmatory and complementary action; it referred to the Uniting for Peace Resolution itself, or to one or more specific applications of it; and it was manifested either through votes or through a form of tacit recognition of the legal capacity of the Organization to act in a certain manner. Owing to this diversity of forms for expressing the members' consent, and also to the successive, complementary, and integrative character of the different phases of this creative process, it would be difficult to determine at what precise moment the new rule came into being.[49] It would seem better to consider the diverse complementary actions of the Council and of the Assembly as an organic whole, formed by the juxtaposed consents of states, to which could be attributed the creation of the new rule.

CONTENT OF THE NEW RULE ON COLLECTIVE SECURITY

The content or object of this new rule, or rather, of this new system of rules, may be formulated thus:

1. The Security Council, having determined that there is a threat to the peace, a breach of the peace, or an act of aggression, may *recommend*[50] the adoption of enforcement measures, includ-

ing the use of armed force, on behalf of the United Nations, and
directed against states or *de facto* governments, *without following the procedures and observing the requirements established in
Chapter VII of the Charter for the use of armed force.* This
means that members can make available to the Council armed
forces in accordance with procedures different from the special
agreements contemplated in Article 43; that plans for the use of
such armed forces need not be drawn up with the assistance of
the Military Staff Committee, as provided in Article 46; and that
the strategic direction of armed forces made available for enforcement action need not necessarily be the responsibility of the
Military Staff Committee, as set forth in Article 47.[51]

2. The General Assembly can *recommend*, when there is
lack of unanimity among the Permanent Members of the Security
Council, and when there has arisen in the Assembly's opinion a
threat to the peace, breach of the peace, or act of aggression, the
adoption of enforcement measures, including the use of armed
force in the event of an armed attack or an act of aggression, on
behalf of the United Nations and directed against states or *de
facto* governments, also without observing the procedures and
requirements of Chapter VII for the use of armed force.

3. Both the Security Council and the General Assembly
may *decide, without* a previous determination that a threat to or
breach of the peace or an act of aggression exists, to create a
United Nations military force to carry out *nonenforcement
functions*, without complying with the procedures and requirements of Chapter VII for the use of armed force; and they may
recommend—but may not legally require—that members contribute contingents to establish it. The functions of a United
Nations Force may range from mere observation and supervision
to the undertaking of typically military operations, such as en-
gaging in battle with armed groups for the purpose of destroying
them as combat units, as occurred in the Congo.[52]

Up to the present there has not been a single instance in the practice of the United Nations that could serve as a legal basis for a new rule authorizing the General Assembly to recommend the use of armed force, without the legal support of the Uniting for Peace Resolution, even for nonenforcement purposes.[53]

BINDING LEGAL EFFECTS OF THE NEW RULES ON COLLECTIVE SECURITY

The legal effect of the new rule, per se, is the broadening of the competence of both the Council and the Assembly to act in a manner different from that originally contemplated in the Charter. The degree to which this competence was enlarged is indicated by the three principles suggested above. It is possible to speak of a legal effect because there has been a modification of a pre-existent legal situation, although, from a different point of view, the change in the competence of the organs constitutes *not the effect but the very content* of the new rule created by the practice of the Organization.[54]

The second effect is of a diverse nature. Actually, it is a question here of a legal effect directly produced by the resolutions adopted by the Security Council or General Assembly on the basis of the customary rule created by their practice, rather than a direct effect of that rule as such. This effect consists in the *temporary suspension of the Charter obligation of members to refrain from the use of force against any state,* in conformity with Article 2(4). That certain Council or Assembly recommendations concerning the use of force should have as an effect the suspension of the Charter obligation not to use it, is a consequence of the new rule created by the practice of the organs.

The purpose of this type of recommendation is to bring about conduct involving the use of force. The legal effect is thus a change in the pre-existent legal situation. What is legally relevant in this context is not the use of force in itself, but rather the question of whether such use of force violates a legal obligation. Since the general Charter prohibition against the use of force was the pre-existent situation, the legal effect contemplated here is the liberation of members from this obligation. The change is brought about *ipso iure*, as an effect of the adoption of the resolution and with respect to all its addressees, and not as a consequence of compliance with the recommendation by each of the states individually.

The reason why this unusual and specific effect can be attributed to the new rule can only be perceived in the case of a recommendation. A later exceptional obligation prevails over a previous general one, especially when it originates in the decision of an organ created by the same instrument that established the general obligation. But it could not be maintained, within the original Charter system, that a nonbinding recommendation could have, per se, the effect of derogating or annulling an express provision of the Charter, especially such a significant one as that prohibiting the use of force. Thus the only basis for justifying this unusual effect is the unanimous or near-unanimous acceptance of a practice, whereby force was in fact used in the name of the United Nations, in compliance with recommendations presumably voted for by members convinced of their legality.

The third effect is present only under certain circumstances. The resolutions of the Council or the Assembly providing for the use of force are usually linked to a situation that may produce a special effect. In Korea, as well as in Egypt, the situation that provoked the intervention of the Organization was an armed invasion. An essential element of the key resolutions in both cases was the United Nations call for withdrawal of the invading forces. In Hungary and in the Congo, the situation was somewhat different in origin, since the initial presence of foreign troops was not the result of an invasion; but the crisis reached the stage of United Nations intervention after both governments had respectively requested the withdrawal of the troops, an act that was one of the crucial factors in the situation. Therefore, the element common to all four cases was the presence of foreign troops; an aggravating influence in the cases of Korea and Egypt was the fact that this presence had its origin in an illegal act of force.

In each of these four cases, the resolutions adopted (whether by the Council or the Assembly) repeatedly requested the withdrawal of foreign troops in emphatic terms appropriate to a compulsory request and not to a recommendation. The imperative calls of the Council in that sense may easily be considered true binding decisions.[55] Their binding force can be based directly on Article 25 of the Charter, although they may have been adopted under Chapter VII.

The resolutions of the Assembly requesting the withdrawal of troops present greater problems. Their binding force is not patent and their basis is less direct and evident. However, admitting that a reasonable margin of doubt exists, it is possible to propound the thesis that peremptory calls by the Assembly for withdrawal of troops have a binding character, that is, that they legally oblige their addressee to carry out the request.

The first pertinent consideration in suggesting this thesis, although not a decisive one, is the imperative language used by the Assembly, which reveals the will and the intention of an order. Obviously, this in itself could not establish the binding force of these resolutions, although it is not completely without legal relevance.

The principal reason on which to base their binding character is the following: the purpose of such Assembly resolutions is to specify, actualize, and apply to a concrete situation the general, pre-existing obligation established by the Charter to refrain from the use of force. The illegal and continued military occupation of another state's territory is, *in itself*, a "use of force against the territorial integrity or political independence of any state" and, as such, a violation of the explicit and unconditional prohibition of Article 2(4). The correlative legal obligation "to refrain" from recourse to force is complied with, in this context, by the immediate cessation of its use, that is, by the immediate withdrawal of occupying troops. This obligation of the Charter is categorical, precise, and by its very nature, requires immediate compliance; it does not allow, as do other provisions of the Charter, an evaluation by the states. Therefore, the Assembly resolutions referred to have a special legal significance. Those requesting the withdrawal of troops constitute, on the one hand, a reaffirmation of that general obligation and an emphatic appeal to comply with it, and on the other hand, a specification of the terms, modalities, and conditions under which the Organization deems the withdrawal should be accomplished in a given case.

As has been indicated, the duty to refrain is unconditional; therefore, the obligation to end the use of force must be, with greater reason, also unconditional and immediate. Thus, the Assembly could not logically establish through its resolutions an obligation greater than that established by the Charter. The conditions, modalities, and arrangements decreed for the withdrawal of troops may reflect political prudence and may be the result of negotiation, as in the case of Egypt but, obviously, in no case may they be more onerous than the unconditional obligation imposed by the Charter. Therefore, they must be considered the expression and the minimal specification of the general Charter obligation, and as such, binding in character.

To the extent that this binding and unusual effect of some Assembly resolutions can only legally occur within the scope of application of the Uniting for Peace Resolution, this effect may be considered a result of the rule created by United Nations practice, which has allowed the Assembly to perform activities not specifically provided for in the original Charter system. But this exceptional consequence of certain Assembly resolutions (the obligation to withdraw troops) does not, in itself, originate in customary practice: out of four instances, this obligation was not complied with in either Hungary or Korea, in spite of the fact that in the latter case, the request to do so was made by the Council. As indicated, this effect rests directly on the general obligation imposed by the Charter, even if the basis for the Assembly's action is found in the Uniting for Peace Resolution.

THE SCOPE OF THE NEW RULE ON COLLECTIVE SECURITY AND THE PRINCIPLE OF THE DOMESTIC JURISDICTION OF STATES

Of the four cases examined, that of the Congo is most related to the problem of domestic jurisdiction. In his recommendations and reports to the Security Council (some of which constituted a basis for its action), the Secretary-General invariably emphasized that the Council's resolutions had not authorized enforcement action against any state in the sense of Article 42 of the Charter, so that the last clause of Article 2(7) was not applicable; and that, consequently, the United Nations Force could not intervene in the domestic affairs of the Congo.[56]

Moreover, as previously stated, although the final aim was the maintenance of international peace by preventing the Congo convulsion from becoming an international conflict, the immediate and direct objective of the United Nations Force was a fundamentally domestic one: to maintain internal law and order and to avoid a civil war. When the situation gradually worsened, the Organization began setting forth new objectives, which complemented previous ones, of a typical internal nature: the convening of Parliament, the formation of a national government, the opposition to secessionist activities, the reorganization of the Congolese army, etc. It is true that the tasks assigned to the Secretary-General and to ONUC for the realization of these domestic aims were not necessarily incompatible with the condition established by the Security Council (resolution of August 9, 1960) that the "United Nations Force in the Congo will not be a party to or in any way intervene in or be used to influence the outcome of any internal conflict, constitutional or otherwise." Without doubt, the Secretary-General likewise correctly interpreted the absence of any reference to Article 42 in the Council Resolutions as an implicit prohibition against intervention in the domestic affairs of the Congo. Obviously, too, the above tasks set by the Organization were necessary in order to re-establish a normal situation and to avoid the internationalization of the conflict. All these facts and considerations may be easily accepted.

However, it cannot be reasonably denied that the intervention ordered by the Security Council related precisely to matters that Article 2(7) considers "essentially within the domestic jurisdiction of any state." Likewise, there is no doubt that the intervention of the Organization was carried out in the absence of the implicit condition provided for in the final clause of Article 2(7), that is, there was no question here of the application of enforcement measures under Chapter VII. All this is true independently of the Secretary-General's legitimate scruples in interpreting and implementing the mandate of the Security Council; the problem was not just one of application. The very aim of the operation, and the way in which it was conceived and organized, as expressed in the decisions of the Council, reveal the clear wish of the United Nations that its military and civil action concern itself with matters that can only be considered Congolese domestic affairs, without its intending to undertake enforcement action in that country.[57]

To recognize this fact does not mean to affirm the illegality of the Organization's intervention. Apart from the problem of the meaning of the term "intervention" in Article 2(7) of the Charter, exhaustively debated since the foundation of the United Nations, it must be stressed that the intervention of the United Nations was requested by the Government of the Congo. This circumstance, however, cannot be absolutely decisive in a situation of constitutional crisis such as the one that prevailed there for some time, not to mention the fact that the Congolese Government and the United Nations did not always agree on the scope of the Organization's action concerning many specific aspects of the operation. But in spite of this, the consent of the Government of the Congo is the principal consideration in affirming the legality of the intervention in conformity with the Charter. Moreover, this consent must be considered one of the essential premises of the entire operation. As Schachter says, "All [Members] subscribed to the principal that it must be left to the Congolese to determine their own political fate and constitutional system within the framework of national unity of the existing Republic of the Congo."[58]

Thus, it cannot be maintained that the Congo operation was an exception to the application of the principle of the reserved domain of states vis-à-vis the international organization. But this experience shows how the traditional distinction between "internal" and "external" matters does not constitute an obstacle to action by the Organization, even if it is not enforcement action, when other decisive factors are present, especially when the situation poses a potential threat to international peace.

ENFORCEMENT MEASURES OTHER THAN USE OF FORCE IN THE NEW RULE ON COLLECTIVE SECURITY

The decisions or recommendations of the Council or the Assembly requesting that Members adopt enforcement measures not involving the use of armed force, such as the severance of diplomatic relations, etc. (Article 41), which are adopted in circumstances similar to those of the resolutions considered earlier, produce, *mutatis mutandi*, equal effects. These consist in suspending other conventional obligations (resulting, for instance, from commercial or communications treaties), which could be binding upon the state that wishes to carry out the enforcement measures, vis-à-vis the state against which they were directed. Such was the case of Assembly Resolution 500 (V), which recommended the embargo on arms and strategic materials against China and North Korea, as well as of the numerous resolutions of the past few years whereby the Council or the Assembly has decided or recommended the adoption of similar measures in relation to South Africa, Portugal, or Rhodesia. The state that, in following one of these recommendations, refuses to fulfill obligations derived from a commercial treaty with the state against which the recommendation is directed, would not incur international responsibility for it. The reasons advanced to explain this effect of resolutions requiring the use of force are equally applicable to resolutions requesting the adoption of other enforcement measures. The Collective Measures Committee specifically studied this matter and came to similar conclusions.[59]

Chapter 4

RESOLUTIONS THAT DETERMINE THE EXISTENCE OF FACTS OR CONCRETE LEGAL SITUATIONS

GENERAL OBSERVATIONS

The subject of this chapter is a second group of resolutions which, although they refer to the external activity of the Organization, may nevertheless produce legal effects that can be characterized as binding. This group constitutes, therefore, a second exception to the legal regime normally applying to resolutions that are the product or result of United Nations activities.

These resolutions do not purport to induce directly certain conduct by the members, either through an invitation or through an order to carry out a concrete action (or to refrain from action). United Nations organs, in the performance of their functions, also make pronouncements as to the existence or nonexistence of certain facts or legal situations. Sometimes the stand taken by an organ in these matters is nothing but the expression of a point of view or opinion from which no legal consequence flows. But on occasion, these pronouncements or estimations have a special characteristic: they are "determinations" from which may derive under certain circumstances—difficult to formulate in a general manner, but considered here in specific cases—legal consequences that cannot be opposed in a juridically significant way by the members.

THE LEGAL FUNCTION OF DETERMINATIONS AND THE LOGICAL STRUCTURE OF LEGAL RULES

In order to perceive why these determinations can have a binding effect, it is necessary to analyze their legal function. That function is to provide the *hypothesis* or *condition* of the rules of law applied, or at times issued, by international organs in the performance of their activities.

Notwithstanding differences of nuance and especially of terminology among authorities on the Theory General of Law, all legal rules comprise two elements: (1) an hypothesis or conditional statement—in other words, the assumption on which the rule rests (what the Roman jurists expressed with the words *si quis*)—sometimes called simply a "juridical fact"; and (2) the consequence that the rule attaches to the realization of that hypothesis or condition, expressed by an affirmative or negative proposition. The connection between the hypothesis or condition and the consequence is precisely that which establishes a legal duty or, as it is sometimes called, a juridical imperative.[1]

The hypothesis or condition of a rule of law can be either a simple fact, such as the birth of an individual or an armed attack, or a legal situation, such as the nationality of a person or the fact that a matter pertains essentially to the domestic jurisdiction of a state.

The second element, the consequence, may assume diverse forms: it may enunciate a positive duty or a prohibition; express the principle of a legal responsibility; constitute an authorization; consist in the modification of a pre-existing legal situaton, such as the nullity of a contract or the applicability of a treaty; or establish (or deny) the legal competence of an organ.

The technical enunciation of a rule of law coincides in most cases neither with the articles of domestic codes nor with each provision of the United Nations Charter or of other international treaties. The elements of a legal rule are usually dispersed among various provisions, but sometimes several rules are included in one provision, and often there are chains of connected rules that form a system.

Article 18 of the Charter (which is far from a model of precision and legal clarity) contains, from a technical point of view, at least three or four articulated rules of law. To illustrate the function and meaning of the Assembly's determinations, one of these rules could be separated and expressed technically thus: "If the Assembly considers that another category of questions, besides those enumerated in paragraph 2, is important [hypothesis] . . . then . . . the decisions adopted in relation to this new category shall be made by a two-thirds majority of the members present and voting [consequence]."

Here, the Charter merely supplied in general terms the hypothesis or condition of the legal rule, or rather, contented itself with providing a basis on which to determine that hypothesis concretely: "If the Assembly considers. . . ." At the same time, it ascribed to an organ (the Assembly) the function of filling that hypothesis or condition, that is, of giving it a precise and concrete content: to establish, to determine specifically whether a certain category of questions (not included in paragraph 2) should be considered "important" in the sense of the rule contained in Article 18. The consequence of such a determination, indicated in the Charter itself, necessarily affects all the members: the obligatory application of the two-thirds majority vote. In other cases, when, for example, the hypothesis or condition is that a certain matter is not within the domestic jurisdiction of the state, the Assembly's determination in that sense results in the establishment of the Organization's competence.

Such cases, in which an organ has the power to determine concretely the hypothesis or condition for the application of a rule, are exceptional. In general, the hypothesis is stated specifically in the legal instrument itself.[2] This last situation is not the subject of this chapter. The resolutions discussed here are those whose function it is to set forth concretely a condition or hypothesis that is undetermined (or insufficiently determined) in the legal rule, in order to make possible the application of the consequence foreseen in such a rule.

As already stated, it is necessary to distinguish, among pronouncements made by United Nations organs concerning the existence of facts or legal situations, two very distinct categories: on the one hand, true legal determinations in the sense in which this term is used here, that is, pronouncements defining the hypothesis or condition of an international legal rule; and on the other, pronouncements that are no more than opinions, estimations, or directives, generally political, which lack the specific juridical function examined here and thus do not give rise to a legal consequence. Only resolutions containing pronouncements of the first type can be characterized as binding.[3]

Thus, the Assembly made a pronouncement in Resolution 637A (VII) which, although it externally resembles a determination, does not constitute the hypothesis of a rule of law: "The right of peoples and nations to self-determination is a prerequisite to the full enjoyment of all fundamental human rights." This is a political appreciation with no binding legal result.

In contrast, many resolutions adopted in connection with Article 73 of the Charter and pertaining to related matters constitute true determinations. According to a rule of law contained in Article 73, if a member has or assumes responsibility for the administration of non-self-governing territories (hypothesis), . . . then . . . it must transmit to the United Nations the information about those territories specified in paragraph (e) (consequence). But the Charter does not state the *content* of the hypothesis in this rule; it does not specify the non-self-governing territories to which the consequence in this rule is linked. In order to apply the rule requiring the transmission of pertinent information—whose observance is in the Assembly's competence—it was necessary for that organ to define and specify the hypothesis or condition to which the consequence is attached, that is, it had to determine the territories concerned. The General Assembly, in effect, has considered that it can make that determination binding by specifically recognizing its competence "to *decide* whether a Non-Self-Governing Territory has or has not attained a full measure of self-government as referred to in Chapter XI of the Charter."[4]

In postulating the binding character of resolutions that contain determinations, it is obviously not meant that these resolutions in themselves legally oblige an addressee to execute a given act, as is the case with Security Council decisions that contain an *order*. The function per se of these determinations is not to elicit certain behavior; they do not express a duty, but rather establish in a definitive manner the hypothesis or condition from which flows a legal consequence, which makes possible the application of a rule of law. They provide only one element of the rule: the hypothesis. The other, the consequence, may be present in the Charter or in another resolution, or may even be implied in the Organization's decision-making machinery as a whole. By its nature, this consequence may be an order to act or not to act, an authorization, or the granting or denial of legal competence to an organ.

But the determination as such is a *pronouncement* of the Organization, which is legally definitive, and against which there is no legal recourse. Inasmuch as it represents the official United Nations position on the existence of a fact or legal situation, it is the only one that the Organization takes into account as the basis for eventual action; thus the individual dissident attitude lacks juridical relevance. In this sense these pronouncements have legal validity, and the resolutions that contain them can properly be characterized as *binding in what they determine*.[5]

THE FUNCTION OF DETERMINATIONS AND THE
PROBLEM OF CHARTER INTERPRETATION

The matter just examined is closely related to the problem of interpreting the Charter. Determinations of the above type, made by United Nations organs, are equivalent in a sense to Charter interpretations. For them to be valid, therefore, the issuing organ must have legal capacity to interpret the Charter.

The Assembly is not authorized to give "authentic" Charter interpretations of a general character with the power to bind the other organs and "authority to establish a precedent." According to the statement accepted by the San Francisco Conference, this type of "authentic and constitutional" interpretation may be equivalent to a revision of the Charter and therefore requires the same procedures as those necessary to amend it.[6]

But it does not follow from the absence of such general authorization conferred upon the Assembly that the members retain the right to make, with legal validity, their own interpretation of the Charter. As Lauterpacht observes with respect to a similar though slightly less general question, the lack of a Charter provision giving any organ the power legally to decide whether a question lies essentially within the domestic jurisdiction of a state, together with the fact that the proposal to confer that power on the International Court of Justice was rejected in San Francisco, are not sufficient reasons to maintain that members are legally authorized to determine the matter by themselves. Lauterpacht rightly characterizes such a thesis as a "manifest absurdity."[7]

In principle, it is not up to the members to interpret the scope of the obligations imposed on them by the Charter; it is up to the organs, which apply the rules of the Charter expressing these obligations. Although the organs may not interpret the Charter in a general, "legislative," manner, they do determine the meaning and scope of its provisions, that is, they interpret them in the process of applying them to concrete cases. This is also an "authentic" interpretation of the Charter, but of a particular—as opposed to a legislative—nature. The interpretation of a Charter rule, implicit in the decision by which the rule is applied in a concrete case, is binding, even though normally it is so only for that specific case.[8] The meaning of the *travaux préparatoires* for the Charter at the San Francisco Conference is clear in this respect. The Report of Committee IV/2 contains the following "conclusions": "In the course of the operations from day to day of the various organs of the Organization, it is inevitable that each organ will interpret such parts of the Charter as are applicable to its particular function. This process is inherent in the functioning of any body which operates under an instrument defining its functions and powers." The same report later adds that, naturally, if an interpretation offered by any organ "is not generally acceptable," it will not be binding.[9]

Unless the expression "*generally* acceptable" is given an unusual and unwarranted meaning, with no basis in the Charter, it probably means, from a strictly technical point of view, acceptable to the majority of the members of the organ in question, in accordance with the voting majority applicable to that organ and to the nature of the matter being treated. Consequently, according to the above conclusion of the San Francisco Conference, *a contrario sensu*, the legal interpretation given by an organ will have binding force when it is "generally acceptable," using this term with the meaning indicated.[10]

THE DETERMINATION OF FACTS OR LEGAL SITUATIONS AND THE JUDICIAL FUNCTION

The function of establishing the hypothesis or condition for the application of certain rules of the Charter, which frequently means specifying the scope of members' obligations, has a certain external similarity to a function of the International Court of

Justice contemplated in Article 36(2c) of its Statute: to determine "the existence of any fact which, if established, would constitute a breach of an international obligation."

It might be thought preferable that these determinations should be made by the Court, especially insofar as they concern legal questions. Actually, the Assembly has consulted the Court with regard to the determination of facts, as will be seen, and it will always be possible to do so when deemed desirable. But this task could not be conceived as a specific or even pre-eminent function of the Court for two main reasons.

The first is the difficulty of distinguishing, especially in the international legal field, between the judicial function and the normal application of international rules. Even in the internal sphere, as is well known, there are serious differences of opinion among authorities on the characteristic and distinctive elements of the three essential functions of the state: the legislative, the executive, and the judicial.[11]

Naturally, these difficulties increase greatly when the same problem arises within a much more decentralized normative order lacking specialized organs for the creation of law, such as the international order. The functions of creating law and of recognizing its existence and applying it (the law-making and law-finding functions) present less pronounced differences in the international sphere than in the domestic one. Apart from the organic and functional insufficiencies of the international order, this is due to the great number of lacunae in international law and to the frequent vagueness of customary law. When the General Assembly, for example, had to distinguish between "codification" and "progressive development of international law," it could do so only in a general way, and warned that it used these terms merely "for convenience."[12] The International Law Commission recognized that in practice it had to do away with this distinction when it drew up the draft conventions on the Law of the Sea.[13] It is significant, likewise, that Lauterpacht gave such importance, over thirty years ago, to the study of ways in which international tribunals, even while remaining within their strictly judicial function, may contribute to the adaptation of law to changing circumstances, either by establishing "regulations" or by proposing recommendations at the request of parties, or even *proprio moto*.[14]

Tammes mentions several interesting cases of international bodies and conventions in which the same organ that normally applies the statutory rules is authorized to settle any disputes of interpretation that may arise: the Constitutions of the IMF and the World Bank, and some of the so-called commodity agreements (on wheat, sugar, and tin), provide that disputes over the interpretation or application of the agreements shall be submitted to the Executive Directors, the Board of Governors, or the Council, as the case may be, for decision. As Tammes points out, it is not easy to determine, in these cases, "whether the essence of the decision is on the judicial or rather on the legislative side."[15]

The above considerations and examples underline the theoretical and practical difficulties of distinguishing clearly between the two different functions. There is also a second important reason for preferring that this type of determination be made by the political organs of the United Nations: the different basic aims of the judicial and the administrative (or executive) function.

The exercise of the judicial function has as its normal prerequisite the existence of a "contention," an exceptional incident that sometimes arises in the process of applying the law; the aim of the judicial function is to resolve this contention in order to re-establish the social peace. The determination of facts or legal situations by the political organs has a different objective: to make possible the execution of a normal function assigned to them by the Charter. The fact that contrary opinions are expressed in the process of formulating a collective decision within an organ does not mean that there is a contention. This is a normal phenomenon in the formulation of decisions by collective organs.

When the Assembly determines, for instance, whether a territory is non-self-governing, it does not do so with a view to ending a dispute, even if there are differences of opinion in the matter, but rather as the necessary prerequisite to carrying out an assigned function, namely, to ensure compliance with the obligation to report as stated in Article 73 (e).

Of course, the Assembly may ask for technical advice by requesting an advisory opinion of the Court, when the fact or situation it must determine is of a legal nature. That was the case, for example, when the Assembly had to make a pronouncement on the legal capacity of the Organization to present an international claim for losses suffered in its service. But the request for an advisory opinion in no way changed the nature of the subsequent determination, which was in the Assembly's competence to make for itself. As the Secretary-General said in a memorandum on this subject: "It would seem that certain questions of *law*, policy, and procedure should be determined by the General Assembly" (Doc. 674 of October 7, 1948). He was referring to questions concerning the United Nations, whose determination was a prerequisite for the exercise of a normal function of the Organization and which could have been legally determined by the Assembly.

EXAMPLES OF RESOLUTIONS THAT DETERMINE FACTS OR LEGAL SITUATIONS

The first category of cases, already examined in part, concerns those Assembly resolutions that determine the status of a territory in order to implement the obligations stated in Chapter XI or XII of the Charter. A typical example is Resolution 1542 (XV) concerning the transmission of information according to Article 73 (e), which refers specifically to Portugal. The Assembly explicitly established that "the territories under the administration of Portugal listed hereunder (Cabo Verde, Angola, Mozambique, etc.) *are* non-self-governing territories within the meaning of Chapter XI of the Charter," and it subsequently declared that "an obligation exists on the part of the Government of Portugal to transmit information under Chapter XI of the Charter concerning these territories and that it should be discharged without further delay."

This resolution corresponds exactly to the theoretical schema. What is more directly of concern here is the Assembly's determination that the enumerated territories are non-self-governing. This determination was equivalent to a concrete interpretation of Article 73; that is to say, it constituted an interpretation implicit in the application of that provision to the particular case of the Portuguese territories. Stated in terms of the theoretical model used here, the aim of the determination was to provide concretely the hypothesis or condition of the legal rule according to which states administering non-self-governing territories must transmit the appropriate information. As such, *this determination of the Assembly is binding.*

The Assembly made the determination in question (Resolution 1542 [XV], first operative paragraph) on the basis of the list of "factors" (approved by Resolution 742 [VII]) that must be considered in deciding whether a territory has reached a full measure of self-government, as well as on the basis of certain "principles" (approved by Resolution 1541 [XV]) for determining whether there is an obligation to transmit information under Article 73(e).[16] These factors and principles are useful guides taken into account by the Assembly in order to make concrete determinations that are obligatory, but such factors and principles in themselves do not bind the Assembly or the member states. They represent, rather, what was characterized above as an authentic *general* interpretation of the Charter which, in order to be directly binding, would require the same procedure for approval as that necessary to amend the Charter. Only a concrete determination of the Assembly, applied to a particular case, can be binding.[17]

Several resolutions concerning South-West Africa are also pertinent. The significant determination, from the point of view under study, refers to the fact that the administration of the Territory, as the Assembly noted "with grave concern," ". . . has been conducted in a manner increasingly contrary to the Mandate" given by the League of Nations to the Union of South Africa (Resolution 1568 [XV]).

The determination by the General Assembly that South Africa has not complied with the obligations of the Mandate establishes the condition or hypothesis of a legal rule, which has the character of a "general principle of law recognized by civilized nations": if one of the parties to a bilateral treaty does not comply with its obligations, the party that does observe its own obligations ceases to be bound by them and may consider the treaty terminated.[18] By virtue of this rule, the General Assembly could, on the basis of its determination, revoke the Mandate; moreover, as the present representative or agent of the organized international community that granted the Mandate, it could re-assume the titles, rights, and powers enjoyed over the Territory when the Mandate was conferred, and could thus proceed to achieve the objective of the Covenant as well as of the Charter—the self-government or independence of the people of the Territory.[19]

Mention was made of other determinative resolutions—those that establish whether certain categories of questions fall under one or the other voting majority provided for in Article 18 of the Charter, and those that determine whether a matter belongs essentially to the domestic jurisdiction of states, thereby establishing or denying the competence of a United Nations organ. Among the latter, the numerous resolutions adopted in relation to the apartheid policy of South Africa are of particular importance.

Sloan gives an interesting example of a hypothetical resolution (since the case has so far not arisen) consisting in the Assembly determination that the circumstances which gave rise to the conclusion of a treaty have changed sufficiently to require its revision.[20] In other words, the Assembly would establish the condition or hypothesis, in a specific case, of the legal rule that expresses the so-called *rebus sic stantibus* doctrine. It is generally considered that Article 14 of the Charter authorizes the Assembly to recommend the revision of international treaties, since it allows it to "recommend measures for the peaceful adjustment of any situation, *regardless of origin....*"[21] Sloan even maintains that "in the absence of judicial settlement a recommendation [of the Assembly] based on the doctrine *rebus sic stantibus* would have sufficient force effectively to release a state from obligations incurred under a treaty."

The magnitude and nature of the changes that have occurred, and especially the impact that the continuation of a situation considered obsolete and unjust by one of the parties could have on "the friendly relations among nations" (Article 14), are matters that can be better evaluated by a political organ than by a judicial one. If, after a recommendation of the Assembly, a legal dispute should arise before an international tribunal, the court would have to give the Assembly's determination all due consideration, as Sloan states. It could be added that the tribunal could do nothing but accept the validity of that determination, especially if it rested on political considerations of a general character.

However, an authorized assessment of the assumption or hypothesis (a radical change in the circumstances) that would give rise to the application of the rule, is not the only pertinent question in deciding whether a state is released from its conventional obligations without incurring international responsibility. The tribunal would likewise have to resolve another essential question: to what extent is the doctrine of *rebus sic stantibus* an indubitable rule of international law, and what is its accepted scope, especially if it is recalled that international tribunals have seldom touched on this question and rarely or never in a conclusive manner.[22] The practice of the League, whose Covenant expressly provided that the Assembly could recommend the revision of treaties (Article 19), was rather negative,[23] and the United Nations has never been faced with a question of this nature.

In any case, the scope and effects of the rule are far from clear, especially as to whether its result is to release a state completely from its conventional obligations or simply to authorize it to request such a release from the other parties.[24] Because of all these factors, Sloan's conclusion that a recommendation of the Assembly would result, *ipso jure*, in releasing the state from its conventional obligations, is doubtful. However, it can easily be accepted that the Assembly's evaluation of whether a radical change in circumstances had occurred would have legal validity inasmuch as it would be an authorized determination of the fact.

Other cases of binding determinations by the Assembly concern representation in United Nations organs when two or more governments claim to be the legitimate representative of a member state. This has occurred in the cases of China, Congo-Leopoldville, and Yemen. The power to deal with this matter corresponds to the functions concerning the structure and internal organization of the United Nations, which are subject in principle, as stated earlier,[25] to the regime of the binding resolution. The Assembly's competence to make binding pronouncements on the legal validity of the representation of member states must be considered a necessary implied power for implementing the Charter provisions concerning the composition of the Assembly (Article 9). The binding effect of the determination does not consist solely in the fact that the government whose credentials have been accepted as valid is the only one that participates in the organs, but also that it is the only one the Organization recognizes as the legitimate government of the member state, with the obvious and important political and legal consequences that that implies. However, the resolution of the Assembly has no legal effect on bilateral relations between the members and the rival governments.

In these matters of representation, what is binding is the specific determination of the Assembly for each particular case, and not its general pronouncements. Thus, Resolution 396 (V) entitled "Recognition by the United Nations of the Representation of a Member State" is more of a general guide without any binding effect.[26]

LIMITS ON THE BINDING CHARACTER OF DETERMINATIVE RESOLUTIONS

The first limitation on the binding nature of the resolutions examined here is the fact that they are valid only in concretely decided cases and that they may not be an obligatory precedent for other cases. The principle *stare decisis* is not applicable. What is binding is only the specific decision, the organ's determination for a particular case; the abstract *ratio decidendi* in itself is not binding. The general interpretation of the Charter or the enunciation of a legal principle, which could be implicit in the way in which an organ acted in a specific case, is not binding in future cases, even by the same organ.

Naturally, precedents are frequently invoked in the United Nations because the logical, juridical, or factual premises on which resolutions are based usually have an objective value transcending the concretely determined case. But United Nations practice does not reveal that the organs respect these precedents as a matter of legal obligation.

The second limitation is the fact that the determination of a fact or legal situation as the hypothesis or condition of a Charter rule must not entail new obligations for the members, nor restrict the pre-existing rights of the states or entities to which the resolutions are directed, nor, in the last resort, bring about a change in territorial status, even *de facto* or provisional, without the consent of the parties concerned.

Resolution 181 (II) on Palestine is a good example of this limitation. In theory, there seem to be good reasons to attribute binding force to Resolution 181. As stated at the time by the representative of the Jewish Agency, although resolutions "which touch the national sovereignty of the Members of the United Nations" are mere recommendations, "the Palestine resolution [is] essentially different, for it concern[s] the future of a territory subject to an international trust. Only the United Nations as a whole [is] competent to determine the future of the territory, and its decision, therefore, has a binding force."[27]

Although Resolution 181 recommended to the United Kingdom, as mandatory power, and to all the other members that they approve and implement the Partition Plan, it also conferred upon the Palestine Commission temporary authority over the Territory and its people. It is significant, however, that the discussions dealt more with the viability and the opportuneness of the proposed measures than with the competence of the Assembly to adopt them. The thesis of the Assembly's lack of competence to carry out the partition of Palestine was upheld by a relatively small minority of members.[28]

The real reason for the nonbinding nature of Resolution 181 (II) is not so much the Assembly's lack of competence to adopt binding resolutions in general, or in particular, to create an organ with the necessary authority to administer a territory on behalf of the international community. The essential reason lies in the fact that resolutions of this type are limited to the determination and concretization of obligations (and related rights) implicit in the Charter for particular cases, and that they may not legally create additional obligations or abolish existing rights.

Resolution 181 exceeded these limitations. The resolution could not be justified by saying, as was maintained, that it filled a politico-legal vacuum. The fact that the Arab and Jewish communities then did not really constitute "subjects" of international law is not sufficient reason to deny the existence of "parties," with internationally protected rights, especially in light of the way in which the United Nations has understood and generally applied the principle of self-determination. The Partition Plan, by its very nature, restricted some of the rights of those entities and created new obligations.[29]

In general terms, resolutions that are not the expression of an agreement among the parties concerned, but that represent rather the will of a majority in a political organ, are inadequate instruments today for settling territorial problems or even for adjusting particular situations. Almost always, these problems entail and reflect a plurality of interests, relatively consolidated, that often give rise to genuine but conflicting rights. Generally, there is no clearly applicable legal rule whose content may be determined through the action of the Assembly, and therefore it cannot truly "apply" a solution.

This is so even with respect to situations in which, as Sloan says, sovereignty is not clearly vested in a member state, in which there exists a "legal vacuum,"[30] or in which—to use Goodrich's related concept—the United Nations has as its task "the creation of a new legal and political order,"[31] as in the cases of the Italian colonies, Korea, and Palestine.[32]

But in reality, the legal vacuum is more apparent than real. The Assembly does not act *ex novo*, since in these situations there still remain some traces of sovereignty vested in the parties, or there exist newborn rights, as was the case in Palestine. In this type of situation, the adequate instrument for a solution can only be a resolution that reflects an agreement among the parties and states principally concerned.

BINDING FORCE AND COERCIVE APPLICATION
OF A RULE OF LAW

In an organization such as the United Nations, the aims and obligations of members can be expressed only in the constitutive agreement in broad and general norms. The task of concretizing and applying them to particular cases belongs to the organs. In doing so, the Organization frequently uses a procedure common to all normative orders: the legislator utilizes an element outside the legal rule in order to establish its content. This occurs, for example, when the law lends binding efficacy to the will of the parties in a contract or to a prevalent commercial usage.

Assembly determinations that set forth the hypothesis or condition of a rule or, in other words, that fill the content of a rule of the Charter, have an identical function. The determination of an international organ, the will of the parties in a contract, or a commercial usage are not in themselves rules, nor do they create any rule; they are not a source of law in the same sense that domestic law or the Charter are. Their object is to *give content* to the legal rule. The legislator sometimes provides only a blank rule, a rule whose content is undetermined and for whose determination he refers to an element outside of the rule: the private will of the parties in a contract, a commercial usage, or the determination of an international organ.

This is the meaning of the General Assembly's determinations of facts or legal situations. They are not binding in themselves or by themselves; they are binding as an element, that is, as the content, of a binding rule of the Charter. Although these determinations are limited to concretizing and applying the rules of the Charter to particular cases, without creating new obligations for the members not implicit in the Charter, they have full legal validity.

The problem of the binding force of determinative resolutions (and, in general, of all resolutions of international organs) is closely related to the problem of the coercive application of international legal rules.[33] It is not considered necessary to examine this question closely here—a question that involves, in the last analysis, nothing less than the problem of the juridical nature of international law. For purposes of the present study, it suffices to indicate broadly, among the diverse conceptions that are logically possible, the premises accepted here as working hypotheses.

It is believed that rules of international law may be characterized as obligatory even when the possibility of applying them coercively, in case of noncompliance, is limited or nonexistent. That is a problem of legal efficacy and not of legal validity. When noncompliance is prejudicial to another state, and other conditions established by general international law are present, there arises an international responsibility. Frequently, the obligatory force of a rule or decision has no effect other than the creation of an international responsibility because of noncompliance. The fact that, in turn, it becomes difficult or impossible in practice authoritatively to establish responsibility and coercively to effect reparation for damage caused, does not make nonbinding the rule not complied with, which gave rise to the responsibility.

The distinction between binding force and coercive application is present likewise in the particular normative system of the United Nations. However, there is an additional element—the outlawing of recourse to the use or threat of force—which bears decisively on the problem of the coercive application of Charter rules, to the extent that it radically restricts the freedom of action that states traditionally enjoyed in making the necessary decisions and in carrying out sanctions on their own. Only the Organization can adopt enforcement measures, either directly or by entrusting them to a regional organization in accordance with Article 53, in case of a threat to or a breach of the peace or an act of aggression. Furthermore, it is doubtful that Security Council enforcement action has the character of a "sanction" under Chapter VII.[34] The only specific sanctions, in a technical sense, provided for in the Charter are few: suspension of the rights and privileges of members (Article 5); expulsion (Article 6); suspension of a member's vote in the Assembly due to arrears in payments (Article 19); and the impossibility of invoking a treaty, which has not been registered previously, before any organ of the United Nations (Article 102). In addition, the Charter authorizes the Security Council "to decide upon measures" in order to give effect to a judgment of the Court (Article 94). This could be considered the only case in which the Organization can act directly as the agent for coercive application of law.[35]

It is obvious that United Nations organs have adopted resolutions considered by them as binding, and accepted by the members as such, in many more cases than those few in which the Organization can take enforcement action or apply sanctions. Many resolutions may not be susceptible to coercive application and perhaps are *leges imperfectae,* but they are binding to the same degree and for the same reasons as the rules of general international law. As expressed by Sloan in a paragraph that explains admirably the *raison d'être* of the legal value of certain resolutions: "The force of a recommendation is not derived from a judgment made in an internal court of conscience, but from a judgment made by an organ of the world community and *supported by many of the same considerations which support positive international law.* The judgment by the General Assembly as a collective world conscience is itself a force external to the individual conscience of any given state."[36]

On the other hand, General Assembly determinations sometimes produce ineluctable effects for the members, from which they cannot exempt themselves, as when, for example, the Assembly applies the sanction of denying a member his vote because of arrears in payments. Here, the mechanics of the decision-making process, through the action of the organs, imply a form of enforced execution of resolutions.

This occurs also in the frequent determinations of the Assembly that a matter submitted to it does not belong essentially to the domestic jurisdiction of a state. The opposition of a minority of members to such a determination has no legal relevance. The objection is legally inoperative, and it cannot prevent the consequence of the determination from occurring, that is, it cannot prevent the Assembly's effective exercise of the competence it assumes to discuss the matter. Not only is the Assembly's determination binding but also, in this sense, *its execution is ineluctable*. In practice, the dissenting minority remains effectively submitted to the will of the majority. From a legal point of view, the decision is definitive, since the minority has no recourse to change it. As Robinson affirms: "The constitutionality of the actions of the organs of the United Nations cannot be challenged. Obviously, no review of the legality or constitutionality of United Nations actions is possible in the absence of an organ to pass judgment on such questions."[37] In these circumstances, to affirm that members retain their freedom of individual judgment in the face of Assembly resolutions when the resolutions contemplated are of a determinative nature, has no meaning, or rather, it amounts to an inexactitude.[38]

Furthermore, outside of those resolutions executed indirectly through the decision-making process and, in a certain way, automatically complied with, as in the example given, the problem of noncompliance with an Assembly determination is, on the whole, similar to lack of compliance with a binding decision of the Security Council made without reference to the specific powers enumerated in Chapter VII of the Charter. Noncompliance with a Council decision of this type, just as noncompliance with an Assembly determination, would not give rise *ipso jure* to the application of enforcement measures. Even if noncompliance should result in an alleged threat to or breach of the peace, the Security Council would not automatically decree enforcement measures merely because a state had not carried out the Council's decision (or the Assembly's determination), as a form of punitive reaction against the illegal act of noncompliance; rather, it would do so discretionally, basing its action on an assessment of whether the objective situation of a threat to or a breach of the peace in fact obtained. In other words, neither Assembly determinations, nor binding Council decisions not based on the specific powers of Chapter VII, are *directly* susceptible of coercive implementation; but this is not sufficient to deprive the latter (or the former) of their binding character.

Chapter 5

RESOLUTIONS WHOSE BINDING FORCE RESTS ON INSTRUMENTS OTHER THAN THE CHARTER

GENERAL OBSERVATION

The General Assembly may, under certain circumstances, make recommendations that produce binding effects on the basis of a special instrument other than the Charter. The exceptional legal foundation that allows the Assembly to adopt binding resolutions may be either an instrument that is and continues to be outside the particular normative system of the United Nations, or one whose provisions become integrated into the Organization's legal order and finally become part of it. An example of the first (perhaps the only one in United Nations practice) was the Italian Peace Treaty of 1947; examples of the second type are the diverse trusteeship agreements.

PRECEDENTS

Since the time of the League of Nations, precedents have not been lacking of cases in which the parties to a controversy bound themselves in advance to accept a settlement recommended by the Council, which meant conferring on that recommendation a binding character. Some of the best known were the following:

The Treaties of Saint-Germain, Trianon, and Neuilly gave the Council of the League certain legislative powers, to be exercised by majority vote, in relation to the modification of certain provisions on minorities applicable to Austria, Hungary, and Bulgaria, respectively.[1] In the matter of Upper Silesia, it was also previously agreed to "accept the solution recommended by the Council of the League." Likewise, in conformity with the Venice Protocol of October 13, 1921 regarding the boundary between Hungary and Austria, the latter agreed to respect the "decision recommended by the Council of the League."

Finally, Article 3(2) of the Treaty of Lausanne provided that the delimitation of boundaries between Turkey and Iraq should be the object of friendly arrangements between Great Britain and Turkey; but if an accord was not reached within nine months, the dispute would be referred to the Council of the League for its decision. As there were doubts concerning the nature of the decision the Council had to make (arbitral award, recommendation, or simple mediation), that organ requested an Advisory Opinion of the Permanent Court of International Justice, which stated in its opinion of November 21, 1925 (Series B, Number 12) that the "decision to be taken by the Council" will be "binding on the Parties and will constitute a definitive determination of the frontier between Turkey and Iraq."

The interest of the Court's Opinion, from the point of view of the matter studied here, is that it presented in a clear and general way the legal possibility of broadening exceptionally the normal competence of an international organ on the basis of an agreement among states authorizing that organ to make binding decisions.[2] The relevant part of the Opinion reads as follows:

There is nothing to prevent the Parties from accepting obligations and from conferring on the Council powers wider than those resulting from the strict terms of Article 15 (of the Covenant), and in particular from substituting, by an agreement entered into in advance, for the

Council's power to make a mere recommendation, the power to give a decision which, by virtue of their previous consent, compulsorily settles the dispute.[3]

THE QUESTION OF THE ITALIAN COLONIES

A similar case arose in the United Nations. According to paragraph 3 of Annex XI of the Italian Peace Treaty, the "Powers concerned" agreed to accept the General Assembly's recommendation in case of nonagreement among themselves about the future of the former Italian colonies, and they agreed to adopt the necessary measures to implement it. Since they did not reach an accord, the Assembly examined the case and finally adopted Resolution 289 (IV), in which were formulated specific *recommendations* concerning each of the former Italian colonies. These recommendations, some of which were adopted by a small majority, were in effect accepted and carried out.

It could be maintained that the Peace Treaty did not give the Assembly the power to adopt *binding decisions per se*, but rather that it obliged the parties, that is, certain states, to accept and carry out the recommendations of the Assembly, which is juridically different.[4] However, in line with the reasoning of the old Permanent Court in the case of the Turkish-Iraqi frontier, the more probable effect of the previous agreement was to confer on the Assembly "powers wider" than those in its normal competence, and to substitute for "the power to make a mere recommendation, the power to give a decision. . . ." The result of denying the objectively binding character of the Assembly's resolution and its validity *erga omenes*, would be that such a resolution would be binding for certain members (the Powers concerned) and not for the rest. It could hardly be admitted that any of the latter members who voted against the adopted resolution, could, because of that fact, legally refuse to recognize the future mapped out for the Italian colonies and refuse to act in conformity with the solution approved by the General Assembly.

Concerning the effect of the resolution on Italy, which was not then a member of the United Nations, it could be maintained that because of the referral of the Treaty to the General Assembly for eventual action, Resolution 289 (IV) probably intended, and had as its result, a limited and specific broadening of the normative system of the United Nations to include Italy.

POSSIBLE APPLICATION OF THIS SOLUTION TO OTHER CASES

The General Assembly's intervention resolved satisfactorily, and with legal finality, a politically difficult matter. It would seem that in this type of problem the previous agreement to invest in the Assembly the power to make final decisions has indisputable advantages and merits. Sloan, in an often-quoted article written in 1948, maintained that this system could even be generalized.[5] Unfortunately, however, United Nations practice has not confirmed his hopes.

The cases of Korea and Palestine were somewhat similar, from a certain point of view, to that of the Italian colonies. In all three cases the Organization furthered the creation of a new permanent politico-legal status, to replace an anomalous and temporary condition and thus to normalize the situation in accordance with the interests of the local population and of international peace. The interest of the whole international community was also manifest in the Korean and Palestinian cases, and the effective intervention of the United Nations seemed clearly desirable. Unfortunately, owing to lack of agreement among the parties, the initial intervention of the Assembly could not develop a decisive and final character.

The Assembly has not been able to act in such a way in connection with boundary disputes or controversies over the condition of minorities. The controversy between Italy and Austria over the condition of the German-speaking population in the province of Bolzano has certain similarities with the cases settled in a binding way by the Council of the League. However, disagreement over whether the political or the legal aspects were dominant, and consequently over which organ should intervene (General Assembly or International Court of Justice) limited the Assembly's role to exhorting the parties to negotiate directly among themselves (Resolution 1497 [XV]).

Another significant case, that of the future of Ruanda-Urundi, is interesting for more than one reason. The Assembly attempted to influence the form the trusteeship territory would assume once it had been granted independence. Faced with the danger that the small and hardly viable territory would be born divided, the Assembly called a constitutional conference "with a view to finding a mutually acceptable formula for the creation of the closest possible form of political, economic, and administrative union" (Resolution 1743 [XVI], paragraph 4). The conference failed, and as the Assembly lacked the capacity to impose its frequently reiterated conviction that "the best future of Ruanda-Urundi lies in the emergence of a single State," the two portions of the territory became independent as separate states.

THE TRUSTEESHIP AGREEMENT AS A FOUNDATION FOR THE BINDING FORCE OF CERTAIN RESOLUTIONS

Other resolutions with binding effects based on an instrument other than the Charter are those adopted by the Assembly and, under its authority, by the Trusteeship Council, in relation to trust territories. The Charter itself does not provide that such resolutions should be compulsorily applied to these territories, but Article 87 (d), states that the two organs may "take these [that is, the measures enumerated in paragraphs (a), (b), and (c)] and *other* actions in conformity with the terms of the Trusteeship agreements" (italics added).

All the trusteeship agreements signed by the United Nations in conformity with Article 79 of the Charter contain a provision, differing slightly for each territory, that establishes the following: the administering authority *undertakes to apply* to the trust territory international conventions, as well as past or future recommendations of the United Nations and of the specialized agencies that may be appropriate to the particular circumstances of the territory and that might lead to the realization of the basic aims of the trusteeship system.[6] The trusteeship agreement is, therefore, the foundation, or instrument other than the Charter, that serves as the legal basis for the obligatory application in the trust territory of recommendations of the United Nations or the specialized agencies.

INTEGRATION OF THE TRUSTEESHIP AGREEMENT INTO THE PARTICULAR NORMATIVE ORDER OF THE UNITED NATIONS

The terms of the trusteeship agreement "shall be agreed upon by the states directly concerned," according to the controversial phrase of Article 79 of the Charter. There has been much discussion as to whether such agreements are treaties between individual states, or between the authority that ceded the territory and the state that assumes its administration, or all the rest of the states, or between the Organization and the states "legally" concerned. None of these interpretations seems completely satisfactory. For purposes of the present study, the most significant aspect of the problem from the legal point of view, is the following:

The Assembly's approval of the trusteeship agreement results in its integration into the normative order of the United Nations. The provisions of the agreement are absorbed, so to speak, by this order and become a complement to the trusteeship principles of the Charter. This integration is permanent as long as the agreement is in force, and is institutional in the sense that the connection is established, ultimately, by the provisions of Article 87(d). But the integration occurs by virtue of the resolutions of the Assembly that approved the agreement. For the members who are not "directly concerned," the only act that relates them to the trusteeship is the resolution approving the agreement. Thus, this resolution produces the legal consequence, for all members of the United Nations, to link them legally to the international trusteeship system for each trust territory.

CONTENT AND SCOPE OF THE OBLIGATION OF THE ADMINISTERING AUTHORITY

On the basis of the provisions indicated above, the administering authorities are obliged to apply the resolutions of the United Nations in the trust territories. In order to clarify the content and scope of this obligation, it is necessary to distinguish two different situations:

Resolutions Not Relating to the Administration of the Territory

The obligation mentioned in the trusteeship agreements to apply recommendations in the trust territories refers to recommendations distinct from those directly concerning the administration of the trust territory; that is, the obligation refers to recommendations of a general nature, directed to all members and relating, for instance, to human rights or general economic or political matters. The obligation to apply United Nations recommendations in the trust territories could not refer to those concerning their administration, since the trusteeship agreements state that the administering authorities shall apply those resolutions that lead to the achievement of the basic aims of the trusteeship system. But resolutions adopted by the Trusteeship Council or the Assembly concerning the administration of the trust territories must necessarily lead, *ex hypothesi*, to the realization of the basic aims of that system; if the obligation mentioned in the trusteeship agreements referred to this type of resolution, the phrase in question would lack meaning.

Concerning recommendations that do not relate to the administration of the territory, the content of the obligation imposed on the administering authority consists, according to Malintoppi, not necessarily in always executing the recommended measures, but rather in *extending* to the trust territory the application of those recommendations that the administering authority applies in its metropolitan territory. If that were not the true content of the obligation, Malintoppi argues, we would have to admit that the administering state would be obliged to execute certain recommendations in the trust territory, but at the same time would not be obliged to carry out these same recommendations in its national territory—which seems inconceivable. The obligation referred to in the agreements is really the pendant of the former "colonial clauses," as would seem to be confirmed by the fact that these agreements likewise establish the obligation to apply international conventions in the trust territories, an obligation that obviously cannot refer to all international conventions, but only to those to which the administering authority is a party. The object of the obligation to extend the application of conventions and recommendations to the trust territories is to avoid discrimination between the inhabitants of these territories and those of the national territory of the administering authority.[7]

The majority of agreements, with some variations, also assign to the administering authority an additional obligation: to include in its periodic reports to the United Nations information concerning the implementation of recommendations formulated by the Trusteeship Council and the Assembly. This is an obligation similar to the one established by the Constitution of the

International Labor Organization (Article 19[6d]) and of other specialized agencies, which does not imply the mandatory execution of the substance of the recommendation; the obligation consists only in reporting on the implementation or nonimplementation of the recommendations.

Resolutions concerning the Administration of the Territory

As for Assembly or Council recommendations that specifically deal with trusteeship administration, the situation is less clear. It is not likely that the above-mentioned provision imposes on the administering authorities a legal obligation to carry out recommendations relating to the administration of the territory. In conformity with Article 79 of the Charter, the trusteeship agreements themselves establish the terms of administration and, therefore, the limits of the obligation assumed by the administering authorities. It can hardly be admitted, therefore, as a question of principle, that the Trusteeship Council or the Assembly has an unquestionable general competence to impose on the administering states obligations greater than those assumed when they signed the trusteeship agreement.

Once this thesis is accepted as a general position, it is also necessary to take into account other factors and considerations in order to specify in each case the scope of these obligations.

THE ADMINISTERING AUTHORITY AS AN AGENT AND ORGAN OF THE UNITED NATIONS

First, consideration should be given to the peculiar position of the administering authority and its special function within the international system of trusteeship administration and supervision. According to the Charter conception, the administering authority acts as an agent of the international community and, indeed, as an organ of the United Nations, accepting as a "sacred trust" the obligation to promote the welfare of the inhabitants of the territories in every possible way. The recommendations addressed to the administering authorities concerning territorial matters are not addressed to them as United Nations subjects, as would be the case for the rest of the members, but rather as agents or mandatories of the Organization. Moreover, these recommendations concern functions that they carry out, not for their own benefit, but for the benefit of the inhabitants whose welfare has been assigned to them by the Organization. These circumstances have considerable relevance in determining the freedom of judgment retained by the administering authorities in relation to such recommendations.[8]

The example best illustrating the nature of the function exercised by the administering authority, as an organ of the system, is the possibility foreseen in Article 81 of the Charter: that the Organization itself might exercise the administration of a trust territory. But there is no essential difference between this case—which has not occurred in practice, although it was seriously considered in the case of the former Italian colonies—and the other cases in which the trusteeship system is applied through negotiated agreements to the diverse categories of territories contemplated in Article 77. The objective of the system is identical, as are the functions of the administering authority in providing for the welfare of the population. In both cases, the authority acts on behalf and under the supervision of the international community, as an administrator and not as a sovereign. The juridico-political link between the authority that exercises the administration and the people of the territory is not direct, as in the case of sovereign states.[9] It derives rather from the normative order of the United Nations and is framed by that order. Therefore, the administrator's character as agent of the international community is the same, whether the territory is subject to the trusteeship system in accordance with Article 77, or whether it is administered by the Organization.

This character of both agent and organ assumed by the administering authority is not in itself a decisive or sufficient reason to conclude that the Organization may impose on it *new* obligations, beyond those established in the trusteeship agreement. The agreement establishes the terms of administration, and any modification requires the consent of the administering authority in conformity with Article 79.[10] But the authority's dual character is an element that must be taken into account, especially when interpreting the scope of its obligations. Given its place within the system, the power to interpret the meaning of its obligations as stated in the trusteeship agreement belongs in principle to the source of its authority, the Organization; in other words, it is up to the Assembly to determine, through its resolutions, the scope and modalities of the obligations assigned to the administering authority.

The General Assembly has exercised its power broadly in this respect. Thus, for example, it adopted Resolution 1605 of April 21, 1961 concerning the "question of the future of Ruanda-Urundi," in which it exhorted Belgium "to observe strictly its international obligations under the Trusteeship Agreement" and specified several of these obligations, despite Belgium's view that they were not stipulated in the Agreement.

Chapter 6

RESOLUTIONS THAT EXPRESS AND REGISTER AGREEMENT AMONG THE MEMBERS OF AN ORGAN

GENERAL OBSERVATIONS

Certain resolutions, few in number, but juridically significant, have as their content an informal agreement, explicit or tacit, among the members of an organ or an international organization. To the extent that a resolution is the result of an agreement, giving it form and registering and externalizing it, the resolution can have binding force. This is true even though the resolution may have been issued by an organ normally lacking competence to take binding decisions in the field to which the resolution pertains.

It is not a question of the different, although related, problem of whether states that vote in favor of an ordinary recommendation are, in principle, legally bound to comply with it, as some authors maintain. This specific question will be considered later in light of the pertinent opinions, and a negative conclusion will be reached. The matter to be examined now is different. The resolutions considered here all have this characteristic trait: from the terms of reference of an organ, or from the charter of an organization (as in the case of some of the specialized agencies), or even from the circumstances under which a resolution is adopted, it can be validly inferred that the main object of these resolutions is to register an agreement among the members. When this occurs, such resolutions are actually instruments that incorporate a form of international agreement lacking the usual treaty form—something similar, it might be said, to a "multilateral executive agreement."

These resolutions have precedents both in the League of Nations and in the inter-American system. Also, the constitutions of some specialized agencies provide for resolutions that are binding only for those members that accept them, in terms suggesting that such resolutions reflect an agreement among them. On the other hand, the United Nations Charter does not contemplate these situations, although there have been a few resolutions that could be included in this category, or that, at least, have some similarity with the theoretical schema outlined above. This is especially the case in matters where practice has shown the limited efficacy of majority resolutions, and where the only viable solution consists in a negotiated agreement among a group of states.

LEGAL BASIS OF THESE RESOLUTIONS; THE CONSENSUAL NATURE OF INTERNATIONAL AGREEMENTS

There is no essential legal obstacle that prevents states from assuming binding agreement through any form they choose to manifest their accord, even through the concurrence of votes within an international organ. International agreements are totally consensual: there is no legal rule that prescribes precise forms for their validity. According to modern international law, mutual consent may be expressed even in unwritten form, through signs or symbols, as in the case of military truces. An oral statement, made by a responsible official on a matter within his competence, has a binding value identical to that of a formal written declaration, as the Permanent Court of Justice recognized in judging the status of Eastern Greenland.[1]

There is no legal reason why a vote in an international organ cannot be, *in principle*, an equally licit and effective way of expressing consent to an agreement, when the circumstances in which it is cast prove that the vote is a clear manifestation of the wish to be bound. In reference to the League of Nations resolution of March 11, 1932 (which will be examined later, in another context),[2] concerning the nonrecognition of changes brought about by violence, Lauterpacht declares: "Probably there is no good reason for denying generally that a State may undertake a binding obligation by consenting to a Resolution of the Assembly. Ratification of a signed treaty is not the only way of assuming binding obligations in International Law."[3]

Obviously, the possibility alluded to by Lauterpacht has one limitation: the vote can only reflect an agreement and bind the state that casts it when the instrument that created the organ does not attribute to this vote a different value, incompatible with the assumption of obligations in the circumstances and conditions under which the vote was cast. This is, of course, the general rule in the United Nations and the specialized agencies. Only exceptionally do instances arise in which a special legal connection is established among the states that cast coincident votes, such a connection being distinct and independent from the legal situation normally created by the vote.

However, as will be seen when an analysis of some examples is attempted, resolutions of this type are sufficiently significant, if not to postulate the existence of a new juridical figure—that of "multilateral executive agreements"—at least to underline the common and characteristic elements of these resolutions and to group them under a separate rubric.

EXECUTIVE AGREEMENTS IN GENERAL
INTERNATIONAL LAW

The situation that, in modern international law, best shows the total absence of prescribed forms for the assumption of international obligations is the vast proliferation of executive agreements or, to use the descriptive French term, *accords en forme simplifiée*. The number and proportion of executive agreements concluded today have considerably increased in comparison to ratified treaties. Thus, in the League of Nations era 53 per cent of all treaties were ratified, but in the United Nations period only 23 per cent have been ratified.[4]

Moreover, the most diverse matters, including extremely important political questions, have been the subject of nonratified treaties—for instance, the Munich Pact, the Yalta Agreements, the Four-Power Agreement of August 8, 1945 for the trial of war criminals of the European Axis, and the Agreements of the Geneva Conference of 1954 that ended the Indochina War.[5] Regarding their respective subject matter, formal treaties and executive agreements can be considered interchangeable instruments. It does not seem possible to infer criteria from international practice for the differentiation of treaties from executive agreements in terms of substance, that is, criteria founded on their diverse nature.[6]

If mutual consent, clearly manifested but lacking any special predetermined form, has full binding efficacy, it may be concluded that, according to *general* international law, nothing prevents mutual consent, when expressed in an international organization through a vote, from having the same effect, unless the *particular* normative order of the organization prohibits it. For this reason, some authors have come to the conclusion that, in principle, states voting in favor of a recommendation are bound *inter se*.

THE NONBINDING FORCE, IN PRINCIPLE, OF
A VOTE IN FAVOR OF A RECOMMENDATION

It has been argued that the General Assembly, although primarily a principal United Nations organ and, as such, an entity with a legal personality distinct from that of its members, is at the same time a conference of individual states. In this latter capacity, the Assembly has certain inherent powers that need not be derived from specific enumeration in the Charter.[7] The member states, when they meet as the Assembly, do not thereby lose their normal legal capacity to bind themselves mutually; and they may, therefore, express their accord by means of coincident votes. Vallat, for instance, is of the opinion that the effect of an Assembly resolution (which determined a threat or breach of the peace or an act of aggression) would be to bind those members who voted in its favor.[8] In a less general, but equally clear and categorical way, Judge Klaested expressed, *a contrario sensu*, the same concept in an individual opinion in which he discussed specifically the effect of Assembly recommendations: "Only if the Union Government (of South Africa) by a concurrent vote has given its consent to the recommendation can that government become legally bound to comply with it."[9] Judge Winiarski, in his dissenting opinion to the Court's advisory opinion in the case concerning certain expenses of the United Nations, expressed, *a contrario sensu*, the same view: "It is apparent that the resolutions approving and apportioning these expenses are valid and binding only in respect of the Member States which have accepted the recommendations."[10]

This extreme position, especially when formulated as a general thesis, is not acceptable because it tends to distort the basic conception and structure of international organizations. It is true that states do not lose their normal capacity to be bound when they act as members of an international body; but in doing so, they act within certain rules and mechanisms *that normally affect the legal meaning of their votes.* Most of all, as Gentile rightly points out, resolutions adopted by international organizations "are not imputed to the individual Members who voted in their favor, but to the organ and to the organization."[11] That is, the resolution is a legal act of the organization and not of the aggregate of its members considered individually. Only when it may be interpreted that the resolution (understood as an act of the organ and not of the members) has as its objective to register and express the coincident consent of the members to bind themselves, because of the circumstances under which it was adopted, can it be affirmed that the resolution incorporates a binding agreement for those who concluded it through their votes.

EXAMPLES OF "EXECUTIVE AGREEMENT-RESOLUTIONS"

In the League of Nations

An advisory opinion of the Permanent Court of International Justice, frequently quoted in this respect ("Railroad Traffic between Lithuania and Poland," Advisory Opinion #21 of October 15, 1931), recognized that a resolution of the Council of the League of Nations had binding force for Poland and Lithuania, precisely because both states had voted in its favor. The Court determined that the participation of both countries in the adoption of the resolution of December 10, 1927, which "recommended that both Governments initiate direct negotiations" with each other, had created between them a legal obligation in that sense.[12]

Another case, quoted by Sorensen, is equally illustrative:

In its advisory opinion concerning the schools of the German minorities in Upper Silesia, the Court [the Permanent Court of International Justice] examined a resolution unanimously adopted on March 12, 1927 by the Members of the Council [of the League of Nations], including Germany and Poland, in which these two countries agreed to accept certain measures concerning the schools. The Court did not think it necessary to inquire whether "the settlement adopted by the Council's resolution constituted a transactional agreement [approved by the Council] between these two Governments only, or whether the respective consent of each one of them, resulting from their participation in the unanimous vote of the Council, left any character of its own to the Resolution." The Court contented itself with stating that the agreement had been accepted by both parties, and that no objection had been made to the fact that the agreement "accepted as such, was valid and binding for both States."[13]

In the Specialized Agencies

The Constitutions of some specialized agencies provide that certain resolutions shall go into force only when they have the consent, express or tacit, of the member states. According to Tammes[14]—whose choice of cases, although made for a different purpose, is nevertheless a pertinent basis for the thesis under study —the method of legislating by tacit consent of the members may be applied, both to certain regulatory powers of such organs as the Assembly of the World Health Organization, as well as to other situations in which it is necessary to modify certain parts of the constitutive instrument of an organization or its annexes. Examples of the first type of case are the following:

1. Article 22 of the Constitution of the World Health Organization states: "Regulations adopted pursuant to Article 21 shall come into force for all Members after due notice has been given of their adoption by the Health Assembly, except for such Members as may notify the Director-General of rejection or reservations within the period stated in the notice." The regulations in question are enumerated in Article 21 and relate to quarantines, nomenclature of diseases, uniform rules on the safety, purity, and potency of biological products, labeling of pharmaceutical products, etc. They come into force only for those states that tacitly manifest their wish to accept them. The legal links

created among the states that voluntarily accept these regulations are exactly the same as those that would have been created if a treaty had been concluded among them. In this case, the approved regulations, or rather, the resolutions that incorporate such regulations, are really nothing less than multilateral executive agreements.

2. "The fact that a Member of the OEEC, at the adoption of a decision by the Council (which has to decide unanimously), is absent or reserves its position, does not prevent the other Members from provisionally applying the decision *inter se*, until it has been accepted by the first member. Failing acceptance, the Council may decide that the decision will be maintained as between the other Members (Article 19 of the Rules of Procedure)."[15]

Examples of the second type of case (amendments to constitutive instruments) are the following:

"The successive Universal Postal Conventions have provided for revision, in the intervals between Congresses, under voting conditions varying according to the importance of the modifications involved. Proposals are circulated and those Administrations that have not notified their vote within a certain period are considered as abstaining (Articles 25-27 of the Convention as revised in 1952).

"Annexes to the Convention on International Civil Aviation, adopted by a two-thirds majority of the Council, are submitted to each contracting State and become effective within a certain period, unless in the meantime a majority register their disapproval with the Council (Articles 54 [I] and 90).

"The Schedule which forms an integral part of the International Convention for the Regulation of Whaling may be amended by the International Whaling Commission, acting with a three-fourths majority, and amendments become effective with respect to the Contracting Governments after a certain period following notification to them, if no Governments present objection. Amendments do not become effective with respect to objecting Governments (Article III[2] and Article V)."[16]

Finally, and still according to Tammes, "Some constitutions make a distinction between the external legislative effects of constitutional amendments and their internal organizational effects; while the latter may become operative for Members without their active or silent consent, an amendment defined as 'involving new obligations for Members' can only become binding upon each Member after he has accepted it"; this situation occurs, for example, in FAO (Article XIX of its Constitution) and in the World Meteorological Organization (Article 28).

In some of the above cases, agreement is established only through subsequent confirmations, express or tacit, of the decision made by an organ. In those cases, it would not be accurate to say that the decision itself registers and incorporates a consummated agreement, although it does represent a *conditional agreement*. In other cases, concurring votes, without need of subsequent validation, are in themselves the expression of the mutual consent by Members that established the multilateral agreement.

In the Inter-American System

The legal phenomenon now being studied may have particular importance and weight in the absence of a constitutive treaty. Such a situation existed among the American states before the Charter of the OAS was signed in 1948, during the time when they acted as a "system." For more than half a century, the American Republics formed a "quasi-international organization," characterized by periodic meetings of a supreme organ (the Conference), by a considerable degree of institutionalization of its activities, by the development and formulation of certain common juridico-political principles, by the creation of permanent organs, and especially, by their common awareness of being a group of nations united by specific links. But these tasks and activities were carried out without the support of a constitutional instrument that would attribute a definite legal value to their common decisions and would regulate the diverse categories, modalities, and scope of these decisions. In such circumstances, the "agreement-resolution" constituted an ideal instrument for the solution of the organizational problems of the inter-American system, in a way similar and parallel to that in which the "declaration," an instrument also of peculiar importance in the same regional sphere, which contained a formulation of certain general common principles, replaced the typical chapter of "principles" included in all constitutive charters.

Those organizational resolutions, so frequent in the inter-American system, created permanent organs, established machinery and rules of procedure, assigned budgetary obligations, etc. All these activities, whose effects continued beyond the duration of the conference that initiated them, were necessarily binding and accepted as such, since, as indicated above,[17] resolutions concerning internal structure and functioning have by nature a binding character. Thus, in the absence of a constitutive treaty that could serve as the legal basis for the attribution of binding effects, the only legal ground on which such binding provisions could have been based was the agreement established among the members who participated in the adoption of the resolution by their affirmative vote. These resolutions were truly international agreements lacking treaty form; they were resolutions that registered and expressed a multilateral executive agreement.

One of the most significant resolutions of this type was Number IX of the Inter-American Conference on Problems of War and Peace (Mexico, February-March 1945), entitled "Reorganization, Consolidation and Strengthening of the Inter-American System."[18] This resolution resolved, *inter alia*, the following: that the Inter-American Conferences shall formulate general inter-American policy and meet every four years; create a Governing Council for the Pan American Union, consisting of *ad hoc* delegates, indicating their rank (ambassadors) and other requirements (they could not be a part of the regularly accredited mission in Washington); determine the functions of the Council, the location of its headquarters, and requirements for the election of its director; create an Inter-American Economic and Social Council and establish four other permanent organs; and finally, recommend that the Governing Council of the Union draft a plan for a preliminary constitutive charter, specifically indicating the different elements that it should contain.

The nature of these functions and activities, the terminology used in this resolution, and the discussions that took place in the Chapultepec Conference prior to the charter's adoption clearly show that the members intended to assume legal obligations when they voted in favor of it, a fact that was indirectly confirmed by their subsequent attitude and by their effective implementation of the resolution. All this occurred before there was any international organization or constitutive charter on which to base the binding force of the resolution. It was indeed a case of an executive agreement-resolution.

THE USE OF AGREEMENT-RESOLUTIONS IN THE UNITED NATIONS

The few resolutions of this type and their heterogenous and rather exceptional character reveal that the multilateral executive agreement does not yet constitute a legal category or phenomenon generally accepted in the theory and practice of an international organization. Its most appropriate field is that of decisions or regulations of a technical nature, since it facilitates the adoption of uniform norms without the difficulties inherent in the elaboration of more formal agreements. Moreover, the conditions that favored this type of resolution in the inter-American system are no longer present to the same extent since the OAS Charter was adopted.

In the United Nations, the possibility of using agreement-resolutions is slight. There have been instances, however, when an agreement negotiated among groups of states has been a more satisfactory solution than a majority voting procedure. This situation is the necessary but not sufficient prerequisite for an agreement-resolution.

An example of the type was the Assembly resolution adopted on February 12, 1946 to deal with "the transfer of certain functions, activities, and assets of the League of Nations." According to its terms, "the General Assembly *'records'* that those Members of the United Nations who are parties to the instruments referred to above *assent by this resolution*, to the steps contemplated below . . ." for the anticipated transfer.

Another significant case arose when the Commission on the Peaceful Uses of Outer Space began its work in 1962 with a changed composition provided for in Resolution 1721/E (XVI), since the previous Commission had not been accepted by the Socialist states, who did not participate in it. From the beginning of its preliminary work, it had seemed evident to almost all members of the Commission that the study of the technical and legal aspects of the use of outer space would result in fruitful, significant, and viable conclusions only if these were accepted by at least the two states that had so far explored outer space. In initial consultations among the members, it was proposed that the substantive decisions of the Commission not be submitted to a vote, but that only those principles or conclusions be adopted that would elicit unanimous or very generalized agreements among the members of the Commission. This, in practice, meant attributing to them the character of agreement-resolutions. Although no one objected to the premises of the proposed solution or to the objectives sought, the majority of members felt that it was not advisable to establish formally that unusual system, since it might set a precedent that could be dangerous in other cases. Finally it was agreed, as a compromise, that the chairman of the Commission should declare at the inaugural session that the Commission "would endeavor" not to take votes and would try to reach conclusions acceptable to all members. That is what actually happened.

The Commission's conclusions in its Report to the Assembly (Doc. A/5181), some of which were explicitly confirmed by that organ (Resolution 1802 [XVIII] of December 14, 1962) or served as the basis for its recommendations, may be considered to be the result of an agreement; and because of the circumstances under which they were adopted, the resolutions that incorporated them may be considered resolutions whose object or content was to express a true multilateral agreement.

However, in this case we cannot speak of a binding force, since the Commission's conclusions were not to be applied directly and immediately, but were merely to serve as proposals directed to the Assembly in a very general way. The fact that a resolution is the expression of an agreement does not suffice to affirm its binding character, which results, also, from the intrinsic nature of the elements agreed upon.

The "Declaration of Legal Principles Governing the Activities of States in the Exploration and Use of Outer Space," unanimously approved by the General Assembly on December 13, 1963 (Resolution 1962 [XVIII]), more closely approaches the theoretical model of the multilateral executive agreement-resolution. The binding force of the principles it incorporates rests on various factors: first, the Declaration had been preceded by other United Nations resolutions which, although less explicit and more limited in scope, nevertheless manifested, when taken as a whole, a clear tendency in the progressive development of one or more legal norms. Second, the Declaration is an expression of a customary practice, especially with regard to the freedom of states to orbit satellites in outer space without prior consent by other states and without objections from them. But above all, the representatives of the two states in the forefront of the exploration of outer space, the United States and the Soviet Union, along with the representatives of numerous other states, have declared in unequivocal terms that their governments "would respect" the Declaration's principles. Manfred Lachs, Chairman of the Legal Subcommittee of the Commission for the Peaceful Uses of Outer Space, attributes such importance to this last fact that he has drawn the following conclusion: "Thus, by expressing their will to be bound by the provisions of the document in question, they consented so to be bound, and there is no reason why they should not be held to it, for their intention seems to be clear—the question of form ceased to be of essence."[19]

Other resolutions whose binding force is due to the fact that they incorporate and register an agreement among Assembly members are those that distributed the vice-presidencies of that organ and the chairmanships of its main committees, as well as the elective members to the Security Council and nine additional members to the Economic and Social Council, according to the principle of geographic distribution. The agreements concern the assignment of a certain number of posts to the different regional groups.

Resolution 1990 (XVIII), after approving the modification of Articles 31 and 38 concerning the composition of the Assembly Steering Committee, *decided* "that the President of the General Assembly, the seventeen Vice Presidents of the Assembly, and the seven chairmen of the main Committees *shall be* elected as provided in the Annex to the present resolution." That Annex indicates that "the seventeen Vice Presidents of the General Assembly *shall be* elected according to the following pattern, subject to paragraph 3 below: a) seven representatives from African and Asian States; b) one representative from an Eastern European State; c) three representatives from Latin American States; d) two representatives from Western European States and other States; e) five representatives from the permanent members of the Security Council." In addition, the same Annex indicates the distribution of the chairmanships of the primary committees.

Article A of Resolution 1991 (XVIII) deals with the increase in Security Council members. After approving, in accordance with Article 108 of the Charter, the amendment necessary to increase the number of Security Council members from eleven to fifteen, the Assembly "[decided] further that the ten non-permanent members of the Security Council shall be elected according to the following pattern: a) five from African and Asian States; b) one from Eastern European States; c) two from Latin American States; d) two from Western European and other States." In Article B, the same resolution (1991 [XVIII]) approved another amendment to the Charter, increasing to twenty-seven the number of Economic and Social Council members, and resolved further, using the same mandatory language as in the case of the Security Council, "that the nine additional members shall be elected according to the following pattern. . . ."

These resolutions were the result of agreements worked out among the different geographical groups. The terminology used reveals the clear intention to adopt definitive, binding decisions, and not mere recommendations; in other words, the resolutions express the Assembly's intention that future elections of persons or states, as the case might be, for such offices, would be carried out precisely on the basis of the geographical distribution agreed upon and established in those resolutions. The Assembly and the members, without exception, have considered and accepted them as imperative resolutions since their adoption. Their binding force cannot rest on the amendment of the Rules of Procedure or on the modification of the Charter, considered in themselves, since both deal only with the increase in the number of members of the organ, not with the geographical distribution of the offices. The binding force of this distribution can have as its sole legal basis the agreement of the members to limit their normal freedom of action in election matters.

Chapter 7

RESOLUTIONS THAT CONTAIN DECLARATIONS OR OTHER PRONOUNCEMENTS OF A GENERAL NATURE

ORIGIN OF THESE DECLARATIONS

This chapter will examine certain resolutions whose principal aim is to confirm the existence of customary rules or to express general principles of law. These resolutions do not all have identical legal value, but their common traits make it possible to typify them in a sufficiently identifiable category. Some of them usually take the form of declarations.

These resolutions are a result of the practice of international conferences at the end of the last and the beginning of the present century. At these conferences, the rule of unanimity prevailed, since (as James Brown Scott explains in the introduction to his work on the Peace Conferences of the Hague) "among equals there is not and cannot be a superior. Hence a State is only bound by the action of the Conference if it consents to it. . . . Majorities and minorities, in the parliamentary sense of the word, are unknown."[1]

As a consequence of this, convention drafts that were not unanimously approved could not be signed *under the auspices of the Conference*, not even among the states that approved them. With the purpose of preserving at least the general principles on which there was a substantial consensus, the conference conceived a "declaration," that is, an instrument that could be approved by a majority and that could give formal expression to those general principles. The declaration thus originated as an intermediate instrument between the binding convention and the *voeux*, frequently employed in the Hague Conferences, which expressed a hope and a wish of the Conference, or requested certain conduct of states as true recommendations do.

The case that best reveals and clarifies the *raison d'être* of declarations arose at the Second Hague Conference of 1907. The states represented there failed to reach agreement on a draft convention establishing obligatory arbitration. Because of the vigorous opposition of a minority headed by the Austro-Hungarian Empire and Germany, the states that favored the draft (31 against 9) did not succeed in having the Conference recognize their right to sign the treaty among themselves, but "sous le drapeau de la Conférence," according to the descriptive phrase of the Russian delegate de Martens. As a compromise, the Conference "decreed" unanimously, although with a few abstentions, an *unsigned* declaration, "which, although it preserves each one of the represented powers' position, allows them all to affirm the principles which they consider as unanimously recognized"; namely, (1) the principle of obligatory arbitration; and (2) the principle that disputes over the interpretation and application of treaties can be submitted to obligatory arbitration without restriction.[2]

The three Inter-American Conferences held prior to the Second Hague Conference had already approved unsigned instruments declaratory of general principles, although the terminology and the parliamentary technique used were not uniform. The First Conference (Washington, 1889-1890) resolved to urge the governments represented to adopt the following declarations: (1) the principle of conquest is eliminated from American public law; (2) the cession of territory under pressure or violence is null. This same Conference recommended that the governments adopt "as principles of American international law" the concepts that foreigners enjoy civil rights equal to those of nationals and that the former have no responsibilities or obligations greater than those of the latter. Finally, the First Conference also "resolve[d] to recommend" that the governments "adopt, declare, and recognize the following principle": that rivers separating different states or flowing through their territories shall remain open for free navigation by the riparian states. The Third Inter-American Conference (Rio de Janeiro, 1906) "resolved" to "ratify adherence to the principle of arbitration."

These inter-American resolutions have the same fundamental aim as the declaration of the Second Hague Conference on obligatory arbitration: to declare certain general principles as the formal expression of an entity, that is, the Conference, rather than of the participating nations individually considered. It is significant, however, that some of the cited inter-American resolutions do not directly impute the declaration of principles to the Conference itself. In this period, the intention to enunciate principles in the name of a collectivity is not yet reflected in an adequate technique: the Conference still contents itself with requesting states to "recognize," "adopt," or "declare" the principles.[3]

The historical circumstances under which declarations originated clearly indicate that their drafters did not attribute to them the same binding character as they did to conventions or to signed and ratified declarations. Nevertheless, they recognized that these instruments had special legal significance because they were declaratory of general principles. An indication of this, for example, is that the Second Hague Conference did not incorporate in an ordinary *voeu* or recommendation the principles on obligatory arbitration, but rather placed them in a *sui generis* resolution, which appears in the Final Act between the signed conventions and declarations on the one hand, and the *voeux* and recommendations on the other.

In his work on the Hague Conferences, James Brown Scott

comments on the legal value of the signed conventions or declarations relating to war, in terms that indicate that for him, not only the *form* of the instrument but also its *content*, whether or not it declared or created legal rules, should likewise determine its legal value. His observations concern the signed declaration, but they are partly pertinent in determining, by analogy, the validity of unsigned declarations, since they refer to the eventual application of conventional rules to a state that is not conventionally bound: a belligerent that had not ratified one of the conventions. He says:

It should, however, be pointed out that the failure of a belligerent to ratify a particular Convention only means that the Convention as such is not binding upon it; it does not and cannot mean that principles of law contained in the Convention may not bind the conduct of the parties. It is, therefore, necessary still further to ascertain whether the provisions of the Convention are merely a codification of international law. In this event the provisions are binding as international law, although the Convention itself, or this part of it, may be ineffective. A careful examination of the Conventions of the two Conferences will show that most of their provisions are declaratory, not amendatory, of international law, and that the failure of one Power or of any number of Powers to ratify them is merely to be regarded as the rejection of a codified text, not as a rejection of principles of international law, which no Power can reject without excluding itself from the society of nations.[4]

THE CONTENT OF DECLARATIONS OR OTHER GENERAL PRONOUNCEMENTS

The essential trait of the resolutions under study here, no matter how they are designated, is that they do not *create* law, but that they *recognize* and *declare* it. Their basic content consists of either customary rules or general principles of law. The purpose of incorporating these customary rules or general principles into resolutions is not to attribute legal value to them (in the sense of converting into a rule or a binding principle something that previously was neither) but rather to fix, clarify, and make precise their terms and scope. A principal function of such resolutions is to serve as a valuable and sometimes irreplaceable means of determining in case of doubt, and of authoritatively verifying, whether a legal norm exists.

As was rightly maintained by the Dutch Government in a memorandum dated August 18, 1950, concerning the Draft Declaration on Rights and Duties of States prepared by the International Law Commission of the United Nations:

The General Assembly does not possess legislative competency universally committing the States concerned. A certain amount of law-creating power cannot be denied to the General Assembly, because in those cases which might give rise to doubt whether a rule belongs already to international law or is still *jus consitituendum*, a formal declaration of the General Assembly might make the rule concerned *enter into* the recognized sphere of positive international law.[5]

D. H. N. Johnson, in spite of his generally rather negative attitude concerning the possibility of attributing binding effects in some cases to certain types of resolutions, nevertheless recognizes that General Assembly resolutions may constitute "elements indicative of the law, which an international court could take into account in determining whether there had been a breach of international law by the State concerned."[6] As will be seen below, several resolutions have in effect been invoked by national or international tribunals as proof of the legal character of a rule.

This function of proving and in some way determining the character as legal rules of certain practices, standards of conduct, or principles that have not yet been unquestionably recognized as positive law, helps fill one of modern international society's obvious needs. The absence of permanent legislative organs and, in general, the unspecialized and uninstitutionalized nature of the process by which international law is created, gives rise to a lack of stability, precision, and definiteness in many nonconventional rules, to frequent contradictions among certain rules, and to the relatively numerous lacunae observed in that normative order. Moreover, as a result of this situation, "substantive international law is still a collection of fragments rather than an integrated system of rules," as Friedman rightly observes.[7]

Perhaps the most serious consequence of the absence of an international legislator is the difficulty faced by the organs that apply international law of knowing when a practice has become a true rule of law and when it is still a potential, embryonic rule, and of knowing whether a principle recognized by some but not all states is a general principle of law in the sense of Article 38 of the Statute of the Court, that is, a true source of law. Regarding nonconventional rules, *there is no sign or criterion, formal and external, that indicates accurately when, under what conditions, and to what extent, the transition from a prejuridical stage to the sphere of true law occurs.* The determination of this dividing line, indispensable for the application of law, and implicitly made each day by governments and international organs and tribunals, may be subject to a markedly subjective appreciation. In a particularly dynamic environment of accelerated changes, such as modern international society's, it is natural that marginal zones should be very extensive and their demarcation most controversial. Thus, it is often necessary to rely on an authoritative determination, with full probative value, to attest to the character of the rules applied by the international community. The eminent author and judge Benjamin Cardozo stated this problem admirably in one of his judgments: "International law, or the law that governs between States," he said, "has at times, like the common law within states, a twilight existence during which it is hardly distinguishable from morality or justice, till at length the imprimatur of a court attests its jural quality."[8]

This function has been traditionally performed by international tribunals and, in a secondary, ancillary, and occasional way, even by national tribunals; Cardozo's phrase refers to the imprimatur of a court. But it cannot be concluded that this function belongs only to tribunals as a matter of principle. There is no essential reason preventing other broadly representative international organs from validly expressing on behalf of the international community what, in the community's opinion, *is* international law at a given moment. Moreover, the function considered here is not jurisdictional from the point of view of substance. It is not a question of *stating* the law with reference to a specific case that has assumed the character of a contention, but of expressing previously, in a general manner, whether a certain practice or principle has acquired the "jural quality" that allows it to be considered a part of the body of positive international law. In this sense, it is not a jurisdictional function, but a function that may be characterized as "quasi-legislative."

The juridical character of a practice or a principle derives ultimately from activities carried out, or attitudes assumed, by the states, and depends on the evaluation made and the meaning attributed by the international community to the activities or attitudes of its members. Therefore, a broadly representative organ, such as the General Assembly, is especially well qualified to examine and evaluate those activities and attitudes and to express, through declarative resolutions, the scope and meaning that the international community ascribes to them. These Assembly resolutions do not *create* law, but they *may authoritatively prove its existence.*

Inversely, an Assembly resolution can be proof that a customary rule is no longer one. If the majority of members of the international community express, through a resolution, their rejection of a customary rule, it is evident that that rule lacks the element of *opinio juris.*

As will be seen later in this chapter, the General Assembly and other international organs have clearly shown, by the general sense as well as by the terms of some resolutions, that they consider themselves competent to make categorical pronouncements on the legal nature of certain principles and practices.

LEGAL VALUE OF DECLARATORY RESOLUTIONS

The foregoing developments forecast the meaning given here to the legal value of declaratory resolutions.

The basic foundation for the binding force or rules or principles that are "declared," "recognized," or "confirmed" by a resolution rests, in the final analysis, on the fact that they *are* customary rules or general principles of law. But the declaratory resolution that incorporates and formulates them has a fully probative legal value. As Jessup states concerning the Nuremberg principles and the crime of genocide, the declarations in which the principles are embodied "are persuasive evidence of the existence of the rule of law which they enunciate."[9] The recognition and formal expression of a customary rule or a general principle of law by the General Assembly constitutes a *juris et de jure* presumption that such a rule or principle is a part of positive international law, that is to say, a legal assumption or fiction that does not allow proof to the contrary, and in the face of which an opposing individual position therefore lacks legal efficacy. Freedom of individual judgment vis-à-vis such a General Assembly resolution would not have greater legal relevance and significance than the opposition of a state to the customary rule incorporated in it; and, as is unanimously agreed, customary laws bind all states whether they have participated in or opposed their development.

The technical distinction between content (customary rule or general principle of law) and vehicle of expression may help to illustrate the legal value of declaratory resolutions. But this distinction is artificial to a certain extent. In reality, one cannot dissociate the binding force per se of a customary rule or a general principle, incorporated in a resolution, from the resolution's probative legal value. The observer is presented with a resolution as a unitary phenomenon. Therefore, in order to evaluate the legal value of a declaratory resolution, it will be indispensable to consider and analyze it as a whole.

In this light, each declaratory resolution presents a different problem. In practice, international bodies include principles of unequal value in their declaratory resolutions, that is, principles that are undoubtedly general principles of law, together with others of a more dubious nature. Sometimes, a restatement of customary law may contain aspects of *lex lata* organically connected to progressive development elements of international law. On the other hand, the terms used and the type of specific action adopted by the Assembly in relation to a body of rules or principles, which are generally in consonance with the content, present important degrees and shadings.

Thus, for example, the General Assembly "affirm[ed]" without reservation the Nuremberg principles (Resolution 95 [I]). On the other hand, it did not approve or adopt the Draft Declaration on Rights and Duties of States; but it considered it "a notable and substantial contribution towards the progressive development of international law and its codification, and as such commend[ed] it to the continuing attention of Member States and of jurists of all nations" (Resolution 375 [IV]).

On a lower level in the scale of various actions taken by the Assembly is the draft of the International Law Commission concerning arbitral procedure. The debates in the Legal Committee of the Assembly revealed that, in the opinion of a majority of member states, its provisions not only did not constitute existing law, but also the solutions it proposed went considerably further than customary law in the field of arbitration. Therefore, the Assembly rejected the suggestion of the International Law Commission that it approve the draft as a declaratory code. The Assembly contented itself with "bring[ing] the draft articles on arbitral procedure contained in the report of the International Law Commission to the attention of Member States for their consideration and use, in such cases and to such extent as they consider appropriate, in drawing up treaties of arbitration or *compromis*" (Resolution 1262 [XIII]).

The shadings in the degree of recognition indicated by the terms of the three resolutions mentioned correspond to and reflect, *grosso modo,* the extent to which their provisions constitute existing law. Although the legal value of a declaratory resolution obviously does not depend on the Assembly's intention, as manifested by its choice of action and by the terms used, this factor is *indicative* of the juridical nature of the "declared" rules or principles, and has, together with other factors, unquestionable relevance in the assessment of their legal value.

The foregoing examples underline the difficulties in determining with any certainty the legal value of declaratory resolutions, and the impossibility of formulating previously any general criterion in this respect. If this is the case with respect to declaratory codes,[10] such as the ones mentioned above, which deal mainly with traditional chapters of international law (except for the Nuremberg principles), the margin of subjective and circumstantial evaluation will tend to increase when the Assembly makes declaratory pronouncements on matters that correspond more closely to political law.

In this field, probably the highest degree of authority is represented by all the resolutions adopted since the time of the League of Nations regarding the outlawing of war and related questions. Of course, their binding force is postulated here only from the point of view of states not bound by convention, since the members of the United Nations are conventionally bound by Article 2(4) of the Charter, which prohibits the use of force. (Some of these resolutions will be considered below.)

On an intermediate level would be the "Declaration on the Granting of Independence to Colonial Countries and Peoples" (Resolution 1514 [XV]). This resolution contains disparate elements with regard to its degree of legal validity. Its essential terms —"[The General Assembly] solemnly proclaim[s] the necessity of bringing to a speedy and unconditional end colonialism in all its forms and manifestations"—are not the equivalent of establishing the specific legal obligation to grant political independence, immediately and unconditionally, to all dependent peoples. But the resolution was at the same time much more than the expression of an ideal; it was the modern interpretation of the principle of self-determination, rendered by the most representative organ of the international community, on the basis of political trends and events since the Charter was signed. The Declaration was a programmatic formulation based on new determinations that could no longer validly be impugned. For example, "lack of preparation in the political, economic, social, or educational fields" will no longer "serve as a pretext to delay independence."

The distinction between "advanced" and "less advanced" nations has disappeared as the legal criterion and basis for the preservation of colonial status. Independence is postulated as the inevitable goal; its advent has ceased to be something completely indeterminate and has become a short-time imperative. The Charter institutions for the protection of dependent peoples have lost their relatively permanent character. Free determination in the decade of the 60s means much more than it did in 1945. The new manner of conceiving the colonial problem, and even the changes that have taken place in the way the United Nations interprets and applies the Charter's institutions, are above all a consequence of changing reality. But the Declaration not only reflects the change that has been wrought; it also symbolizes and concretizes a new politico-juridical conception: the definite repudiation and end of colonialism.

As will be seen, the Declaration of Human Rights also lies on an intermediate level in the scale of binding force, inasmuch as some of its provisions establish rights, universally or almost universally recognized as human rights, whereas other provisions express only a common ideal.

On a lower level, purely from the point of view of legal value, would fall certain general declaratory Assembly resolutions whose aim is to set a political objective, such as those postulating that disarmament must be "general and complete" and subject to effective control. This type of resolution may have great political importance, but from a legal point of view it has no relevance whatsoever.[11]

Obviously, the legal value of declaratory resolutions allows for a wide range of shadings. There are no tangible, clear, juridical criteria that demarcate with precision the zones of binding force. Hazy, intermediate, transitional, embryonic, inchoate situations are not infrequent. The concepts of "embryonic norm," of quasi-legal rule, or, as Sloan appropriately defines it, of "nascent legal force" of some Assembly resolutions,[12] are suitable and sometimes inescapable expressions for faithfully describing the amorphous and mobile reality of this legal sector. The categorical and radical distinction, in this field, between what is absolutely binding and what is not, as Lauterpacht demanded, for example, is a manifestation of an exaggerated juridical formalism.[13] To determine the legal value of this type of resolution by means of *a priori*, schematic, and strict criteria, implies failure to take into account the multiform variety and complexity of the underlying international reality, which must necessarily be reflected in the juridical superstructure. Aside from treaty provisions, international rules are not marked by formal and external signs that give unquestionable evidence that they are or are not in force, as occurs with most internal laws. Therefore, the use of the classical criteria and methods of domestic law to evaluate the binding character and force of international rules is rather artificial.

An eloquent proof that nuances are indispensable when considering the legal value and the binding force of certain Assembly resolutions was offered by Lauterpacht himself some years after his call for a definite distinction between binding and nonbinding resolutions. In an individual opinion annexed to an advisory opinion of the International Court of Justice, in 1955, Lauterpacht admitted the pertinence of certain distinctions, nuances, and other factors, such as the cumulative effect of a state's noncompliance with reiterated recommendations or the quasiunanimity of votes received by a resolution. These factors could not have the least relevance, or indeed, any sense at all, within a formalistic conception: a resolution is binding or not binding, and no greater distinctions are necessary. However, Lauterpacht made a very subtle presentation of the problem of the legal value of certain Assembly resolutions, which reveals its extreme complexity. The pertinent lines read:

An administering State (of a trusteeship territory) may not be acting illegally by declining to act upon a recommendation or series of recommendations on the same subject. But in doing so it acts at its peril when a point is reached when the cumulative effect of the persistent disregard of the articulate opinion of the Organization is such as to foster the conviction that the State in question has become guilty of disloyalty to the Principles and Purposes of the Charter. Thus an Administering State which consistently sets itself above the solemnly and repeatedly expressed judgment of the Organization, in particular in proportion as that judgment approximates to unanimity, may find that *it has overstepped the imperceptible line between impropriety and illegality, between discretion and arbitrariness, between the exercise of the legal right to disregard the recommendation and the abuse of that right, and that it has exposed itself to consequences legitimately following as a legal sanction.*[14]

INTER-AMERICAN DECLARATIONS

Declarations of general principles have had great importance in the development of the inter-American system and community. Since the First Conference (Washington, 1889-1890), the American States have adopted numerous declaratory resolutions, sometimes of political postulates and frequently of general principles of law, which have contributed to the precision and consolidation of a certain number of inter-American rules for more than half a century. At times, the objective of the inter-American declaratory resolution has been the incorporation into the regional system of a universal principle;[15] on other occasions, inversely, the American states first formulated principles that, with time, acquired universal validity. Thus, the First Inter-American Conference declared that wars of conquest were "unjustifiable acts of violence and spoliation," and that territorial cessions were null if they were made under threat of war or pressure of armed force, thus anticipating by more than forty years the formulation of the Stimson Doctrine.

For some time, a number of Latin American authors considered that the principles enunciated by the Inter-American Conferences constituted a body of doctrine sufficiently coherent, identifiable, autonomous, and specific as to characterize it as "American international law."[16] Today, in any case, the majority of those that may be considered principles of law have universal character. Moreover, the study of the legal value of the inter-American declarations is now only of historical interest, since all the great principles they declared have already been incorporated in the Charter of OAS and in other Conventions signed in Bogotà in 1948.

The three most important conferences, with regard to declaratory resolutions adopted, were the Inter-American Conference for the Maintenance of Peace (Buenos Aires, 1936), the Eighth Inter-American Conference (Lima, 1938), and the Inter-American Conference on Problems of War and Peace (Mexico, 1945). The latter even attempted to enunciate systematically all those norms "which the American states have been incorporating in their International Law since 1890, by means of Conventions, Resolutions, and Declarations" (Resolution VIII).[17]

The principles formulated in this last resolution are of unequal legal value; some are political pronouncements or even general political evaluations that can hardly be considered norms. The restatements of principles from the other two conferences, as well as those from another resolution of the same 1945 conference (Resolution XI), are substantially the same in content.[18]

Inter-American recommendations and nondeclaratory resolutions of general principles have not generally been considered
binding. However, as indicated above,[19] the Inter-American Conferences adopted, from the outset, resolutions creating permanent
organs or relating to other organizational aspects that transcended
the duration of the conference that adopted them, without the
support of a constitutive treaty. The important results of the
Lima Conference of 1938 were incorporated exclusively into
resolutions and declarations, including the "declaration" that established a consultation system in order to consider situations
where continental peace or security or the territorial integrity of
any American Republic were endangered (Declaration of Lima).
It is likely that the delegates to the Conference "felt that all signing members [of the Final Act] would undertake to fulfill the
commitments assumed under the resolutions and declarations."[20]

Resolution IX of the Conference on Problems of War and
Peace (Mexico, 1945) created periodic organs, such as the Regular Meetings of the Ministers of Foreign Affairs, as well as permanent ones, such as the Council of the Pan American Union,
with specific functions and permanent headquarters; and it even
laid the foundation for the future Organization of American
States through a simple resolution of the Conference. The terms
of this resolution would have been meaningless if its framers had
not considered it binding. As already shown,[21] perhaps the only
possible legal basis for the binding force of this and similar resolutions consists in considering them the expression of multilateral
executive agreements.

In relation to declarations as such, the earlier observations
concerning the legal force of resolutions of this type are also
valid for the inter-American system. From the terms of the inter-
American declarations discussed here, it is impossible to infer
uniform criteria. However, it might be generally stated that the
American states were perhaps more conscious than the members
of contemporary universal bodies of the fact that they were utter-

ing binding pronouncements, at least when they recognized and affirmed legal principles. The American jurist Charles Fenwick, who for many years was the principal legal counselor of the Pan American Union, states that, in numerous cases, inter-American declarations "have been regarded *de facto* as creating binding obligations," in the sense that a state that does not comply with them may be called to account for its conduct by the other parties of the declaration.[22]

Some inter-American declaratory resolutions have been invoked by international and national tribunals as convincing proof of the existence of an international rule. Thus, the resolution of February 18 of the Sixth Inter-American Conference (Havana, 1928) entitled "Aggression,"[23] was used by the Nuremberg Tribunal, together with some resolutions of the League of Nations Assembly and other instruments, to strengthen the interpretation given by the Tribunal to the Pact of Paris, that a war of aggression was not merely illegal, but also criminal. Moreover, the U.S. Department of Justice invoked before the U.S. Supreme Court resolutions of the Inter-American Conferences of Lima (1938) and Mexico (1945), as well as a resolution of the United Nations General Assembly, as proof that "the enforcement of racial restrictive covenants is contrary to the public policy of the United States."[24]

DECLARATORY RESOLUTIONS CONCERNING THE OUTLAWING OF WAR AND RELATED MATTERS

The declarations and other instruments concerning the outlawing of war at the time of the League of Nations are of special interest to the subject considered here. In spite of the fact that the basic purpose of those instruments is met today by the United Nations Charter, it is interesting to examine them because, in the opinion of some, those declarations and instruments are indicative of the existence of a customary rule prohibiting the use of force, which would bind nonmember states if its existence could be proved.

Article 16 of the Covenant of the League contained the essentials of a system of collective security. However, in order to strengthen the Covenant, attempts were made, almost from the start, either to provide for more effective guarantees to assist the states threatened by the use of force, to prohibit in a more categorical way the recourse to war, or to complement collective security with an effective system of peaceful settlement of disputes. During this period, bilateral and multilateral agreements for this last objective multiplied. The *United Nations Systematic Survey of International Disputes, 1928-1948* lists 234 treaties for the peaceful adjustment of disputes made during that period. Several of them also contained definitions of aggression.

The most significant declarations and general instruments for abolishing the use of force and strengthening the Covenant were the following:

The first was the "General Act for the Pacific Settlement of International Disputes," adopted by the League Assembly on October 2, 1924, which, besides providing for mutual guarantees against aggression, established a binding system of measures for the peaceful settlement of disputes. Although 48 states favored its adoption in the Assembly, only 19 later signed it, and in the end the Act did not have the necessary number of ratifications to come into force. Both the Act and the Locarno Treaties of 1925 were forerunners of the United Nations Charter system, to the extent that their parties agreed not to have recourse to war, except in self-defense or in execution of an action taken in compliance with the Covenant. Although the machinery provided for in the Act for the pacific settlement of disputes did not become operative, the value of the General Act was considerable as a precedent that contributed to the development and consolidation of the principle that a war of aggression is an international crime.

The League Assembly also adopted important resolutions in

this respect. The first, of September 25, 1925, sponsored by Spain, clearly established that a war of aggression was an international crime. The report of the First Commission observed that this notion was not yet a part of positive law.[25] The second, adopted on September 24, 1927 on the basis of a Polish initiative, established, *inter alia*, "that all wars of aggression are and shall always be prohibited." After indicating, furthermore, that a means of peaceful settlement must be used in any kind of dispute, the resolution *declared* "that all Member States of the League are under the *obligation* of conforming to these principles." Its drafter, Mr. Sokal of Poland, explained, however, that the proposal did not constitute a juridical instrument but a moral rule that should prepare the way for the establishment of a general norm of positive law in the future.[26] In spite of this opinion, the terms of the resolution reveal a clear acceptance by the members of a legal obligation.

Another resolution of special interest was that of February 18, 1928, introduced by Mexico and adopted by the Sixth Inter-American Conference in Havana. According to its terms, the Conference considered that "war of aggression constitutes an international crime against the human species" and "resolved" that "any aggression is considered illegal and is therefore prohibited."

The most important link in this chain of declarations and conventional instruments was the Kellogg-Briand Pact, signed in Paris on August 27, 1928. In Article I, the parties "condemn[ed] recourse to war for the solution of international controversies, and renounce[d war] as an instrument of national policy . . ."; in Article II, the parties agreed to seek solutions for their disputes only by peaceful means. The instrument, still in force,[27] was almost universally adhered to since only four states of all those comprising the international community prior to the Second World War did not adopt it.[28] In the years following its signature, numerous bilateral and multilateral treaties reaffirmed the obligations of the Kellogg-Briand Pact.

The Judgment of the Nuremberg Tribunal illustrates the legal effect of declaratory resolutions. None of the nonconventional declarations mentioned above created a new obligation by itself; but the analysis of several of them, together with the Kellogg-Briand Pact and the General Act of Geneva, allowed the Tribunal to reach the conclusion that the principle, according to which a war of aggression is a criminal act, was a part of international law. In other words, the declarations were interpreted as an expression of international law.

It is true that the Kellogg-Briand Pact did not state that wars of aggression were criminal, nor did it establish tribunals to try their initiators; but this was equally true of the Hague Conventions of 1907 on land warfare, and that did not prevent tribunals in the past from trying those accused of violating their provisions. Furthermore, although the Pact established only very general principles, "the customs and practices of States which gradually obtained universal recognition [as well as] the general principles of justice applied by jurists and practiced by military courts,"[29] were also part of the law of war. The Nuremburg Tribunal considered that the Kellogg-Briand Pact ought to be interpreted in the light of the legislative history that preceded it, and in this connection specifically described, as elements demonstrative of the scope of the Pact, the Geneva Protocol, the resolution of the League Assembly of September 24, 1927, and the resolution of February 18, 1928 of the Sixth Inter-American Conference in Havana.[30]

What the Tribunal said concerning the Geneva Protocol is particularly revealing, since, as indicated, it never entered into force as a conventional instrument, and the reasoning of the Tribunal is applicable *mutatis mutandis* to other nonconventional instruments: "Although the Protocol was never ratified, it was signed by the leading statesmen of the world representing the vast majority of the civilized states and peoples, and may be regarded as strong evidence of the intention to brand aggressive war as an international crime."[31] The Tribunal concluded in this respect:

All these expressions of opinion and others that could be cited, so solemnly made, reinforce the construction which the Tribunal placed upon the Pact of Paris (Kellogg-Briand Pact), that resort to a war of aggression is not merely illegal, but is criminal. The prohibition of aggressive war demanded by the conscience of the world finds its expression in the series of pacts and treaties to which the Tribunal has just referred.[32]

THE OUTLAWING OF THE USE OF FORCE AS A RULE OF GENERAL INTERNATIONAL LAW

In light of the foregoing considerations, it could be asked, what is the present status of the rule that prohibits the recourse to force for those states not conventionally bound because they are not members of the United Nations? In other words, does this rule presently constitute a rule of general positive international law, which therefore has universal application?

This is a difficult question, and the publicists' opinions in this respect are far from uniform. It is thought that the answer should be in the affirmative for the following reasons:

First, as Brownlie convincingly shows,[33] the practice of states until 1945 is proof that a true customary norm had been created, in the sense that the use of force as an instrument of national policy, as distinct from its use in self-defense, was illegal. The existence of this rule is not denied by the invasions and wars of aggression that took place, nor by the failure of the collective security system of the League (the states did not think that the League's failure made the Axis aggression legal), nor the maintenance of certain forms of neutrality, nor certain acts of recognition and acceptance of conquest (such as the *de jure* recognition by Great Britain of Italian sovereignty over Ethiopia), all of which were, on the whole, exceptional. The wars of aggression were started by a minority of members of the international community; it would be absurd to think that the legal effect of these aggressions consisted in annulling the Kellogg-Briand Pact, instead of considering them a violation of that Pact. Actually, "the majority of States vindicated the Pact by taking action against a minority of aggressor States." By 1942, the war against Germany and its allies was considered by many governments to be a war of collective defense and of sanction against an aggressive and antijuridical attitude that constituted a common danger.

Moreover, no state denied the illegality of recourse to war, and governments that committed acts of aggression tried to justify their actions through legal arguments. The *jus ad bellum*, which general international law recognized prior to the Kellogg-Briand Pact, was never invoked as legal justification for recourse to war. It is true, as Brownlie says, that "the customary rule which existed by 1939 did not create a sharply defined *modus operandi* for those concerned with the appreciation of international law. There was no general agreement on the precise meaning of the terms used in instruments and diplomatic practice relating to the use of force. This still creates serious difficulty, but it is absurd to suggest that because there is a certain degree of controversy the basic obligation does not apply to the more obvious instances of illegality."[34]

Second, even on the assumption that one might not admit the existence of a customary rule prohibiting recourse to force, effective both before the Second World War and today, this question could and should also be examined from a different point of view.

When a principle may so vitally affect the entire international community, as is the case today with the outlawing of the use of force, it can hardly be maintained that its legal character depends only on juridico-formal elements. In examining whether or not the principle is a binding rule of positive law, it would be inconceivable to deny the relevance of considerations such as the simple reflection that the right to use force may mean, in today's world, the right to destroy humanity. To admit that a state, because it is not a member of the United Nations, could make use of force without actually violating the normative order of international society is repugnant to the conscience of humanity. As the Nuremberg Tribunal stated: "The prohibition of aggressive war [was] demanded by the conscience of the world."

These ethical and political considerations are not foreign, in the last analysis, to the notion of "general principles of law recognized by civilized nations." The same ethical motives and reasons of social solidarity that inspired the provision outlawing the use of force in the United Nations Charter support numerous domestic legal provisions in all civilized nations. In the past, when the impact of war on the fate of humanity was infinitely less strong than now, it was understandable to conceive of war as a *right* (in spite of the distinction made by many eminent philosophers and lawmakers between just and unjust wars). But international solidarity has a radically different dimension and meaning in the nuclear age. The magnitude of the interests involved, the essentially different form of social solidarity, must necessarily be reflected in new common legal principles. Within a broad conception of the "the general principles of law recognized by civilized nations," adapted to the needs of the atomic era, there is undoubtedly a place for the principle of outlawing the use of force in international relations.

Third, the United Nations Charter categorically establishes the principle that the members "shall refrain . . . from the threat or use of force" (Article 2[4]). There exists no need to invoke the notion of "international community," represented by the United Nations, nor is it necessary to equate the "law of the

Charter" with general international law to accept the considerable influence that the incorporation of this principle in the Charter may have on its legal status as a universal rule of positive law. The essential reason for that impact is the universal scope of the Organization, which becomes more of a reality each day. There are already over 120 members, nearly every new state now enters the Organization almost automatically, and the independent states that are not members (counting the divided states as single entities) do not number more than half a dozen.

As supporting elements in favor of this thesis, the following two subsidiary arguments could be invoked (neither of which is decisive in itself): the first is based on the provision of Article 2 (6) of the Charter, according to which "the Organization shall *ensure* that States which are not members of the United Nations act in accordance with these Principles so far as may be necessary for the maintenance of international peace and security." As Kelsen states, this provision "may be interpreted to mean that the Charter imposes at least the most important obligations of the Members also upon non-Members, and that means that the Charter claims to have the character of general international law."[35] The second argument is that the Organization has consistently followed the practice of addressing recommendations to nonmember states.[36]

Georges Scelle, on the basis of the solidarist conception of law that still has a good number of supporters, formulated an appealing thesis on the "expansive force of legislative treaties," applicable especially to constitutive treaties such as the Covenant of the League or the Charter of the United Nations. According to Scelle, "the expansive force of the legislative treaty derives from its conformity to objective law and to social solidarity, and from the implicit or explicit recognition of this conformity by the international community. The inherent defect—the non-participation of all the competent governments in the legislative act, in accordance with the customary rule of unanimity—will be remedied by that recognition." Moreover, he adds later, "this inherent defect, in a society in which the specialization of functions is still uncertain and in which the governments fulfill a necessary social function, could not, in our opinion, give rise to the fundamental nullity of an objective normative order truly corresponding to the general interest. To express our thought fully," he adds, "the compliance with public order, even in an incorrect fashion, may at times be preferable to a formalistic respect of procedures."[37]

THE NONRECOGNITION OF THE VALIDITY OF TERRITORIAL ACQUISITIONS ACHIEVED THROUGH ILLEGAL USE OF FORCE

A related principle, which is also of some interest from the point of view of the legal value of declaratory resolutions, is the principle of nonrecognition of the validity of territorial changes brought about through the illegal use of force. As indicated above, this principle had its origin in the inter-American sphere: it was first formulated at the 1889 Inter-American Conference in Washington. Subsequently, several inter-American conferences reiterated it, either in resolutions or in conventional instruments.[38] The Charter of OAS enunciates it in a clear and categorical way in Article 17.

This principle was applied when Japan undertook military operations in Manchuria. The United States Secretary of State, Henry L. Stimson (whence derives the name Stimson Doctrine), sent a note to the governments of Japan and China stating that the United States would not recognize any situation or treaty brought about by means contrary to the Pact of Paris. After a fruitless call on Japan by the members of the League, the Assembly unanimously adopted (with the exception of the Japanese vote) on March 11, 1932, the well-known resolution according to which "it is incumbent upon[39] the Members of the League of Nations not to recognize any situation, treaty or agreement which may be brought about by means contrary to the Covenant of the League of Nations or the Pact of Paris."

The correct interpretation of its scope and legal value probably is the following: the resolution is binding because it is declarative of the obligation contained in Article 10 of the Covenant by which the members agreed to guarantee the territorial integrity and the political independence of the other members. The minimum duty of the guarantor is not to recognize any transgression against the territorial integrity or the political independence of the guaranteed state. The resolution thus fixed the minimum scope and content of the obligations of Article 10, without adding any new obligation.[40]

It may also be asked whether the principle of nonrecognition is at present a part of general international law and whether all States consequently have a legal obligation not to recognize the validity of territorial acquisitions achieved by the illicit use of force.

There is no doubt that the principle is binding for the American states *inter se*, since they have conventionally accepted it. Moreover, the American states have applied the principle on two occasions: the first was the Declaration of August 3, 1932, put forth by nineteen American states in relation to the Chaco War, stating that they would not recognize territorial changes made by nonpeaceful means or the validity of territorial acquisitions "obtained through occupation or conquest by armed forces."

The second, of greater significance, was the signing of a "Convention on the Provisional Administration of European Colonies and Possessions in the Americas" during the Second Meeting of Consultation of Ministers of Foreign Affairs (Havana, July 1940). The consideranda of the Convention invoked "the principle of American International Law" that "the acquisition of territories by force cannot be permitted" as the motive and foundation for declaring: "If a non-American state shall directly or indirectly attempt to replace another non-American state in the sovereignty or control which it exercises over any territory located in the Americas, thus threatening the peace of the Continent, such territory shall automatically come under the provisions of the Convention and shall be submitted to a provisional administrative regime, whose general outlines are the object of the Convention."[41]

With regard to non-American states, the situation is less clear. The United Nations Charter does not oblige the members to "guarantee" the territorial integrity and the political independence of the other members, as did the League Covenant. But the principle of nonrecognition could at present be interpreted as a necessary legal corollary to the principle of the prohibition of the use of force. Indeed, according to the principle of the criminality of wars of aggression, declared by the Nuremberg Tribunal and "affirm[ed]" by General Assembly Resolution 95 (I), recognition might even be considered criminal complicity.[42]

Moreover, it would seem that in spite of several flagrant cases of recognition of the results of conquest, before and after World War II, such cases are few; and it can be maintained, with Brownlie, that "the existence of a coherent body of doctrine and practice on the legal status of resort to force lead[s] to the conclusion that an obligation of non-recognition exists."[43] In support of this thesis (although this is not a decisive reason in itself), the "Draft Declaration on the Rights and Duties of States," formulated by the International Law Commission and declared by the Assembly to be "an outstanding and important contribution to the progressive development of international law and its codification" (Resolution 375 [IV]), includes this principle among the duties of states (Article 11).

There are also doubts as to the nature of nonrecognition. In the light of provisions of the Charter, nonrecognition cannot be interpreted as a *sanction* in the same sense as an embargo, the severance of relations, or other measures provided for in Article 41. The duty of nonrecognition is rather the result of a juridico-political evaluation of a given situation, which is normally made by each state individually. If, as a result of that evaluation, the conclusion is reached that the change in a situation was the consequence of an illicit use of force, the legal duty of not recognizing the change exists, on the basis of and in compliance with a rule of general international law.[44]

Moreover, if the evaluation in question was made by the Security Council or the General Assembly or, in other words, if either of these organs had determined that a territorial acquisition had been made as a consequence of the use or the threat of force, this determination would be obligatory, since its object would be to concretize and apply a legal rule to a specific case, and the members would have the duty of nonrecognition.

THE NUREMBERG PRINCIPLES AND THE CRIME OF GENOCIDE

Other related resolutions, declaratory of general principles, concern the Nuremberg Principles and the crime of genocide.

The General Assembly approved on December 11, 1946, Resolution 95 (I), by which the Assembly "affirms the principles of international law recognized by the Charter of the Nuremberg Tribunal and the judgment of that Tribunal." In its Resolution 177 (I) of November 21, 1947, the Assembly entrusted to the International Law Commission the tasks of "formulating" the above principles and drafting a code of offenses against the peace and security of mankind, in which the function of the Nuremberg Principles would be clearly indicated.

The task of formulating them does not derogate from or diminish the authority of the previous affirmation of these principles by Resolution 95 (I). The unquestionable meaning of that Resolution is that the Assembly *confirmed* the principles of the Statute and of the judgments of the Nuremberg Tribunal *as an expression of international law*. Their formulation must be interpreted within the Assembly's objective of performing a broader task of codification. In the context of a general and systematic code of crimes against peace and security (which eventually would have to be complemented by the statute of an International Criminal Court and perhaps by a definition of aggression), the Nuremberg Principles required a formulation technically suitable for permanent legislation, different in form but not in substance from the judicial expression given to them by the Court and confirmed by the Assembly. When the Assembly examined the formulation of the International Law Commission,[45] practically all the delegations that took a stand in the matter accepted the formulated principles as part of international law.[46]

Resolution 96 (I) affirmed "that genocide is a crime under international law which the civilized world condemns; and for the commission of which principals and accomplices . . . are punishable." Resolution 180 (II) reiterated the concept in similar terms, and Resolution 260 (III) approved the text of the Convention for the Prevention and Punishment of the Crime of Genocide and opened it for signature. These three resolutions are declaratory of the legal principles they express, including those contained in the Convention approved by the Assembly. This organ "affirmed" them (Resolution 96), "declared" them (Resolution 180), and "approved" them (Resolution 260) as an expression of international law. The International Court of Justice categorically recognized this in its Advisory Opinion of May 28, 1951. After examining the origins and antecedents of the Convention, the Court, referring specifically to Resolution 96 (I), concluded that "the first consequence arising from this conception is that the principles underlying the Convention are principles which are recognized by civilized nations as binding on States, even without any conventional obligation."[47]

Thus, the observation made concerning the legal value of these resolutions is applicable to the Nuremberg principles and the crime of genocide: the resolutions are binding, not in the sense that they have *created* new obligations, but in the sense that they are the expression and the legally irrefutable proof of general principles of law that are obligatory.

THE UNIVERSAL DECLARATION OF HUMAN RIGHTS

The legal value of the Universal Declaration of Human Rights has been a matter for discussion ever since it was drafted. Much has already been written on the subject.

The prevailing opinion is that the great majority of members who participated in its drafting did not intend to create a binding document, that is, to impose on states the international legal obligation to respect and guarantee the rights expressed in the Declaration, so that the states that violated them would incur an international responsibility. With differences of nuance and even of conviction, and invoking different arguments, only the representatives of France and Belgium and, to a lesser degree, Lebanon, Panama, and Chile maintained—and even then with some reservations—the binding force of the Declaration. The impression gained by reading the debates of the Third Committee and of the General Assembly in 1948 is confirmed and strengthened by the very wording of the document and by the circumstances under which it was adopted.[48]

The two principal arguments presented in favor of the binding force of the Declaration are the following:

1. Articles 55 and 56 of the Charter state the obligation of the members to respect "the fundamental freedoms for all." But these articles do not specify what those fundamental freedoms are. The Declaration would thus be an "authentic interpretation" of Articles 55 and 56, a determination of the content and scope of the obligations stated in those articles.[49]

2. Some provisions of the Declaration have long constituted "customary rules of nations and were consequently recognized as unwritten international law."[50]

Neither of the two arguments is convincing. As indicated earlier, the *travaux préparatoires* at the San Francisco Conference clearly prove that no United Nations organ is authorized to make, in a general way, that is, through general, abstract pronouncements, "authentic interpretations" of the Charter, which is what the Universal Declaration would be equivalent to if it were accepted that its legal function is to fill the content of Articles 55 and 56 of the Charter.[51]

With regard to the second argument, it is not exact to say that there existed a customary rule imposing an *international* obligation on members to respect individual rights, even the most obvious ones, such as the "right to life, liberty, and security of person" (Article 3 of the Declaration). As Lauterpacht rightly states, existent customary law was exactly the opposite, that is, it held such matters to be within the domestic jurisdiction of states.[52]

Therefore, from a strictly legal point of view, the Universal Declaration of Human Rights is not a binding document to which one may attribute the effect of creating obligations for the states; nor can one ascribe to it the character of a resolution declaratory of pre-existent customary rules. However, once this position of principle is accepted, some considerations concerning the legal significance, actual and potential, of the Declaration, must be kept in mind.

If the "general principles of law recognized by civilized nations" are understood to be those legal principles that may be inferred by induction from a considerable number of national juridical systems that establish them—and this is one of the most widely accepted meanings of this concept—it is undeniable that some of the principles of the Universal Declaration are of that nature.[53] Most national constitutions guarantee at least the classical individual rights. Other rights, particularly those of a social and economic nature, such as the right to an adequate standard of living, to protection against unemployment, to the application without exception of the principle of equal pay for equal work,

etc., are not granted by the majority of states; and their incorporation into the Declaration represents, at least for the time
being, the expression of a common ideal to be achieved in the
future. But with regard to certain "fundamental freedoms," the
Declaration may be interpreted as the expression of general principles of law.

The expression of such principles in the Universal Declaration is not equivalent, per se, to an international obligation of the
states to respect the fundamental freedoms forming the substance
of these principles. But the Universal Declaration, conceived as
the expression of general principles of law, does constitute an
essential element which, along with others, has had a decisive influence on the derogation of the old customary rule, according
to which respect for human rights was a matter within the domestic jurisdiction of states.

Independently of the extent to which Article 2(7) originally may have covered the protection of human rights in the
opinion of the framers of the Charter, there is no doubt that
the adoption of the Declaration has greatly contributed to
strengthening the view that this matter is no longer outside the
international sphere and thus exempt from international action.
Since 1948, United Nations organs have almost invariably asserted their capacity to discuss and make recommendations on the
protection of human rights, frequently invoking the Declaration
as a basis both for maintaining their competence and for addressing specific recommendations to states on these matters. At times,
the recommendations have referred to the Declaration in terms
implying that, "if it does not create direct legal obligations on the
part of United Nations Members and organs, its provisions at least
impose upon them the necessity of being guided in their conduct
by these provisions."[54]

Finally, it is also significant that a large number of international treaties, national constitutions and laws, and judgments of
both national and international tribunals, subsequent to the Dec-

laration, have explicitly invoked it.[55] In an especially pertinent case, heard before the District Appellate Court of California (Fujii v. the State), the court maintained that the provisions of the "Alien Land Law," which prohibited the acquisition of land in California by foreigners not eligible for citizenship, were "incompatible [not only with the Charter but also] with Article 17 of the Universal Declaration of Human Rights, which proclaims the right of all to own property." Although it is true, the court said, that the Declaration is not a treaty that imposes obligations on the United States, it "underlines the purposes and guarantees of the Charter."[56]

NOTES

Chapter 1: Introduction

1. A. J. P. Tammes, "Decisions of International Organs as a Source of International Law," *Recueil des Cours de l'Académie de Droit International,* XCIV, 270 ff.

2. The Conference rejected by 26 votes to 1 a Filipino proposal that would have permitted the General Assembly to enact rules of international law that would become binding for the members of the Organization once they had been approved by a majority vote in the Security Council (*Documents of the United Nations Conference on International Organization* [UNCIO], 22 vols. (New York and London, UN Information Organization, 1945), IX, 70). Furthermore, the San Francisco Conference did not recognize any organ's power to give authentic interpretations of the Charter *in a general way*, because it was thought that they entailed a form of international legislation. It can be clearly inferred from the Conference discussions, on the other hand, that the power of interpretation only arises in relation to the *application* of a Charter provision to a given, specific situation, and resides in the organ that applies such a provision (UNCIO, *Documents,* VI, 509 and XIII, 703–12).

3. See in this connection Rosalyn Higgins, *The Development of International Law through the Political Organs of the United Nations* (London, 1963).

4. Clive Parry, *The Sources and Evidences of International Law* (Manchester, 1965), p. 22. Parry attributes this effect even to the single "Declaration on the Granting of Independence to Colonial Countries and Peoples" (Res. 1514 [XV]).

5. A modest but illustrative case of this gradual transition is the following: although the Expanded Program of Technical Assistance and the Special Fund of the United Nations are financed through voluntary contributions, at least the administrative expenses, which make possible the execution of such voluntary programs, have a binding character owing to their inclusion in the regular budget of the United Nations.

6. Parry, *Sources and Evidences,* p. 113.

7. See Chap. 7 of this book.

8. Parry, *Sources and Evidences,* p. 113.

9. This course of reasoning becomes less convincing when the Court applies a resolution originating, not in a principal organ established by the original treaty, but in a subsidiary organ created in turn by the resolution of another organ. Treaties and resolutions are, in addition, substantially different sources, as is indicated by the fact, among others, that resolutions do not have parties (Tammes, "Decisions of International Organs," p. 269).

10. Besides the Dutch writer A. J. P. Tammes, already mentioned, the following authors have studied this problem: F. Blaine Sloan, "The Binding Force of a 'Recommendation' of the General Assembly of the United Nations," *British Yearbook of International Law,* XXV (1948), 1–33; G. Piatrowski, "Les Resolutions de l'Assemblée Générale des Nations Unies et la portée du droit

conventionnel," *Revue de droit international*, XXXIII (1955), 111–25, 221–42; G. M. Razi, " La Compétence de l'Assemblée Générale de l'ONU," *Revue de droit international pour le Moyen Orient*, II (1952–1953), 36–66; D. H. N. Johnson, "The Effect of Resolutions of the General Assembly of the United Nations," *British Yearbook of International Law*, XXXII (1955–1956), 97–123; P. F. Brugière, *Les Pouvoirs de l'Assemblée Générale des Nations Unies en matière politique et de sécurité* (Paris, 1955); M. Virally, "La Valeur juridique des recommandations des organisations internationales," *Annuaire français de droit international* (1956), pp. 66–97; A. Malintoppi, *Le Raccomandazioni internazionali* (Milan, 1958).

11. Virally, "La Valeur juridique," p. 72. Notwithstanding, in giving a general definition, Virally characterizes the "recommendation" as an "invitation" (p. 94).

12. Malintoppi, *Le Raccomandazioni*, p. 18, n. 30.

13. *Ibid.*, p. 25. In examining their legal nature, Malintoppi observes that recommendations (for the purposes of his study) have only a negative aspect: " . . . for an act to have the nature of a recommendation, it is necessary that no obligatory effect be directly attached to it consisting in the execution of its content by its addressee" (p. 94, n. 1).

14. Sloan, "The Binding Force of a 'Recommendation'," p. 7.

15. *Ibid.*, p. 10.

16. In a separate opinion annexed to the advisory opinion of the International Court of Justice in the Corfu Channel Case, the seven dissenting judges invoked "the normal meaning of the word recommendation, a meaning which this word has retained in diplomatic language, as is borne out by the practice of the Pan-American Conferences, of the League of Nations, of the International Labor Organization, etc." (ICJ, *Reports of Judgments, Opinions, and Orders* [1948], p. 32). This meaning is, of course, of a nonbinding invitation.

17. Functions not consisting of requests to addressees will be illustrated in following sections of this chapter.

18. Malintoppi, *Le Raccomandazioni*, pp. 93 ff.

19. Amos J. Peaslee, ed., *International Governmental Organizations*, 2nd ed. rev., 2 vols. (The Hague, 1961), I, 468. Malintoppi, for the reasons mentioned above, believes that these acts do not have the nature of "recommendations," but rather of "directives" (*Le Raccomandazioni*, p. 13). R. Monacco describes the ECSC recommendations as "quasi-obligatory" (quoted by Malintoppi, *Le Raccomandazioni*, p. 14, n. 23).

An interesting and revealing fact in this connection is that identical resolutions, binding in their goals but permissive in the means for realizing them, are also provided for in the 1957 Treaty of Rome that created the European Economic Community (Article 189), where they already are called "directives." In accordance with Article 189, the Council and the Commissions shall adopt: "regulations" of general application, binding in every respect and directly applicable to each member state; "directives," binding for the member state to which they are addressed as to the result to be achieved, while leaving to domestic agencies a competence as to the forms and means; "decisions," binding in every respect for the addressee named therein; and nonbinding "recommendations" and "opinions." Article 161 of the treaty that created the European Atomic Energy Community (EURATOM) is identical (Peaslee, ed., *International Governmental Organizations*, I, 574, 436).

The resolutions adopted by the International Civil Aviation Organization are also interesting in this respect. Article 37 of the 1944 Chicago Convention establishes both "international standards" and "recommended practices." Even though the Convention does not distinguish clearly between them, and authorities are not in agreement, it may be considered, according to Malintoppi, that "international standards" are in principle binding rather than recommendatory, despite the existence of certain escape clauses. "Standards" are considered by the ICAO Assembly to be "necessary" for the development of aerial navigation, while "recommended practices" are considered "desirable." The latter, in accordance with the Organization's practice, are merely recommendations that must be submitted to the competent national authorities to be taken into account (Malintoppi, *Le Raccomandazioni*, pp. 198 ff.).

20. Concerning the practical efficacy of resolutions, see Gabriella Rosner Lande, "The Changing Effectiveness of General Assembly Resolutions," in R. A. Falk and S. H. Mendlovitz, eds., *The Strategy of World Order*, 4 vols. (New York, 1966), Vol. III.

21. The nature of enforcement measures is examined in Chap. 3 of this book.

22. Tammes, "Decisions of International Organs," p. 333.

23. Malintoppi, *Le Raccomandazioni*, p. 49 ff.

24. Such as Sloan's, which assimilates the moral value of recommendations to a "nascent legal force" ("The Binding Force of a 'Recommendation'," p. 32), or Lauterpacht's, which links compliance with recommendations to the principle of good faith (dissenting opinion annexed to the Court's advisory opinion entitled "Voting Procedure on Questions Relating to Reports and Petitions Concerning the Territory of South-West Africa," Advisory Opinion of June 17, 1955, ICJ, *Reports* [1955], p. 120). These explanations are examined in greater detail in Chap. 7 of this book.

25. Malintoppi himself limits the scope of his thesis. He recognizes that there does not exist any direct correlation between the rejection, even if systematic, of recommendations, and the violation of the obligation that is the basis of the covenant. There does not exist a true legal obligation to observe recommendations. The violation of the covenant does not consist in the rejection of recommendations per se, but in the clear and evident will of a state to place itself outside the covenant. The rejection of recommendations can be a proof of it, but that will can be manifested in other ways. One cannot equate systematic rejection of recommendations with a violation of the covenant (*Le Raccomandazioni*, p. 331).

26. See notes 13 and 14 of this chapter. The conclusion that Sloan reached in 1948 concerning the practice of the organs has been clearly confirmed and strengthened since then.

27. The Secretary-General, in his report of 1960–1961, said the following: "To the extent that more respect, in fact, is shown to General Assembly recommendations by the Member States, they may come more and more close to being recognized as decisions having a binding effect on those concerned, particularly when they involve the application of the binding principles of the Charter and of international law" (General Assembly, *Official Records*, 16th Sess., *Supp. 1A*, p. 3).

28. A good example of the difficulty in disassociating in practice the notions of legal validity and effective compliance with international rules of law is the following: during the two Geneva Conferences on the Law of the Sea, those who maintained that the three-mile rule (regarding the width of territorial sea) was no longer a rule in force based their argument precisely upon the fact that a great number of states had abandoned it. In other words, they maintained that the rule had no legal validity because it was not being ob-

served. The partisans of the three-mile limit, however, interpreted the same fact in a diametrically opposed way: they maintained that acts of noncompliance had no other meaning except that of being violations of a rule of law, which in no way affected its existence as a rule of law, that is, its validity.

29. The criterion of classification used here to distinguish two important categories of resolutions is far from precise. For one thing, the distinction between "internal" and "external" activities does not rest directly on the Charter, nor does the degree to which an activity contributes, more or less directly, to the achievement of United Nations purposes constitute a scientific criterion of classification. Nevertheless, it conveys with sufficient approximation an important difference concerning the objectives of two large groups of resolutions, and is therefore useful as an initial guide to systematize the heterogeneous variety of resolutions that constitute the basic material of this study.

30. See section entitled "Use of the Term 'Obligatory Force'" earlier in this chapter.

Chapter 2: Resolutions pertaining to the Structure and Operation of the United Nations

1. D. Anzilotti, *Cours de droit international*, French trans. (Paris, 1929), p. 295.

2. For a detailed discussion of this subject, see Lazar Focsaneanu, "Le Droit interne de l'Organisation des Nations Unies," *Annuaire français de droit international* (1957), pp. 315–49.

3. A. Verdross, *Derecho Internacional Público*, Spanish trans. (Madrid, 1955), pp. 6, 7 (italics in original). Madame P. Bastid, in a work published in 1931 entitled *Les Fonctionnaires internationaux*, also placed this aggregate of rules within an enlarged concept of international law. The Mexican Judge Roberto Córdova, in his dissenting opinion annexed to an advisory opinion of the International Court of Justice, maintained that "International administrative law and international criminal law may form part of a wider concept of the law of nations, but they certainly concern the relations between a State and individuals and therefore they have no room within the interpretation of the words 'international law' as used in Article 38 of the Statute of the Court" ("Judgments of the Administrative Tribunal of the I.L.O. upon Complaints Made against the U.N.E.S.C.O.," Advisory Opinion of October 23, 1956, ICJ, *Reports* [1956], p. 165).

4. Focsaneanu, "Le Droit interne," p. 319.

5. The first two Inter-American Conferences (Washington, 1889–1890, and Mexico, 1902), for example, created by means of resolutions an organ called the "International Office of American Republics," which was to constitute "a permanent center of information and exchange of ideas" among the American Republics, and which in time became the Pan American Union; an Intercontinental Railway Commission; and another commission to study the production and consumption of coffee. See *International Conferences of American States, 1889–1936* (Washington, 1938).

6. See Chap. 7 of this book (section relating to inter-American declarations).

7. Tammes, "Decisions of International Organs," p. 305.

8. "Competence of Assembly regarding Admission to the United Nations," Advisory Opinion, ICJ, *Reports* (1950), p. 8.

9. *Ibid.,* p. 9.

10. *Ibid.,* pp. 7, 8 (italics added).

11. The election of judges to the International Court of Justice by the joint action of the Security Council and the General Assembly also constitutes a complex act, composed of two constitutive elements that are simultaneous, concurrent in their content, and paired, in the sense that in isolation they cannot effect the election.

12. Malintoppi, *Le Raccomandazioni,* p. 11.

13. In practically all cases of admission, the Security Council has not deemed it necessary to make an express pronouncement as to whether the candidate satisfies the conditions set by the Charter, even in the consideranda of the resolutions it has adopted, contenting itself with recommending the candidate's admission to the Assembly. Nevertheless, there have been cases that specifically illustrate and confirm the existence of these two components (the expression of a wish and of a judgment) within the logical and juridical schema of the Council's resolution: (1) the resolution relating to the admission to membership of Israel, whose operative part reads: "[The Council] *decides* in its judgment that Israel is a peace-loving state and is able and willing to carry out the obligations contained in the Charter" (Security Council, *Official Records,* 4th Year, No. 17, pp. 8, 9); and (2) the resolution relating to the admission of Indonesia, whose operative part also states: "The Security Council finds that the Republic of Indonesia is a peace-loving state which fulfills the conditions laid down in Article 4 of the Charter, and therefore recommends to the General Assembly. . . . " (Security Council, *Official Records,* 5th Year, No. 45, p. 28).

14. See Chap. 4 of this book.

15. *Agreements between the United Nations and the Specialized Agencies and the International Atomic Energy Agency* (Doc. ST/SG/14), pp. 35–36 (italics added).

16. At its first Assembly, the ICAO approved an amendment to its constitutive convention (as a result of Resolution 39 [I] of the United Nations General Assembly concerning Spain) to the effect that those states that had been expelled from the United Nations or whose exclusion from the specialized agencies had been recommended by the Assembly would *ipso facto* cease being members of ICAO. The amendment itself provided a procedure for eventual readmission. If, on the other hand, the rights in the United Nations of an ICAO member are suspended, suspension in ICAO is not automatic but will take place only if accompanied by a request from the United Nations, which would also be obligatory for ICAO.

17. *Agreements between the United Nations and the Specialized Agencies,* p. 23.

18. The Charter does not use this terminology, nor has it been used in the practice of the organs of the United Nations. Legislative acts are generally called "statutes," as in the case of the Statute of the International Law Commission, or "rules of procedure," as in the case of the General Assembly. Nevertheless, the term "legislative" is usually employed to refer to the function generically. Thus, in their oral statements before the International Court of Justice in the case of the Administrative Tribunal, various states alluded to the legislative competence of the Assembly or to the legislative character of the organ (Tribunal Administratif des Nations Unies, ICJ, *Reports:* United

States, p. 317; Greece, p. 353; Holland, p. 379; and the Secretary-General's representative, Mr. Stavropoulos, p. 307).

19. The Articles of the Charter relating to this function are the following: 7(2), 21, 22, 29, 30, 68, 72, 90(1) and 101(1).

20. "Effect of Awards of Compensation Made by the U.N. Administrative Tribunal," Order of January 14, 1954, ICJ, *Reports* (1954), p. 61. It could be affirmed, in addition, that the International Court of Justice, applying in this matter the theory of implied powers, simultaneously applied by analogy, with regard to the Organization, the doctrine that the sovereign state limits itself by virtue of the law it creates. Regardless of the theoretical bases of this doctrine, on which authorities on the Theory General of the state do not agree, and regardless of the name given to it, its validity and its applicability to international organizations can easily be recognized.

21. "Reparation for Injuries Suffered in the Service of the United Nations," Advisory Opinion, ICJ, *Reports* (1949), p. 174.

22. This aspect of the Court's Opinion confirms the general thesis previously presented concerning the relationship between the validity and the efficacy of international legal rules. See Chap. 1 of this book, section on non-recommendatory resolutions.

23. See above, n. 20.

24. The Secretariat is the only principal organ to which the Charter does not attribute the power to adopt in certain cases provisions of a general character vis-à-vis the member states. Moreover, the Secretary-General's political function is limited to calling the attention of the Security Council, in accordance with Article 99, and to performing the functions entrusted to him by the other principal organs, in accordance with Article 98. It is difficult to accept, therefore, that according to the Charter the Secretary-General has, even within the widest and most dynamic conception of his functions, a primary legislative competence, that is, a competence to adopt legislative acts in a substantive (as opposed to an organic and formal) sense, legally valid for member states, as do the other principal organs. There is no doubt that he has an autonomous (not delegated) power to adopt regulations in the administrative sphere that constitutes his responsibility in accordance with the Charter, which provides for the proper functioning of the Secretariat through general provisions. He also enjoys, vis-à-vis member states, a delegated regulatory power when the other principal organs grant it to him, as in the aforementioned case of the Flag Code and in many others. But he lacks, in principle, an autonomous legislative competence vis-à-vis member states. However, it must be recognized that the situation is not absolutely clear. It is not impossible for some general provisions adopted autonomously in the administrative sphere to have, at least indirectly, legal effects for member states from which they cannot possibly escape. And although it is difficult, for the above general reasons, to accept in principle the possibility of applying the doctrine of implied powers to the Secretariat, doubts can arise, as will be seen subsequently, at least in the case of the registry and publication of treaties.

25. Hans Kelsen, *The Law of the United Nations* (London, 1950), pp. 194, n. 5, 200. Since the work was published in 1950, the author probably could not take into account the Advisory Opinion of the Court in 1949, entitled "Reparation for Injuries Suffered in the Service of the United Nations."

26. The United States Supreme Court, in the MacCulloch vs. Maryland Case, developed a similar thesis in the following terms: "Let the end be legitimate, let it be within the scope of the Constitution, and all means which

are appropriate, which are plainly adapted to that end, which are not prohibited but consist with the letter and spirit of the Constitution, are constitutional" (cited by Paul Reuter, *International Institutions*, trans. by J. M.
Chapman [New York, 1958], p. 229).

27. The well-known Article 1 of the Swiss Civil Code states: "In the
absence of an applicable legal provision, the Judge decides in accordance with
customary law, and in the absence of custom, in accordance with the rules
that he would create if he had to act as a legislator."

28. Leland M. Goodrich and E. I. Hambro, *Charter of the United
Nations: Commentary and Documents*, 2nd ed. rev. (Boston, 1949), p. 184.

29. "Certain Expenses of the United Nations" (Article 17[2] of the Charter), Advisory Opinion of July 20, 1962, ICJ, *Reports* (1962), p. 151.

30. Certain resolutions concerning the maintenance of international peace
and security are discussed in Chap. 3 of this book. As will be indicated
there, the Court recognized that the measures adopted by the Assembly (and
also by the Security Council in the case of the Congo) when creating and
employing military forces in Egypt and in the Congo, did not constitute
respectively enforcement actions in the sense of Chapter VII of the Charter,
so that such measures could legally have been recommended by the Assembly
(or by the Council in its case) without observing Articles 42 ff. of Chapter
VII. By doing so, the Court helped clarify, and in a certain measure con-
solidate, the concept of "peace-keeping operations."

From the point of view of the subject matter of this chapter, the consequence of the Court's recognition of the Assembly's competence to organize
a noncoercive operation for the maintenance of peace is the following: the
substantive resolution that gave rise to the financial consequence held to be
obligatory was a legally adopted resolution. The Court went even further:
it indicated that even in a case in which "the action was taken by the wrong
organ, it was irregular as a matter of that internal structure, but this would
not necessarily mean that the expense incurred was not an expense of the
Organization. Both national and international law contemplate cases in which
the body corporate or politic may be bound, as to third parties, by an *ultra
vires* act of an agent" (*ibid.*, p. 168).

Judge Winiarski argued against this conception of the Court in a dissenting opinion: "The Charter has set forth the purposes of the United
Nations in very wide, and for that reason too indefinite, terms. But—apart
from the resources, including the financial resources, of the Organization—it
does not follow, far from it, that the Organization is entitled to seek to
achieve those purposes by no matter what means. The fact that an organ of
the United Nations is seeking to achieve one of those purposes does not
suffice to render its action lawful. The Charter, a multilateral treaty which
was the result of prolonged and laborious negotiations, carefully created
organs and determined their competence and means of action. The intention
of those who drafted it was clear: to abandon the possibility of useful action
rather than to sacrifice the balance of carefully established fields of competence, as can be seen, for example, in the case of the voting in the Security
Council. It is only by such procedures, which were clearly defined, that the
United Nations can seek to achieve its purposes" (*ibid.*, p. 230).

31. *Ibid.*, p. 159.

32. *Ibid.*, pp. 159, 160.

33. *Ibid.*, pp. 175, 178.

34. "Reparation for Injuries Suffered in the Service of the United Nations";
see the section on the doctrine of implied powers of the organization in this

chapter. In the same sense, see also John G. Stoessinger et al., *Financing the United Nations System* (Washington, 1964), p. 149.

35. "Reparation," p. 158.

36. With the exception of the Security Council's resolution of February 21, 1961, on the Congo, which is discussed in Chap. 3 of this book.

37. "Reparation," p. 234.

38. *Ibid.*, p. 287 (italics in original).

39. *Ibid.*, p. 209.

40. The nature and scope of resolutions grouped, for the purposes of this study, under the heading "determinative" resolutions, are examined in Chap. 4 of this book.

41. "Reparation," p. 213 (italics in original).

42. *Ibid.*, pp. 213, 214.

43. As demonstrated, for example, by the prolonged inaction of the United Nations in the Vietnam War.

44. Judge Fitzmaurice himself recognizes, in the final paragraphs of his opinion, that it is not easy to distinguish clearly and consistently between the two types of functions, and that at present the humanitarian functions are not less important (if less imperative) than the political ones ("Reparation," pp. 214, 215).

45. Stoessinger et al., *Financing the United Nations System*, p. 153.

46. See Chap. 1 of this book, section on nonrecommendatory resolutions.

47. Kelsen, *The Law of the United Nations*, pp. 699, 703, 704.

48. *Repertory of Practice of United Nations Organs*, 5 vols. (New York, 1955), V, 297–98.

49. The Regulations for the United Nations Joint Staff Pension Fund, adopted by Resolution 248 (III) and amended by Resolution 680 (VII), also refers to an aspect of working conditions and has, therefore, the same basis and legal scope as the Statute of the Personnel.

50. *Repertory of Practice*, V, 239–40.

51. *Ibid.*, pp. 235–36.

52. "Effect of Awards of Compensation Made by the U.N. Administrative Tribunal," Advisory Opinion of July 13, 1954, ICJ, *Reports* (1954), p. 59.

53. ICJ, *Pleadings, Oral Arguments, Documents*, "Effect of Awards," p. 295.

54. The International Court of Justice recognized it in the aforementioned advisory opinion when it distinguished between an organ's mode of creation and its nature. To the argument of the United States that the Administrative Tribunal was a subordinate organ established by the Assembly to help it in the fulfillment of its own functions, whose decisions could not bind the Assembly because that would make it a principal organ subordinate to its subsidiary, the Court said:

"This view assumes that, in adopting the Statute of the Administrative Tribunal, the General Assembly was establishing an organ which it deemed necessary for the performance of its own functions. But the Court cannot accept this basic assumption. The Charter does not confer judicial functions on the General Assembly and the relations between staff and Organization come within the scope of Chapter XV of the Charter. In the absence of the establishment of an Administrative Tribunal, the function of resolving disputes between staff and Organization could be discharged by the Secretary-General by virtue of the provisions of Articles 97 and 101. Accordingly, in the three years or more preceding the establishment of the Administrative Tribunal, the Secretary-General coped with this problem by means of joint administrative machinery, leading to ultimate decision by himself. By establishing the Administrative Tribunal, the General Assembly was not delegating the performance of its own functions: it was exercising a power which it had under the Charter to regulate staff relations. In regard to the Secretariat, the General Assembly is given by the Charter a power to make regulations, but not a power to adjudicate upon, or otherwise deal with, particular instances.

"It has been argued that an authority exercising a power to make regulations is inherently incapable of creating a subordinate body competent to make decisions binding its creator. There can be no doubt that the Administrative Tribunal is subordinate in the sense that the General Assembly can abolish the Tribunal by repealing the Statute, that it can amend the Statute and provide for review of the future decisions of the Tribunal and that it can amend the Staff Regulations and make new ones. There is no lack of power to deal effectively with any problem that may arise. But the contention that the General Assembly is inherently incapable of creating a tribunal competent to make decisions binding on itself cannot be accepted. It cannot be justified by analogy to national laws, for it is common practice in national legislatures to create courts with the capacity to render decisions legally binding on the legislatures which brought them into being.

"The question cannot be determined on the basis of the description of the relationship between the General Assembly and the Tribunal, that is, by considering whether the Tribunal is to be regarded as a subsidiary, a subordinate, or a secondary organ, or on the basis of the fact that it was established by the General Assembly. It depends on the intention of the General Assembly in establishing the Tribunal, and on the nature of the functions conferred upon it by its Statute. An examination of the language of the Statute of the Administrative Tribunal has shown that the General Assembly intended to establish a judicial body; moreover, it had the legal capacity under the Charter to do so" ("Effect of Awards," p. 61).

55. Resolution 174 (II).

56. Maurice Hauriou, who has been called the "apostle" of the doctrine of the institution, thus summarized his essential conception toward the end of his life: "An institution is an idea-undertaking [*idée d'oeuvre*] which lives juridically and develops within a given social *milieu*. For the realization of this idea, a power is organized which provides it with organs; and among the members of the social group interested in the fulfillment of the idea are generated manifestations of solidarity [*de communion*] directed by the organs and regulated by procedures" (Hauriou, "La Théorie de l'institution et de la fondation," *La Cité moderne et les transformations du droit*, Cahiers de la Nouvelle Journée, IV (1925), 2 ff.).

57. Tammes, "Decisions of International Organs," p. 307.

58. This result has often been achieved through the "double veto" (See P. F. Brugière, *Droit de veto* [Paris, 1952], pp. 154 ff.). In the case of Laos, the Security Council voted 10 to 1 (USSR) in favor of the view that a draft resolution creating a fact-finding subcommittee was of a procedural nature, and the President of the Council ruled that, under Article 29 of the Charter, he was bound to accept that view since that Article appeared under the Charter heading of "Procedure." In spite of the USSR representative's protests, the Council then proceeded to adopt the resolution creating the subcommittee by the same majority of 10 to 1 (*Yearbook of the United Nations, 1958–1959* [New York, 1959], p. 63).

59. *Repertory of Practice*, I, 679 ff.

60. Resolution 111 (II) and *ibid.*, pp. 682–83.

61. *Repertory of Practice*, IV, 50.

62. The legal value of resolutions that request the transmission of information by virtue of Article 73 (e) of the Charter is examined in Chap. 4 of this book.

63. The legal value and scope of declarations and other resolutions that express general principles are considered in Chap. 7 of this book.

64. Chapter X of the Charter; Articles 85 (2) and 87; and Article 98, respectively.

65. Texts of the different agreements can be found in Peaslee, ed., *International Governmental Organizations*.

66. Independently of the intrinsic merits of the two theses as to the substance of the matter, the example cited illustrates the disadvantages of geographic distribution as the sole criterion for the integration of organs. The solution in similar cases would seem to consist in the Assembly giving the organs a composition congruent to their terms of reference. The position of the different states in regard to an issue is a criterion juridically pertinent (besides geographical distribution) for establishing the composition of organs. Of course, this solution is not feasible when tasks are entrusted to permanent organs whose composition is established beforehand.

67. Tammes, "Decisions of International Organs," p. 316 (italics in original).

68. Georges Scelle, *Précis de droit des gens*, 2 vols. (Paris, 1932–1934), I, 51 ff. and II, 10 ff.

69. See Chap. 5 of this book.

*Chapter 3: Certain Resolutions concerning International
Peace and Security*

1. Chapter VI concerns the "pacific settlement of disputes"; Chapter VII, "action with respect to threats to the peace, breaches of the peace, and acts of aggression"; and Chapter VIII, "regional arrangements."

2. *Repertory of Practice*, II, 19–25, 41–49.

3. It was argued during the debates that the tasks proposed for the Council (particularly that of assuring the integrity and independence of the territory and of appointing a Governor responsible to the Council and subject to its instructions) were not covered by the specific powers conferred on the Council by Chapters VI, VII, VIII and XII. The Council accepted the responsibilities assigned to it on the basis that its action is not restricted to the specific powers described in those Chapters (in accordance with the view held by the Secretary-General), but that Article 24 confers upon it authority to maintain peace and security in a sufficiently broad manner to permit it to accept the tasks derived from the Trieste agreements (*Repertory of Practice*, II, 21).

4. The interpretation of Article 24 was brought up indirectly in connection with the elimination or inclusion of the question of Iran on the Council's agenda. Iran withdrew the claim that had given rise to the question before the Council; various members declared that, unless the Council specifically exercised the investigative functions provided in Articles 33, 34, and 36 of the Charter (Chapter VI), it could not continue dealing with the

dispute once the claim had been withdrawn. The Council rejected the resolution that expressed this viewpoint, on the basis of a report of the Committee of Experts of the Council, according to which the Charter had invested in the Council, especially by virtue of Article 24, important political functions; therefore it had to be concluded that, even after the parties had reached an agreement, circumstances might subsist that could arouse fears concerning the maintenance of peace, so that the matter should remain on the agenda (*Repertory of Practice*, II, 20).

5. At its 416th Session (March 10, 1949), the Council examined a report of the Commission on Indonesia, which referred to the noncompliance by the Netherlands with Resolution S/1234 of January 28 of that year. That resolution had called upon the Netherlands, as well as on Indonesia, first, to cease all military operations, and second, to free all political prisoners. In discussing the report, it was argued that Resolution S/1234 was not imperative, since the Council could not take "decisions" on the substance of disputes, but could only make recommendations. The majority maintained, however, that the resolution had to be complied with and, to this effect, the Council sent telegraphic instructions to the Commission on Indonesia, indicating that the Commission should assist the parties in reaching agreements for "the implementation of the Council resolution of January 28, and in particular paragraphs 1 and 2 of the operative part thereof" (cessation of military operations and freeing of political prisoners) (Security Council, *Official Records*, 4th Yr., 421st Mtg., March 23, 1949, p. 5). The Security Council's instructions can also be interpreted as a new recognition of its authority to take mandatory decisions beyond the specific powers mentioned in Article 24(2).

6. *Repertory of Practice*, II, 22, 47–49.

7. See Chap. 4 of this book.

8. The International Court of Justice, in its Advisory Opinion of July 20, 1962, helped clarify the legal scope of the Security Council's resolutions on the Congo by establishing, negatively at least, what such resolutions are not. It said: "It is not necessary for the Court to express an opinion as to which article or articles of the Charter were the basis for the resolutions of the Security Council, but it can be said that the operations of ONUC did not include a use of armed force against a State which the Security Council, under Article 39, determined to have committed an act of aggression or to have breached the peace. The armed forces which were utilized in the Congo were not authorized to take military action against any State. The operation did not involve 'preventive or enforcement measures' against any State under Chapter VII and therefore did not constitute 'action' as that term is used in Article II" ("Certain Expenses of the United Nations," p. 177).

9. The connection between certain internal aspects of the Congo situation and international peace could support the interpretation that measures such as the convening of Parliament and the maintenance of internal public order are based directly on the specific powers of the Council defined in Chapter VII. Thus, Fouad A. M. Riad ("The United Nations Action in the Congo and Its Legal Basis," *Revue Égyptienne de droit international*, No. 17 [1961], p. 29) maintains that various measures ordered by the Council resolution of February 21, 1961 (S/4741) rest on Article 40 of Chapter VII, which states that the Council may take provisional measures in order to prevent an aggravation of the situation.

10. The Security Council's resolution of August 7, 1963, on the same question, may possibly be different. On the one hand, the Council recognized unambiguously that "the situation in South Africa is seriously disturbing

international peace and security." Then, on the basis of this recognition (among other things), the Council requested that all members stop the sale and shipment of arms, munitions, and military vehicles to South Africa. A proposal to establish an economic boycott as well, which would have been a sanction under Article 41, did not receive the necessary majority for its approval. However, the outlawing of the sale of military materiel may be considered a "partial interruption of economic relations" and would thus fall under Article 41, thereby permitting it to be considered a sanction, or it may be interpreted as a provisional measure, under Article 40, in order to prevent an aggravation of the situation.

Almost all speakers attributed great importance to the military preparations that South Africa had undertaken and to the necessity of preventing a worsening of the situation, so that the second interpretation probably came closer to the viewpoint of the majority. In any case, regardless of which basis is accepted (the resolution does not refer to any article of the Charter), it would seem correct to say that the Council adopted the resolution within the general framework of Chapter VII of the Charter and not merely on the basis of Article 25. Nevertheless, the British representative distinguished between a situation that "has engendered international friction" (as in South Africa, in his opinion), and "one which constitutes a threat to the peace." The considerandum of the resolution did not reproduce the terms of Article 39—a fact of some significance. However, the rest of the members did not seem to support the British delegate's interpretation that "for [the Council] to move to action under Chapter VII of the Charter would be to exceed [its] powers under the Charter" (Security Council, *Official Records*, 18th Yr., 1054th Mtg., August 6, 1963, pp. 19, 20).

11. For the opposite view, that is, that the scope of Article 25 has not been defined by practice, see Tammes, "Decisions of International Organs," p. 344, and Kelsen, *The Law of the United Nations*, p. 95.

12. This problem will be studied more closely when the consequences of the various applications of the Uniting for Peace Resolution are examined (see the section entitled "Analysis of the Uniting for Peace Resolution in the Light of Charter Provisions" in this chapter).

13. Kelsen, *The Law of the United Nations*, p. 96. Alf Ross (*Constitution of the United Nations* [Copenhagen, 1950]) also reaches the conclusion that Security Council recommendations have the same binding force as decisions, on the basis of the representative nature of the Council, that is, on the basis of the fact that the members recognized, in conformity with Article 24, that the Security Council "acts on their behalf" (p. 71). It would have to be concluded, consequently, Ross affirms, that "single Members are bound by the decisions of the Council, having thus waived the right, for instance, to resist, politically, a recommendation by the Council for the settlement of a dispute or the like."

Besides certain reservations that could be made regarding the legal significance and scope of the "representative" nature of the Council, it is difficult to accept the premise upon which Ross bases his argument. The affirmation that the members renounced the right to oppose, politically, the Council's recommendations would seem contrary to the entire structure of the Charter. If it were so, the Charter would not have established the legal possibility for the Council to make both recommendations and decisions, but only for the latter. The members are certainly obliged to conform to the purposes of the Charter, but precisely in the way those purposes are interpreted by the competent organs and by means of those instruments to which the Charter attributes the effect of binding them.

14. Kelsen, *The Law of the United Nations*, pp. 732 ff.

15. *Ibid.*, p. 294.

16. Kelsen offers an additional argument in favor of the thesis that the Council's enforcement measures are of a political nature and do not constitute "sanctions": the fact that the Council, once it has determined that a threat to or breach of the peace or an act of aggression has occurred, can have recourse, in accordance with Article 39, either to enforcement action or to recommendations (*ibid.*, p. 733). However, the same author, as indicated, bases his interpretation that the recommendations adopted by the Council in accordance with Article 39 are not "recommendations" but true binding decisions, *precisely on the fact that the Council's enforcement measures can be considered sanctions.*

17. Malintoppi, *Le Raccomandazioni*, pp. 125 ff.

18. The Security Council's resolution of April 9, 1947 recommended that Albania and Great Britain submit their dispute to the International Court of Justice. Great Britain maintained in her initial *requête* that the recommendation of the Council bound the parties, in accordance with Article 25 of the Charter, and that therefore the Court should consider itself competent according to the terms of the first paragraph of Article 36 of the Statute, even in the absence of an express agreement between the parties to refer the case to the Court. Albania, in a preliminary exception relating to competence, argued that Article 25 referred only to decisions of the Council, and that a recommendation could not have the effect of binding the parties, and therefore could not serve as a basis for the Court's competence. Subsequently, Great Britain no longer insisted upon its initial argument, but was content to maintain that a letter from the Albanian government to the Court constituted a tacit agreement for the purpose of establishing competence. The Court accepted this and declared its competence, without, however, pronouncing on the point that is of interest here—whether or not the Security Council's recommendation had the binding effect attributed to it. However, a separate opinion by seven judges examined this point specifically and reached a negative conclusion (ICJ, *Reports* [1947], p. 31).

19. Moreover, this case does not constitute an unequivocal precedent because of a certain doubt about the legal nature of the June 25th resolution, considered in itself, independently of its connection with the following one of June 27th. The doubt arises from the fact that, in spite of the imperative terms the Council used ("calls upon"), it could be maintained that the Authorities of North Korea were not legally bound, since that entity was not a member of the United Nations. As will be seen in Chap. 7 of this book, certain authors consider (contrary to the opinion here maintained) that the obligation not to have recourse to threat or use of force (Article 2[4] of the Charter) is at present of a conventional nature only.

20. Kelsen, *The Law of the United Nations*, p. 932.

21. Kelsen clearly recognizes this (*ibid.*, p. 967); but in his anxiety to "play the devil's advocate with himself," in Arangio-Ruiz's clever phrase (quoted by Malintoppi, *Le Raccomandazioni*, p. 140), Kelsen observes that the principle of interpretation (according to which the particular prevails over the general) "is only a possible [principle], not an obligatory principle of interpretation, unless it is laid down as a rule of law."

It is difficult to comprehend the requirement that a principle of interpretation of treaties, such as the one cited, be established as a rule of law in order to accept its unquestionable applicability. The old Permanent Court of Justice (*Cases of the Mavrommatis Palestine Concessions*, series A2, p. 31) as well as the present International Court of Justice ("Admission of New Members," ICJ, *Reports*, [1947–1948]) accepted and applied the principle *lex specialis derogat generali*, without requiring that it be established as a rule of law. The principle is applied daily without any difficulty whatsoever by all national courts in the sphere of internal law, even though only some codes specifically enunciate it. Furthermore, it can be considered that this canon of interpretation is nothing but the legal translation of an evident logical principle. If the reason for Kelsen's reticence to pronounce himself categorically could be carried to its last logical consequence, it would have to be concluded that neither the rules of syllogisms or sophisms are "obligatorily" applicable in interpreting treaties, unless they had been established (who knows where) as rules of law.

22. *Ibid.*, p. 964.

23. *Ibid.*, pp. 962–63.

24. This "determination" is inescapable and imperative, even though the Uniting for Peace Resolution avoids the use of the verb "to determine," contenting itself with saying: "in any case where *there appears to be* a threat to the peace . . . etc., the General Assembly shall consider the matter immediately with a view to. . . ."

25. René de Lacharrière, "L'Action des Nations Unies pour la sécurité et pour la paix," *Politique Étrangère* (September–October 1953), pp. 317 ff. Lacharrière points out that a classical or natural system of collective security based upon the collective and spontaneous reaction of the members of a group in favor of the victim of an aggression can function effectively only if the following two elements are present: first, a relative homogeneity among the members of the group, and second, sufficient fragmentation of real power factors to prevent any individual member from curbing or stopping the concerted action of the rest. The fundamentally bipolar division of political and military power in postwar international society does not favor the normal operation of a system of collective security; thus it had to be structured on the *agreement* of the Great Powers, and the voting system of the Security Council reflects this situation. Without agreement among the Great Powers, it is illusory to suppose that if aggression occurs there will be forthcoming, in favor of the victim, collective and spontaneous aid from all the members of the society. The victim of the aggression will normally have at his disposal only the assistance of his own camp, and will have to oppose a coalition of about equal force. In the last instance, there is not much difference between that situation and collective self-defense.

In Korea, exactly this situation arose: world opinion "was not moved either way by the formality of a vote in the General Assembly: the American action would have had more or less the same number of supporters and the same adversaries throughout the world if it had been undertaken simply as the exercise of collective self-defense" ("L'Action des Nations Unies," p. 332). On the other hand, it is clear that self-defense constitutes merely a provisional solution in cases of emergency; Article 51 permits it "until the Security Council has taken measures necessary to maintain international peace and security." However, the lack of a positive Council resolution—because of either a veto or the inability to obtain the necessary majority—confirming the legitimacy of the measures taken initially for self-defense, *cannot have as a legal effect their* necessary cessation. In such a case, the victim of the aggression and the states that succor it will be able to continue exercising the right of collective self-defense. The absence of a Council decision "is not equivalent to the condition under which the exercise of the right of self-defense must cease, namely that the Security Council has taken the necessary measures to maintain international peace and security" (Kelsen, *The Law of the United Nations*, p. 803). For the exercise of self-defense to cease, it is necessary to have a *positive* Council decision to the effect that the invoked right is nonexistent or has been improperly exercised, which is very different from the Council's not succeeding in adopting a decision confirming the action initially undertaken. For precisely that reason, *the consequence of the veto cannot be that the victim of aggression will remain in a defenseless state.*

26. Eduardo Jiménez de Arechaga, *Derecho Constitucional de las Naciones Unidas* (Madrid, 1958) pp. 204 ff. Josef L. Kunz ("Sanctions in International Law," *American Journal of International Law* [April 1960], p. 336) comments in a curious way on Jiménez de Arechaga's position. He criticizes Arechaga's enthusiasm for the Uniting for Peace Resolution, as well as his "typically Latin American" belief that it will produce "the transcendental consequence to democratize the Charter" and "to heal the essential vice of the San Francisco product." All this is of course impossible to maintain, asserts Kunz, both from the legal and from the practical points of view. It is impossible to maintain from the practical point of view, because "the strong and growing Afro-Asian bloc, always helped by the Soviet bloc and some other countries, can now—in contrast to 1950—prevent the reaching of the necessary two-thirds majority." Apparently, according to Kunz, the democratization of the Organization does not consist in the adoption of resolutions desired by the majority, but rather in the adoption of resolutions that a *certain* majority desires—specifically, by what can be inferred from his words, a majority that is constituted by states other than those of the Afro-Asian bloc, the Soviet bloc, and other groups of states.

27. Its single recommendation was of a general nature and consisted in calling upon the members to maintain, within their national forces, elements that could be made available for action as units of the United Nations, in case of eventual emergency, "on the recommendation of the Security Council or the General Assembly."

28. *Repertory of Practice*, II, 340–41.

29. It is possible that one of the considerations taken into account to authorize the prosecution of the military operations was the following: ". . . an attempt to free all of North Korea from Communist control [would facilitate] the carrying out of the objective of the Assembly of a unified, independent, and democratic Korea as suggested in its resolution of November 1947" (Leland M. Goodrich and Anne P. Simons, *The United Nations and the Maintenance of International Peace and Security* [Washington, 1955], p. 469).

30. Kelsen, examining the United Nations Participation Act, adopted by the 79th Congress of the United States in 1945, calls attention to the fact that the government of the United States probably at that time considered "enforcement actions taken by the Security Council in conformity with Article 41 or Article 42 as the only enforcement actions of the United Nations in which a Member was supposed to participate under the Charter" (*The Law of the United Nations*, p. 933).

31. General Assembly, *Report of the Collective Measures Committee*, 6th Sess., *Supp. 13*, p. 25.

32. Goodrich and Simons, *The United Nations and the Maintenance of International Peace,* p. 457.

33. Paragraph 12 of the final report of the Secretary-General to the Assembly (Doc. A/3302) on the plan to establish an emergency force defined the functions of the force as follows: "When a cease-fire is being established, to enter Egyptian territory *with the consent of the Egyptian Government,* in order to help maintain quiet during and after the withdrawal of non-Egyptian troops, and to secure compliance with the other terms established in the resolution of 2 November 1956 . . . [the Force] would be more than an observers' corps, but in no way a military force temporarily controlling the territory in which it is stationed; nor, moreover, should the Force have military functions exceeding those necessary to secure peaceful conditions on the assumption that the parties to the conflict take all necessary steps for compliance with the recommendations of the General Assembly" (italics added).

34. Interpreted literally, the terms of the resolution, "The Security Council requests that the United Nations take immediately all appropriate measures, etc." have no meaning. On the one hand, the Security Council is an organ of expression of the Organization, through which the latter manifests its will; on the other, the United Nations can only take measures through its organs. Presumably, the terms used mean that the Council instructs the organ previously authorized by it, that is, the Secretary-General, to take urgent measures, making use of the United Nations Force, etc.

35. See above, n. 9.

36. See below, n. 52.

37. There is no doubt whatsoever that the Council Members were fully aware that they were voting a direct application of the Uniting for Peace Resolution, inasmuch as the voting was preceded by a debate in which Great Britain and France argued unsuccessfully that the calling of the emergency meeting of the Assembly was improper procedure because the conditions set for it by the Resolution had not been fulfilled (*U.N. Review* [November 1956], pp. 14 ff.).

38. "Certain Expenses of the United Nations," ICJ, *Pleadings* (1962), p. 154.

39. *Ibid.,* p. 399. Derek W. Bowett rightly observes that "as the Soviet Government was aware that the whole basis of Resolution 377 (V) was the provision of enforcement measures by the Assembly, it may perhaps be thought that this explanation lacks conviction" (*United Nations Forces* [London, 1964], p. 295, n. 6).

40. General Assembly, *Official Records,* 1st Emergency Special Sess., 563rd Mtg., p. 77 (representative of Czechoslovakia) and 567th Mtg., p. 127 (Mr. Kuznetsov, USSR).

41. Rumania (A/3302/Add. 7); Czechoslovakia (A/3302/Add. 6 and 19).

42. Poland proposed, with the support of the USSR, that Czechoslovakia be included in the Consultative Committee (General Assembly, *Official Records,* 1st Emergency Sess., 567th Mtg., p. 108).

43. Security Council, *Official Records,* 5th Yr., 520th Sess., November 8, 1950, p. 7.

44. The Armistice of July 27, 1953 was signed by "Lt. General William K. Harrison, United States Army Senior Delegate, United Nations Command Delegation" and by "General Nam Il, Korean People's Army, Senior Delegate, Delegation of the Korean People's Army and the Chinese People's Volunteers." Subsequently it was confirmed by "General Mark W. Clark, United States Army, Commander-in-Chief, United Nations Command," for

the one side, and by "Marshal Kim Il Sung, Democratic People's Republic of Korea, Supreme Commander, Korean People's Army," for the other side (S/3079, pp. 1, 26).

45. In reality, the Soviet Union and the members of the Socialist bloc voted against Resolution 711A (VII) as a whole, which approved the Armistice, but that resolution (adopted by 43 votes in favor, 5 against, and 10 abstentions) in its recommendatory part referred solely to the question of calling a political conference to solve the Korean question peaceably. The Soviet Union voted against the resolution because it objected to the criterion adopted for the composition of the conference. But the first paragraph of the preamble contained the following clear approval of the Armistice: "The General Assembly: 1. *Notes with approval* the Armistice Agreement concluded in Korea on 27 July 1953, the fact that the fighting has ceased, and that a major step has thus been taken towards the full restoration of international peace and security in the area." This and the three other preambulatory paragraphs were voted on separately. The paragraph that approved the Armistice was adopted by 59 votes in favor, none against, and no abstentions (*Yearbook of the United Nations, 1953*, p. 127).

46. On the diverse meanings of acquiescence and its effects in international law, see I. C. MacGibbon, "The Scope of Acquiescence in International Law," *British Yearbook of International Law*, XXXI (1954), 143 ff.

47. MacGibbon observes that "[acquiescence] . . . constitutes a procedure for enabling the seal of legality to be set upon rules which were formerly in process of development and upon rights which were formerly in process of consolidation. . . ."; he later adds: "The influence of acquiescence may similarly be observed in the assumption by international organizations of functions for which their constituent instruments provide no warrant. . . ." (*ibid.*, pp. 145, 146–47).

48. Sir Gerald Fitzmaurice makes a distinction, pertinent to the question examined here, between two separate situations: the acquisition of rights by prescription for a State requires undoubtedly a considerable unfolding of time. On the other hand, "a new rule of customary law based on the practice of States can in fact emerge very quickly, and even almost suddenly, if new circumstances have arisen that imperatively call for legal regulation. . . ." ("The Law and Procedure of the International Court of Justice, 1951–1954: General Principles and Sources of Law," *British Yearbook of International Law*, XXX [1953], 31).

Little has been written on the influence of time upon the creation of customary law in the particular framework of international organizations. In opposition to the viewpoint expounded in the text, Krzysztof Skubiszewski, one of the few authors who have studied the subject, considers that "time is the decisive factor in the creation of customary law, and only a small number of the present international organizations can point to a record of long activity, i.e., preceding the Second World War. Therefore, at the present moment one must still say that the contribution of international organizations to the law-creating processes is more visible and tangible in the field of written law" ("Forms of Participation of International Organizations in the Law-Making Processes," *International Organization* [Autumn 1964], p. 792).

49. Malintoppi (*Le Raccomandazioni*, p. 153) is of the opinion that the new rule that has emerged as a result of the application of the Uniting for Peace Resolution, according to which the pertinent Assembly resolutions have had the legal effect of suspending the obligation not to have recourse to force, was born with the approval of the first resolution (498 [V]) adopted on the

basis of the Uniting for Peace Resolution, which declared China to be an aggressor. The main reason for this, according to Malintoppi, was the considerable number of votes it obtained, inasmuch as only the five states of the Soviet bloc opposed it; the majority achieved was sufficient, therefore, to satisfy the necessary condition of general application. Malintoppi also considers very significant the fact that certain countries representative of an "intermediary opinion," such as Sweden, for example, that had expressed doubts about the constitutionality of the Uniting for Peace Resolution even though they were in agreement with the objective pursued, did not express any scruples during the debate and vote on the first application of that resolution.

Piero Ziccardi ("L'intervento collettivo delle Nazioni Unite e I nuovi poteri dell'Assemblea Generale," *Contributi allo studio dell'organizzazione internazionale* [Padua, 1957], p. 178), for his part, maintains, perhaps with better reasons, the view that the rule was born as a result of the Suez crisis, when quasi-unanimity of acquiescence was achieved.

As already observed, the quantitative and qualitative evaluation of the will of the members, or, in other words, of the generality of acceptance, must be interpreted in the light of the structure and principles of the particular normative system involved. Given the essential features of the Charter's collective security system, which in the last instance reflect the political reality of the postwar world, it would not be an exaggeration to affirm that a new rule of such importance could not have taken form, with pretenses of universal validity, while a minority so politically important as the Soviet bloc, notwithstanding its small number of votes, persisted in violently intransigent opposition to it. Malintoppi does not exclude the possibility, by way of theoretical hypothesis, that the new practice of a majority could have created a rule in force only among certain members. This thesis, however, is difficult to support, given the constitutional nature and the necessarily universal application of the rules on collective security. As he himself recognizes, moreover, if that hypothesis were correct, it would have resulted in the breakdown of the entire system. The creation of a rule of restricted application would have resulted in a situation similar to that existing if a group of states had formulated reservations on the Charter provisions regarding collective security, which obviously is absurd.

50. If we accept as valid Kelsen's theory, examined above, that the Council cannot, according to the Charter, *recommend* the adoption of enforcement military measures, but only *decide* that they should be taken, the new rule formulated here would also have modified, in this specific respect, the original Charter system.

51. In the Korean operation, military plans and strategic direction of the forces were entrusted to a command whose chief was designated by a member. Other formulas would undoubtedly be possible within the new rule created by the Organization's practice; the essential modification brought about by the Korean operation was fundamentally negative: the nonutilization of the Military Staff Committee.

As to the request of the Council that the members put at its disposal armed forces, in the absence of the agreements contemplated in Article 43, the Organization's practice indicates that this is a matter exclusively for *recommendations*. Neither practice nor, of course, the Charter, can provide a basis for maintaining that the Council may oblige the members, by a *decision*, to place at its disposal armed forces for a specific action, unless the members had previously given specific consent, by virtue of the special agreements of Article 43.

52. According to some, these operations, which have been called "peacekeeping operations," constitute an autonomous and *sui generis* phenomenon,

which has arisen from the Organization's practice and which lies between enforcement action on the one side and peaceful solution of disputes on the other, within a broad concept of the peace-keeping function of the United Nations. The Brazilian Foreign Minister expounded this thesis in the General Assembly in 1964 in the following terms: "It is possible to acknowledge that the peace-keeping operations have emerged as a new and vigorous concept, altogether different from the enforcement measures contemplated in Chapter VII of the Charter. As a living instrument the Charter was not incompatible with this development, but the difficulties which have so far arisen, and of which the question of financing is merely one aspect, seem to indicate that this new concept should be incorporated into the Charter as soon as possible.

"This could be done by means of the inclusion of a new chapter entitled 'Peace-Keeping Operations,' which could be placed between the present Chapters VI and VII. We would thus have a graduated crescendo: 'Pacific settlement of disputes,' 'Peace-keeping operations,' and 'Action with respect to threats to the peace, breaches of the peace, and acts of aggression.'

"Peace-keeping operations would thus be conducted on the territory of one or more states, members of the United Nations or not, at their request or with their consent. They would be undertaken by military contingents, preferably designated in advance and supplied chiefly by medium and small powers; their only objective would be to preserve peaceful conditions, in contrast to operations falling under Chapter VII to be undertaken against the will of one or more States, transgressors of international order, to impose the will of the international community represented by the United Nations. This certainly does not exclude, during peace-keeping operations, recourse to coercive action in given circumstances and for a limited period of time. Such an amendment of the Charter could provide, in more precise terms, for a method of financing for both coercive and peace-keeping operations" (1289 Plenary Session).

Bowett, who has studied in detail these peace-keeping operations, identifies nine diverse situations in which a United Nations Force could be used with nonmilitary purposes: (1) Cease-fire, truce, and armistice functions entrusted to "observer" groups; (2) frontier control; (3) interpositionary functions; (4) defense and security of United Nations zones or areas placed under United Nations control; (5) maintenance of law and order in a state; (6) plebiscite supervision; (7) assistance and relief for national disasters; (8) preventions of international crimes; and (9) disarmament functions (*United Nations Forces*, pp. 267 ff.).

53. Both Guenter Weissberg and Derek Bowett believe that although the Uniting for Peace Resolution made possible the convening of an emergency session of the General Assembly to deal with the case of Egypt, that resolution was not the constitutional basis for the establishment of the United Nations Force (UNEF). With differences of emphasis and detail, both believe that the establishment of that Force (as well as the one for the Congo, UNOC), was legally based on the inherent powers of the Organization. Bowett attaches considerable importance to the fact that, as the Court recognized, the operations in Egypt and in the Congo were not, respectively, an "action" in the sense of Article 11(2) of the Charter; that is, they did not constitute an enforcement action, but were rather the "measures" contemplated in Article 14, and which the Assembly, therefore, was authorized to take. Furthermore, he adds, if the Charter is interpreted according to the principle of "effectiveness" of treaties, it cannot be accepted that the provisions contained in articles 39, 42, 43, 46, and 47 are a legal impediment to the Assembly's organization and employment of such military forces.

For reasons given in the text (see "Analysis of the Uniting for Peace Resolution in the Light of Charter Provisions" in this chapter), it is submitted that the Assembly could not have had such powers, *ab initio*, solely on the basis of the provisions of the Charter. Therefore, it is thought that the Uniting for Peace Resolution represented not only a procedural mechanism to convene an emergency session of the Assembly, but also an essential element of the legal basis on which rests the validity of the operations and forces employed in Egypt and the Congo for the maintenance of peace, but with a noncoercive purpose. This, in spite of the fact that the kind of operation contemplated by the framers of the Uniting for Peace Resolution was rather an enforcement operation, of the Korean type. As an old legal aphorism says: "He who can do more, can do less." The Secretary-General, when referring to the problem of the constitutional basis of UNEF, stated in his second report (Doc. A/3302, par. 9), that the Force would operate on the "basis of a decision adopted according to the terms of . . . Uniting for Peace Resolution," (See Guenter Weissberg, *The International Status of the United Nations* [London, 1961], pp. 109, 112; Derek W. Bowett, *United Nations Forces*, pp. 98, 295–98, 307–12).

54. The effect of the new rule may be characterized as binding, not in the sense that it imposes a specific duty on someone to do or not to do something, but because, by its very nature, it is an "organizational" rule whose essential purpose is the distribution of legal competences. But it constitutes, nevertheless, a determination that the Assembly or the Council may recommend the use of armed force, under the conditions mentioned, to which the opposition of a minority has no relevance; that is, such opposition lacks legal efficiency to impede the fulfillment of the given determination. In other words, dissenting members cannot prevent the exercise by either organ of its enlarged competence. In this sense, such determination is obligatory. Piatrowski ("Les Résolutions de l'Assemblée Générale") maintains that the Uniting for Peace Resolution is binding in one respect, to the extent that it modifies the rules of procedure of the Assembly, thus creating a general obligation for all the members on the basis of Article 21 of the Charter. This effect is certain, yet undoubtedly it is of an indirect and secondary nature. The rules of procedure of the Assembly could not in themselves constitute sufficient legal basis for altering the distribution of competences established by the Charter between the two principal organs.

55. Excluding the fact that, in the case of Korea, the People's Central Government did not represent China in the United Nations and that Korea was not a member, so that Article 25 of the Charter was not directly applicable to them.

56. Oscar Schachter, "Preventing Internationalization of Internal Conflict: A Legal Analysis of the United Nations Congo Experience," *Proceedings of the American Society of International Law*, 57th Annual Meeting (April 1963), pp. 216 ff.

57. This observation could not validly be distorted by arguing that the very fact of an intervention in internal matters proved that the United Nations action necessarily was of an enforcement nature, in view of the terms of the last part of Article 2(7). The argument would be tautological. On the other hand, however, one can admit, with the International Court of Justice, that the action undertaken was not an enforcement action, and at the same time recognize, as a question of fact, that the Organization acted in connection with matters which undoubtedly belonged to the domestic affairs of the Congo.

58. Schachter, "Preventing Internationalization of Internal Conflict," p. 220.

59. General Assembly, *Official Records*, 6th Sess., *Supp. 13*. Opposed to this view is Malintoppi (*Le Raccomandazioni*, p. 263).

Chapter 4: Resolutions That Determine the Existence of Facts or Concrete Legal Situations

1. Among others, the following authors adopt basically this schema: N. M. Korkounov, *Cours de théorie générale du droit* (Paris, 1914), pp. 194 ff.; Claude du Pasquier, *Introduction à la théorie générale et à la philosophie du droit*, 3rd ed. (Neuchâtel, 1948), pp. 89 ff.; Ernest Roguin, *La Science juridique pure*, 3 vols. (Paris, 1923), I, pp. 82 ff.

2. Thus, for example, the same Article 18 contains this other rule: When the General Assembly must decide questions relative to "the maintenance of international peace and security, the election of the non-permanent Members of the Security Council, . . . the admission of new Members, . . . the suspension of the rights and privileges of membership, etc." (hypothesis) . . . then . . . the applicable voting system will be that of the two-thirds majority (consequence).

3. Of course, the model of a binding determination is Article 39 of the Charter: if the Security Council determines the existence of a threat to the peace, breach of the peace, or act of aggression (hypothesis) . . . it will make appropriate recommendations or decisions in accordance with Articles 41 and 42 to maintain or restore international peace and security (consequence). These determinations and the problems they gave rise to were studied in relation to certain resolutions concerning the maintenance of international peace and security (see Chap. 3 of this book). In connection with such determinations, the legal capacity of the organ (the Security Council) to make obligatory determinations is expressly established in the Charter. This chapter examines more closely certain determinations of the Assembly not directly based on a provision such as Article 39, but which are, nevertheless, binding for reasons adduced in the text.

4. This sentence appears in the texts of both Resolution 748 (VIII) on ceasing the transmittal of information stipulated in Article 73(e), in relation to Puerto Rico, and Resolution 849 (IX) on the same question in connection with Greenland (italics added).

5. Later in this chapter, attention will be given to the limits on this power to determine, as well as to the related but distinct problem of the coercive application of this type of resolution.

6. Report of the Rapporteur of Committee IV/2 of the San Francisco Conference (UNCIO, *Documents*, Doc. 933, XIII, 710), as well as Summary Records of the 12th Sess. of Committee IV/2 (UNCIO, *Documents*, Doc. 664, XIII, 634).

7. Hersch Lauterpacht, *International Law and Human Rights* (New York, 1950), p. 181.

8. Kelsen, *The Law of the United Nations*, Preface, p. xv.

9. The French text uses the phrase: "n'est pas acceptable pour l'ensemble des membres" (UNCIO, *Documents*, XIII, 710, 720).

10. Often, the purely technical or legal meaning of the term "generally acceptable" will prove insufficient. Politically, the necessary majority must clearly include all the significant members in a given case. Not infrequently, this will be in the end the decisive factor in proving whether the pronouncement of an organ is, or remains, binding. A case in point was the determination by the Assembly, not accepted by some of the large contributing members, regarding the binding apportionment of UNEF and ONUC expenses (see Chap. 2 of this book, section entitled "Resolutions concerning the Financing of the United Nations").

11. For example, according to Merkl and Kelsen, authors of the famous theory of the step formation of law (*Stufentheorie*), the only possible distinction among the state's functions is an *organic* one, not one based on different subject matter, inasmuch as the latter distinction would have to be based on an opposition between the creation and the application of juridical norms. In their conception, however, every act that creates law is at the same time an act that applies a hierarchically higher rule; thus, every norm is at the same time the application of another norm. Consequently, it is not possible to distinguish functions of creation from functions of application of law and, therefore, there is no basis for a *material* distinction among the state's functions (Roger Bonnard, "La Théorie de la formation du droit par degrés dans l'oeuvre d'A. Merkl," *Revue du droit public* [1928], pp. 668 ff.).

12. Article 15 of the Statute of the International Law Commission.

13. General Assembly, *Report of the International Law Commission*, 11th Regular Sess. *Supp. 9* (A/3159).

14. Hersch Lauterpacht, *The Function of Law in the International Community* (London, 1933), Chap. 15.

15. Tammes, "Decisions of International Organs," p. 273, n. 1.

16. The "factors" approved in 1953 (Resolution 742 [VII]) were divided into factors indicative of: independence; other separate systems of government; the free association of a territory, on equal footing, with the metropolitan or another country, or as an integral part of one of them, or in some other form. The "principles" of 1961 (Resolution 1541 [XV]) recognized that the obligation to transmit information fell into the sphere of international obligations and established various standards or guides (geographical separation between the territory and the administering nation; ethnic and cultural differences; and other elements of administrative, political, juridicial, economic, and historic nature) for determining whether the obligation to transmit information existed.

17. The annex to Resolution 1541 (XV) is entitled "Principles which should guide Member States in determining . . . etc." The title adequately reflects the guiding nature of the principles, but is equivocal concerning the addressee. In reality, the principles are guides for the Assembly. The title means, presumably, that states should be motivated by these principles in their behavior as members of the Assembly and its subsidiary organs; however, one could not attribute to the title the meaning that members responsible for the administration of these territories have the right, in the last instance, to decide whether or not they must transmit the information, because in that case the title would be contrary to the content of the document.

18. See William Edward Hall, *Treatise on International Law*, ed. by A. Pierce Higgins, 8th ed. (Oxford, 1924), p. 409; L. F. Oppenheim, *Inter-*

national Law, ed. by H. Lauterpacht, 7th ed., 2 vols. (New York, 1950), I, 853; Sir Arnold McNair, *The Law of Treaties* (London, 1961), pp. 492 ff.; Green H. Hackworth, *Digest of International Law*, 8 vols. (Washington, 1940–1944), V, 346; Charles Cheyney Hyde, *International Law*, 2nd rev. ed., 3 vols. (Boston, 1945), II, 389; H. Accioly, *Tratado de Derecho Internacional Publico*, 3 vols. (Rio de Janeiro, 1945–1946), Spanish trans., II, 512 ff.; D. Anzilotti, "Corso di diritto internazionale," in *Opere di Dionisio Anzilotti* (Padua, 1955) I, 383–84.

19. The representative of Mexico argued in favor of this thesis in the following way before the Fourth Committee of the General Assembly (*Summary Records*, November 28, 1961):

"The Mandate which the League of Nations had given the Union of South Africa to administer the territory of South-West Africa constituted an international treaty and, like any other international treaty, it was subject to the usual rules with regard to its fulfillment. The fact that there was no express provision in the text of the Mandate for action in the event of the Mandatory Power failing to fulfill its obligations faithfully did not mean that such failure did not entail normal legal consequences. Indeed, scarcely any international treaties included a specific clause providing for rescission on the grounds of non-fulfillment. It would be absurd to claim that the League of Nations, in granting a mandate, had renounced the right to supervise the activities of the Mandatory and had left it free to fulfill its obligations or not, at its discretion, or that it had renounced the normal right of a party to a treaty to demand its revocation if the other party did not fulfill its obligation. The very nature of the Mandate, under which the Mandatory Power accepted the 'sacred trust' of promoting the well-being of the dependent people of the territory, reinforced the argument that the League could not have renounced the normal legal methods for controlling the fulfillment of the treaty."

After attempting to demonstrate that South Africa had violated time and again the various obligations of the Mandate, the representative of Mexico examined a second point that had to be proved, in the following terms:

"The second point which required to be demonstrated was the link between the legal situation existing at the time the Mandate had been granted and the present situation. South Africa's argument was that the Mandate had lapsed as a result of the demise of the League of Nations, on the grounds that if one of the parties to a treaty ceased to exist legally the treaty lapsed. The International Court of Justice had, however, spoken indirectly but clearly against that argument. In its Advisory Opinion of 1950, it had maintained that the need for international control continued to exist despite the disappearance of the League. The Court had concluded that the United Nations could legally exercise the functions of supervision which the League had previously exercised in relation to the administration of the Territory and that South Africa was under a legal obligation to submit to the supervision of the General Assembly and to present annual reports, and also to allow the submission and examination of petitions from elements representing the people of the Territory. In other words, the Court had clearly confirmed the international legal status of the Territory despite the fact that one of the two parties to the Mandate no longer existed. That meant that South Africa's obligations as a Mandatory Power still existed. The Court had limited itself to defining the scope of those obligations, but the essential point was the legal grounds upon which it had based itself in declaring that South Africa was still under an international obligation to perform certain acts. The fact that the Court recognized that the Union of South Africa had certain international obligations with regard to the Territory of South-West Africa, whereas it had no such international obligations with regard to the people of its own territory, showed that the legal basis of those international obligations and the grounds for the international status of the Territory was the international act which had created that international status, and that that status was still valid despite the fact that one of the parties no longer existed. In other words, if the obligation derived from the Mandate continued to exist, it was not legally possible to deny that the Mandate itself was still in force and was still the legal basis of the international status of the Territory.

"The legal position was somewhat complex because it was not a question of applying the usual methods governing the transmission of rights and duties. In the arrangements made in 1946 for the liquidation of the League of Nations no provision had been made for the transfer to the United Nations of the mandates granted by the League. Moreover, South Africa had not concluded a trusteeship agreement with the United Nations and the Court had recognized by a small majority that it was not obliged to conclude such an agreement for South-West Africa. Thus, in order to find the legal basis for the Court's opinion, it was necessary to resort to ideas, which, though they did not belong to positive international law in its narrowest sense, nevertheless constituted its foundation.

"The key idea was the concept of the international community or community of nations. Fundamentally, the party which had granted the Mandate had not really changed or disappeared; what had happened was that its international agent had been replaced by another. To take the analysis of the situation a little further, it must be agreed that in reality the League had not been the real mandator but only its agent or representative, so that its demise could not affect the existence of the Mandate. The basis of the Court's reasoning was that the real mandator had been the organized international community, i.e., the association of countries which had constituted the League and which at that time had represented the large majority of the countries in the international community. That organized internationational community had been one of the parties to the Mandate and the League had been the instrument acting on its behalf. When the League had been dissolved, it had been succeeded in its capacity as the embodiment of the international community by the United Nations. There had been no formal transfer of the Mandate because there had been no change in the two parties to the Mandate; only the instrument representing the mandator had changed. Had that not been so, the International Court could not legally have recognized the continuance of the international status of the Territory and the continuance of South Africa's obligations once the League of Nations had disappeared."

Referring to the question of the legal consequences of the revocation of the Mandate, the representative of Mexico indicated that "it would mean that the international community which had conferred the Mandate on the Union of South Africa would resume all the rights which it had had at the time the Mandate had been granted. It would resume all the rights and titles concerning the Territory which might be necessary to achieve the objective laid down by the Covenant of the League and by the Charter of the United Nations, namely, to promote the well-being and progress of the people and to prepare them for self-government or independence. Once the United Nations had resumed those powers, the selection of one or more methods to attain that objective would be a political rather than a legal problem and would depend upon the decision of the Assembly. For the moment, it was sufficient to stress that when the Mandate was revoked, jurisdiction over South-West Africa would be vested in the United Nations."

20. Sloan, "The Binding Force of a 'Recommendation'," p. 29.

21. *The Charter of the United Nations*, Hearings, U.S. Senate, Committee on Foreign Relations, p. 67 (italics added).

22. Georg Schwarzenberger, *International Law*, 3 vols. (New York, 1949), I, 55–56, 200–202, 364.

23. Oppenheim, *International Law*, I, 358, 359.

24. *Ibid.*, pp. 846–50, especially p. 847.

25. See Chap. 2 of this book.

26. Moreover, this resolution is so vague that even as a guide it has very little value. Its essential operative part is reduced to recommending that when the question arises, it should be considered "in the light of the Purposes and Principles of the Charter and the circumstances of each case."

27. A/C.1/SR 127.

28. Goodrich and Simons, *The United Nations and the Maintenance of International Peace*, pp. 245 ff., especially p. 247.

29. On the other hand, the reservations of the United Kingdom, both in the presentation of the case and during the course of its development, helped to prevent Resolution 181 from becoming binding. It did not accept restriction of the rights it enjoyed as administering authority, as long as the Mandate was in force, but maintained its right to exercise undivided control over Palestine, and did not accept the gradual transferral of authority to the United Nations Commission and to the Provisional Government Councils provided for in the resolution. Virally considers the attitude of the United Kingdom an important influence in the denial of the binding effect of Resolution 181; also important in his view is the fact that, at the moment it was adopted, "the situation in that territory had already given rise to a dispute that concerned third States" (*ibid.*, p. 86).

Concerning the part of the resolution by which the Assembly "called upon" the Security Council to adopt the necessary measures provided for in the plan for its execution, the impression is clearly gained from the Council debates that it did not consider the Assembly's request binding.

30. Sloan, "The Binding Force of a 'Recommendation'," p. 24.

31. L. M. Goodrich, "Development of the General Assembly," *International Conciliation*, No. 471 (March 1951), pp. 262 ff.

32. The question of the future of the Italian colonies is considered below in another category: those resolutions whose binding force rests on a legal instrument other than the Charter.

33. For many authors, an essential element of any legal order is the possibility of applying its rules coercively, by means of physical force if necessary. For some, general international law is law only in the measure that it permits sanctions: war and reprisals. This view, however, is far from unanimous. The degree to which this situation has changed since the United Nations Charter has been in force and, in general, the entire problem of the existence of sanctions in the different international organizations, as well as their nature and functions, are also matters of discussion (see Kunz, "Sanctions in International Law," pp. 324 ff.).

34. See Chap. 3 of this book.

35. Kunz, "Sanctions in International Law," p. 331.

36. Sloan, "The Binding Force of a 'Recommendation'," p. 32 (italics added).

37. Jacob Robinson, "Metamorphosis of the United Nations," *Recueil des Cours* (1958), p. 567.

38. This inaccuracy becomes a tautology when it is argued that these determinations are not binding *because* the members preserve their individual freedom of judgment.

Another reason for considering that the Assembly and not the individual members has the power to determine questions such as those examined (whether a territory is non-self-governing in the sense of Article 73, or whether a question lies within the domestic jurisdiction of a state, etc.) is that if the decision remained in the hands of the state concerned, that state would become *judex in re sua*. Tammes' contestation of this argument ("Decisions of International Organs," p. 353) does not appear to be very convincing: "Against this objection, it may be observed that the principle referred to is not a logical, but a practical rule; it does not say that it is impossible that a person should objectively interpret the law in his own cause. Applied particularly to international persons, one finds that this requirement which in the case of single individuals would mean a superhuman condition of mind, can be, and not infrequently is, satisfied by a State."

Chapter 5: Resolutions Whose Binding Force Rests on Instruments Other Than the Charter

1. Tammes, "Decisions of International Organs," p. 283.

2. Besides deciding for the first time that the votes of the parties to a dispute should not be considered in computing unanimity.

3. Manley O. Hudson, ed., *World Court Reports*, 2 vols. (Washington, 1934), I, 739.

4. Malintoppi, *Le Raccomandazioni*, p. 59, n. 31.

5. Sloan, "The Binding Force of a 'Recommendation'," p. 18.

6. Trusteeship agreement for Togo under British administration (Article 7); for Cameroon under British administration (Article 7); for Tanganyika under British administration (Article 7); for New Guinea under Australian administration (Article 6); for Togo under French administration (Article 8); for Cameroon under French administration (Article 6); for Ruanda-Urundi under Belgian administration (Article 7); for West Samoa under New Zealand administration (Article 7); for the Pacific Islands under American administration (Article 14); for Nauru under joint British, Australian, and New Zealand administration (Article 6); for Somalia under Italian administration (Article 12). In the agreements on New Guinea, West Samoa, and Nauru, the obligation of the administering authority is conditioned by its own opinion regarding the compatibility of conventions and recommendations with the circumstances in the territory and with the attainment of the objectives of the trusteeship system. The agreements vary also with respect to the applicability of recommendations of the specialized agencies and with respect to other details.

7. Malintoppi, *Le Raccomandazioni*, pp. 164–67.

8. Reference was made (Chap. 2 of this book), when dealing with a related subject, to Professor Georges Scelle's well-known theory on the *dédoublement fonctionnel*, according to which the state sometimes acts, in the absence of organs of the international community, as an agent of that com-

munity. This revealing doctrine helps in understanding how and why the administering state acts as an organ of the international trusteeship system, even though in reality it is not necessary to resort to it as a basis for the thesis expounded here. The Charter provisions relating to the aims of the system, to the obligations of the administering authorities, and to the system of international supervision exercised by the Organization, combined with the provisions of the agreements made thus far, which, as has been indicated, are integrated into the normative order of the Organization, suffice to justify the thesis that an administering state assumes the functions of an organ of the United Nations (see Tammes, "Decisions of International Organs," pp. 356–59).

9. The direct juridico-political link referred to is nothing but the "nationality."

10. The character of agent and organ is not necessarily incompatible, from a juridical point of view, with the fact that the Organization cannot unilaterally modify the provisions of the trust administration. This legal situation is certainly heterodox, but it is not unknown. In private law there exists the institution of the irrevocable mandate, which resembles such a situation. In the same way, a certain parallel, or at least an analogy, might be found to this situation, described in Chap. 2: as recognized by the International Court of Justice, the General Assembly is obliged to carry out the decisions of the Administrative Tribunal of the United Nations, in spite of the fact that the Tribunal is a subsidiary organ of the Assembly.

*Chapter 6: Resolutions That Express and Register Agreement
among the Members of an Organ*

1. Series A/B. No. 53, p. 71.
2. See Chap. 7.
3. Oppenheim, *International Law*, ed. by Lauterpacht, I, 139, n. 1. The opinion quoted encompasses two distinct but related questions: first, the legal possibility of states assuming conventional obligations through an unusual method of expressing consent, that is, by the vote; the second refers to the question of treaty ratification. Lauterpacht's view on the second question is that ratification is a normal but not absolutely necessary procedure (p. 815). According to other points of view, especially more recent ones, the old rule under which, in the absence of a contrary provision, it was presumed that ratification was necessary for a treaty to enter into effect has undergone a change. According to António de Luna García (*El Poder Exterior* [Madrid, 1962], p. 24), the following rule is in the process of formation: "Treaties enter into effect in accordance with the expressed or clearly implicit will of the parties, and in case of silence, by signature." The main reason for this rule, according to Luna García, is the small and decreasing number of treaties that are ratified today.
4. Luna García, *El Poder Exterior*, p. 24.
5. Claude Chayet, "Les Accords en forme simplifiée," *Annuaire français de droit international* (1957), p. 5.
6. The question of the legal distinction between a treaty and an executive

agreement is closely related to the problem of the internal validity of the latter. Generally, state constitutions declare that all treaties or certain types of treaties are subject to the approval of a legislative body and to subsequent ratification. Consequently, there arises in certain countries the problem of knowing which international agreements that are not "treaties" in the sense of the constitution involved, can be entered into validly without parliamentary approval. Solutions vary considerably according to constitutional provisions and, above all, to practice. Thus, for example, in accordance with custom in Great Britain, only the following types of treaties require parliamentary approval: (1) those that require a modification of internal law; (2) those for whose execution the Crown must be invested with powers not yet recognized by customary law; (3) those that entail a financial obligation; and (4) those that involve cession of British territory. For reasons of political expediency, the Crown is wont to consult Parliament, *ex abundanti cautela*, before ratifying certain important treaties, even though it is not specifically obliged to do so (McNair, "L'Application et l'interprétation des traités d'après la jurisprudence brittanique," *Recueil des Cours*, XLIII (1933), 251 ff.).

In the United States, in addition to certain matters less frequently considered appropriate for executive agreement—such as military agreements, preparatory and provisional agreements for entering into a future treaty, or protocols for the interpretation or execution of treaties—the more numerous and important executive agreements are those based on a law of Congress that authorizes the Executive to negotiate them with other powers on such matters as commercial treaties. One of the arguments invoked in favor of the constitutionality of executive agreements in the United States is the following: The American Constitution refers in one part to "treaties" (Article II, Section 2), and elsewhere to "agreements and compacts" (Article I, Section 10, paragraph 3), submitting them to different legal regimes. The States of the Union can in no case conclude the first, whereas they can enter into the type with Senate approval. This single consideration is not enough to establish directly the validity of the "executive agreement" not approved by the Senate, yet it does underline the constitutional existence of two distinct types of international agreements, subject to different treatment. The next step was simple: "While Article II, Section 2 of the Constitution authorizes the President by and with the advice and consent of the Senate to make *treaties* with foreign nations, it does not say that no other form of international agreement shall be concluded by the President" (Hackworth, *Digest of International Law*, V, 397). In countries in which the Constitution provides a clearly uniform system for all international agreements, such as Mexico, the problem of justifying the internal validity of the executive agreement is more difficult.

Notwithstanding the internal legal difficulties sometimes raised by the executive agreement, it performs a function so important and obvious that, as already seen, there is increasingly frequent recourse to this simplified form of international contracting. To solve the problem of distinguishing agreements from treaties, the latter are generally described merely as those international accords that require the approval of the legislature for their validity, whereas on the other hand, executive agreements are defined as international accords that do not require such approval. This purely formal and external characterization is exact, but when it is used, as is sometimes done, to justify the constitutionality of executive agreements, it is tautological: the validity of an executive agreement not approved by the legislature would be a consequence (and not a cause) of its being different from a treaty.

From the international point of view, on the other hand, the executive agreement poses no problem as far as its legal validity is concerned. It is an almost universal customary development and today no one doubts its binding character.

7. Sloan, "The Binding Force of a 'Recommendation'," p. 22.

8. F. Vallat, "The General Assembly and the Security Council of the United Nations," *British Yearbook of International Law* (1952), p. 74.

9. "Voting Procedure on Questions Relating to Reports and Petitions Concerning the Territory of South-West Africa," ICJ, *Reports* (1955), p. 88.

10. "Certain Expenses of the United Nations," ICJ, *Reports* (1962), p. 233.

11. F. C. Gentile, "Competenza del Consiglio di Sicurezza e dell' Assemblea Generale in materia di mantenimento e ristabilimento della pace," *Comunicazioni e studi*, Instituto di diritto internazionale e straniero della Università di Milano (Milan, 1953), V, 327.

12. Series A/B, No. 42, p. 116. Text reproduced in Hudson, ed., *World Court Reports*, II, 755. For Ian Brownlie (*International Law and the Use of Force by States* [London, 1963], p. 72, n. 5) this opinion is distinguishable (probably in the sense that it recognized that a recommendation could produce an unusual binding effect) "because of the existence of the dispute and the particularity of the assent given to a resolution dealing with that dispute." In effect, these special factors give such a recommendation the character of an expression of agreement and establish its binding effect for the two parties.

13. Sorensen, *Les Sources du droit international* (Copenhagen, 1946), p. 68.

14. Tammes, "Decisions of International Organs," p. 345, nn. 1, 2.

15. *Ibid.*

16. *Ibid.*, p. 346.

17. See Chap. 2 of this book.

18. *International Conferences of American States*, 2nd Supp., (1945–1954, Washington, 1956), pp. 20–24 of the Spanish edition.

19. Manfred Lachs, "The International Law of Outer Space," *Recueil des Cours*, CXIII (1964), 98.

Chapter 7: Resolutions That Contain Declarations or Other Pronouncements of a General Nature

1. *The Hague Conventions and Declarations of 1899 and 1907*, ed. by James Brown Scott, 2nd ed. (New York, 1915), Introduction, p. x.

2. Final Act, *ibid.*, pp. 27–28. Previously, the Hague Conference had used the same term, "declaration," to designate three instruments *signed and subject to ratification*, which, from a legal point of view, are distinguishable in no way from a true convention: declarations dealing respectively with the outlawing of (1) projectiles or explosives discharged from balloons; (2) the use of asphyxiating or deleterious gases; and (3) the use of dumdum bullets. The 1907 Conference issued another *signed* declaration prohibiting the discharge of projectiles from balloons. The 1856 Paris Conference also used the term "declaration" to designate conventional instruments. Only the nonconventional declaration, that is, the genuine "resolution-declaration" is discussed in this chapter.

3. Another significant difference between the first three Inter-American

conferences and the Second Hague Conference lies in the practical finality that was sought by means of the declaration. As noted, the Hague Conference conceived of this instrument as a means for expressing certain general principles, accepted by all, when it was not possible to achieve unanimity concerning their detailed formulation within a convention. On the other hand, at the conference prior to the Inter-American Conferences, the rule of unanimity did not prevail in the same way. The rules of procedure of the First Conference contain no applicable rule on the voting system, but the rules of procedure of the Second (Article 21) as well as of the Third (Article 17), establish that "the reports or proposals that the Conference may examine shall be considered approved when the affirmative vote of an absolute majority of the Delegations represented is obtained. . . . "

4. Scott, *The Hague Conventions*, p. xi.

5. General Assembly, *Documents*, 6th Regular Sess., *Annexes*, item 48 of the Agenda, p. 9 (italics added).

6. Johnson, "The Effect of Resolutions of the General Assembly," p. 118.

7. Wolfgang Friedmann, *Law in a Changing Society* (Berkeley, 1959), p. 56.

8. New Jersey v. Delaware, 291 U.S. 383 (1933). Cited by Sloan, "The Binding Force of a 'Recommendation'," p. 33.

9. Philip C. Jessup, *A Modern Law of Nations* (New York, 1948), p. 46. This work was published shortly before the Convention for the Prevention and Sanction of the Crime of Genocide (December 9, 1948) was concluded.

10. The General Assembly thus far has not favored the system of the declaratory code. Besides the three matters indicated in the text, there was the possibility of using this procedure in the following cases:

The Draft Code of Offenses against the Peace and Security of Mankind prepared by the International Law Commission (General Assembly, *Official Records*, 6th Regular Sess., *Supp. 9* [A/1858]); the definition of aggression; the suggestion made in 1959 before the Sixth Committee of the Assembly by the Special Rapporteur of the International Law Commission for the Law of Treaties (Sir Gerald Fitzmaurice), that the principles eventually approved in relation to that subject be incorporated in a declaration (A/C.6/SR 601); the suggestion made by the representative of the United States before the Sixth Committee of the Assembly in 1958, that the Draft on Diplomatic Intercourse and Immunities prepared by the International Law Commission be incorporated in a code approved by the Assembly, instead of in a treaty; and the proposal of South Africa at the first United Nations Conference on the Law of the Sea that the Draft Articles on the High Seas also be incorporated in a declaration. In none of these cases was the procedure of the declaratory code adopted. The first two (the Draft Code of Offenses against the Peace and Security of Mankind and the definition of aggression) never reached the point at which the form of the instrument is given careful examination, inasmuch as the Assembly's reticence was due rather to considerations of substance. In the Drafts on Diplomatic Intercourse and Immunities and on the High Seas, it seemed probable that in both cases (as indeed occurred) the respective conventions would be successfully adopted and that that type of instrument was preferred to the declaration. The Convention on the High Seas indicated in its preamble that "the States party to this Convention . . . recognizing that the United Nations Conference on the Law of the Sea . . . adopted the following provisions (i.e., the body of the treaty) as generally declaratory of established principles of international law, have agreed as follows: . . . "

On one occasion, the Assembly discussed the theoretical question (of special interest here) concerning the legal value of these declaratory codes in general, as compared with the convention. The delegate of Poland (Prof. Manfred Lachs) expressed the opinion in the Sixth Committee that if the principles of the Law of Treaties were not incorporated in a treaty, but in a code, "that code would fall under paragraph 1 b and not paragraph 1 a of Article 38 of the Statute of the International Court of Justice" (General Assembly, *Official Records*, 14th Sess., 6th Comm., 603rd Mtg., September 29, 1959, p. 14). Actually, one source is not superior to the other, nor is there a question here of "promotion" to a hierarchically higher category. With the exception of a few isolated opinions, such as those of J. Spiropoulos or Karl Strupp, most authors agree that the sources of international law are not enumerated in the first three paragraphs of Article 38 in order of juridical hierarchy. The order of enumeration corresponds to the logical and juridical principle that the specific, the particular, or the exceptional prevails over the general; the enumeration of these three sources goes from the particular to the general. The process carried out by the International Court of Justice when it decides a case is nothing but the application of this logical principle: first, it decides whether there exists a bilateral treaty between the parties that could be applicable to the case; second, whether there exists a multilateral treaty applicable; and third, whether customary law is applicable, and, in the last instance, some general principle of law. But this is not a question of hierarchy or of greater or lesser legal value. A code that incorporates true customary rules in force or authentic general principles of law would not possess a lesser degree of "juridicity" than a treaty of identical content.

11. Except to the extent that it may constitute a working directive for an organ.

12. Sloan, "The Binding Force of a 'Recommendation'," p. 32.

13. Lauterpacht criticizes precisely the concept of "nascent legal force" that Sloan uses (*International Law and Human Rights*, p. 413).

14. "Voting Procedure," ICJ, *Reports* (1955), p. 120 (italics added).

15. Principles concerning arbitration, previously embodied in the three Hague Conventions of 1899, were incorporated into the regional sphere by a Protocol of Adhesion approved by the Second Inter-American Conference (Mexico, 1902). Article 1 states: "The American Republics represented at the International Conference in Mexico which are not signatories of the three Conventions signed at the Hague on July 29, 1899, recognize the principles enunciated in those Conventions as forming part of American public international law."

16. The specifically "inter-American" nature of certain principles claimed by some enthusiastic and zealous Pan-Americanists is rather doubtful. Thus, J. M. Yepes enumerates as rules of "Latin-American international law" the embodiment of the norm *pacta sunt servanda* as the basis of international law; the principle of self-determination of peoples; "the existence of a certain form of civilization based on respect for the individual, on freedom of thought, on the law of contract, and on an international morality of a binding and objective nature," and other similar rules (*Philosophie du Panaméricanisme et organisation de la paix: le droit Panaméricain* [Neuchâtel, 1945], pp. 86–87).

17. Such rules are the following: (a) the outlawing of territorial conquest and the nonrecognition of all territorial acquisitions achieved through violence (First Inter-American Conference, 1889–1890); (b) the condemnation of the intervention of a state in the internal or external affairs of another (Seventh Inter-American Conference, 1933, and the Inter-American Conference for the

Maintenance of Peace, 1936); (c) the recognition that all wars or threats of war affect directly or indirectly all civilized peoples and endanger the great principles of liberty and justice that constitute the ideal of America and the basis of its international policy (Conference for the Maintenance of Peace); (d) the system of mutual consultation to seek procedures for peaceful co-operation, in case of war or a threat of war among American countries (Conference for the Maintenance of Peace); (e) recognition that any act likely to disturb the peace in America affects all the American nations, individually and collectively, and justifies the initiation of procedures of consultation (Conference for the Maintenance of Peace); (f) the adoption of conciliation, arbitration, or international adjudication to resolve all differences and disputes among the nations of America, whatever their nature or origin (Conference for the Maintenance of Peace); (g) recognition that respect for the individuality, sovereignty, and independence of each American state is the essence of the inter-American order, supported by the continental solidarity that has been manifested historically and upheld by declarations and treaties in force (Eighth Inter-American Conference, 1938); (h) the affirmation that respect for and faithful observance of treaties is the indispensable norm for the development of peaceful relations among states, and that treaties can be revised only by agreement of the parties (Declaration of American Principles, Eighth Inter-American Conference); (i) the proclamation of their common interest and of their determination to increase their solidarity, coordinating their respective attitudes through the procedure of consultation, and using the means that in each case are prompted by the circumstances, whenever the peace, security, or territorial integrity of the American Republics appears threatened by acts of any nature whatsoever (Declaration of Lima, Eighth Inter-American Conference); (j) the declaration that any attack by a non-American state against the territorial integrity or inviolability, or against the sovereignty or the political independence of an American state, would be considered an act of aggression against all American states (Declaration XV of the Second Meeting of Consultation of the Ministers of Foreign Affairs, Havana, 1940) (*International Conferences of American States*, 2nd Supp.).

18. Other principles not incorporated in Resolution VIII of the Conference on Problems of War and Peace are the following: "Forced collection of debts is unlawful" (Resolution XXVII of the Conference for the Maintenance of Peace, Buenos Aires, 1936). On the basis that "residents considered as foreigners, according to local law, cannot collectively claim the status of minorities . . . ," the Third Meeting of Consultation of the Ministers of Foreign Affairs (Rio de Janeiro, 1942) declared that it reiterated "the principle of American public law, according to which foreigners residing in an American State are subject to the jurisdiction of that State, it being unlawful for the governments or the organizations of the countries of which those foreigners are nationals, to interfere, directly or indirectly, in national life for the purpose of directing their situations or activities" (Resolution XX). Resolution XXII of the Third Meeting of Consultation declared that "the principle that international conduct should be motivated by the 'good neighbor' policy is a norm of international law of the American Continent." The resolution did not define what "good neighborliness" consisted in; in any case it can be considered only a political practice or posture, hardly a general principle of law. The Conference on Problems of War and Peace adopted another resolution (XI) that also enunciated inter-American principles, in a way quite similar to Resolution VIII of the same conference, adding however, among other things, the following (paragraph 11): "The American States reiterate their fervent ad-

herence to democratic principles, which they consider essential for the peace of America." The formulation of this principle was important because it served as an antecedent to Article 5(d) of the Charter of the Organization of American States, which reads: "The solidarity of the American States and the high aims which are sought through it require the political organization of those States on the basis of the effective exercise of representative democracy." Finally, the same resolution (XI) of the Conference on Problems of War and Peace contains in paragraph 12 an affirmation that cannot be characterized as a principle, and that underlines the declamatory tone and the unrealistic nature of many inter-American pronouncements: "The American man cannot conceive of living without justice, just as he cannot conceive of living without liberty."

19. See Chap. 2 of this book.

20. Ann V. W. Thomas, *The Organization of American States* (Dallas, 1963), p. 67.

21. See Chap. 6 of this book.

22. Charles Fenwick, *International Law*, 3rd ed. rev. (New York, 1948), p. 79.

23. *International Conferences of American States, 1889–1928* (New York, 1931), p. 441. The text of this resolution will be examined later in this chapter.

24. Sloan, "The Binding Force of a 'Recommendation'," p. 28.

25. J. Ray, *Commentaire du Pacte de la Société des Nations selon la politique et la jurisprudence des organes de la Société* (Paris, 1930), pp. 74, 75.

26. Piatrowski, "Les Résolutions de l'Assemblée Générale."

27. The International Military Tribunals of Nuremberg and of Tokyo deemed it to be so. Concerning this particular, and for a detailed study of the Pact, see Ian Brownlie, *International Law and the Use of Force by States*, pp. 74–92, 113–14.

28. El Salvador, Uruguay, Bolivia, and Argentina; Argentina did not sign because of the U.S. reservation regarding the applicability of the Monroe Doctrine.

29. *Judgment of the International Military Tribunal for the Trial of German Major War Criminals*, p. 40.

30. The Tribunal also referred to a Draft Treaty of Mutual Assistance prepared by the League of Nations in 1923, which, however, did not receive sufficient support from governments; the draft, which had been approved in principle by 18 states, was abandoned. The Tribunal's Judgment did not mention, on the other hand, another treaty, which at the time had certain importance: the Antiwar Treaty of Non-Aggression and Conciliation, signed in Rio de Janeiro on October 10, 1933. This treaty was open to the accession of all states; the 21 American states and 11 European states became parties to it.

31. *Judgment*, p. 40.

32. *Ibid.*, p. 41.

33. Brownlie, *International Law and the Use of Force by States*, pp. 107–11.

34. *Ibid.*, p. 111.

35. Kelsen, *The Law of the United Nations*, p. 76.

36. *Repertory of Practice*, I, 462.

37. Georges Scelle, *Précis de droit des gens*, II, 374, 375. Later, examining specifically the scope of Article XVII of the Covenant of the League of Nations, he declares that the purpose of that Article is "to generalize throughout the worldwide international community the procedures for settling disputes that are in force within the restricted community of the League of Nations." The author then asks himself: "Does this intention really not create

obligations for non-Member States? We would not venture to assert this,"
he replies, "since it must be recognized that the objective Law of the entire
international community prohibits recourse to war in order to assert a national
aim, as declared by the Kellogg-Briand Pact, which is one of those *treaties of
expansive force* that we have spoken about, and it can be maintained that an
international organization with universal vocation, such as the League of
Nations, virtually has competence to make this general international norm
respected" (p. 378).

38. Antiwar Treaty of Non-Aggression and Conciliation (Rio de Janeiro,
1933); Convention on the Rights and Duties of States (Montevideo, 1933);
Resolutions of the Inter-American Conferences of Buenos Aires (1936), Lima
(1938), and Mexico (1945). See above, nn. 17 and 18.

39. In French: "sont tenus."

40. Oppenheim, *International Law*, ed. by Lauterpacht, I, 138, 139. In
addition to the reason given in the text, Lauterpacht considers that the resolution bound "with special force" those members of the League that expressly
accepted it. For an argument against the binding force of the resolution, see
the frequently cited study, which appeared in the *British Yearbook* of 1935,
pp. 157 ff., signed with the initials H. A. S. (H. A. Smith), entitled "The
Binding Force of League Resolutions." In the same issue of the *British Yearbook* appears a short article by Brierly on the above resolution, also denying
its binding force.

41. *International Conferences of American States*, 1st Supp., 1933–1940,
pp. 373–77.

42. Verdross examines the League's resolution of March 11, 1932, in
relation to the illegality of compulsion exercised against a state. He declares
that "this principle was confirmed by the judgment of the Military Tribunal
of Nuremberg of October 10, 1946, which characterized as 'a crime against
peace' the compulsion exercised against the President of Czechoslovakia,
Hacha, to obtain the signing of the German–Czech Treaty of March 15, 1939,
even though the Tribunal had verified that Hacha had not been threatened
with personal harm, but that he had been forewarned of the bombardment
of Prague in case of his negative reply. This case thereby constitutes a
classical example of juridico-international compulsion against a State, and at
the same time, a confirmation of the relevance of illegal compulsion against a
State as such" (A. Verdross, *Derecho Internacional Público*, p. 151).

43. Brownlie, *International Law and the Use of Force by States*, pp. 418–
19.

44. J. Kunz ("Sanctions in International Law," p. 324) maintains that
nonrecognition is not a legal sanction, but rather "an attitude which needs
a sanction." Although his first affirmation is correct, the principle of nonrecognition is more than an "attitude." It implies a legal obligation for states,
whose nonexistence could not be proved by the fact that the obligation is
not accompanied by a sanction.

45. *Yearbook of the International Law Commission*, 1949.

46. With the exception of the representatives of Egypt, Venezuela, and
Pakistan (A/C.6/SR 234, 235, and 236). Among the members of the International Law Commission the following expressed doubts, reservations, or
frankly contrary opinions: R. Córdova (Mexico), R. Alfaro (Panama), and
M. Hudson (U.S.A.).

47. "Reservations to the Convention on the Prevention and Punishment
of the Crime of Genocide," Advisory Opinion, ICJ, *Reports* (1951), p. 23.

48. For a selection of the principal opinions expressed in this connection, both before the Third Committee and the General Assembly, as well as by different authors, see Nehemiah Robinson, *The Universal Declaration of Human Rights* (New York, 1958), pp. 33–63.

49. This argument was advanced by France (A/C.3/SR 92), Chile (A/C.3/SR 91 and SR 156), China (A/C.3/SR 91), and Lebanon (A/C.3/SR 91). Along the same lines was the opinion of the President of the Third Committee in 1948, Dr. Charles Malik of Lebanon (*U.N. Bulletin* [July 1, 1949], p. 519). Prof. Cassin of France went even further in a statement before the Economic and Social Council: he maintained that the Declaration was "a complement of the United Nations Charter . . . a clarification of the Charter, and an organic act of the United Nations, with all the legal validity of such acts" (E/SR 215, p. 18).

50. Opinion of the Belgian representative before the Third Committee, Prof. Dehousse (A/C.3/SR 108).

51. See Chap. 4 of this book. As indicated there, this unauthorized function is different from the Charter interpretation normally made by each organ in *applying* concretely to a particular case a provision of the Charter.

52. Lauterpacht, *International Law and Human Rights*, p. 407.

53. B. Mirkine-Guetzevich, "L'ONU et la doctrine moderne des droits de l'homme," *Revue générale de droit international public* (April–June 1951).

54. Nehemiah Robinson, *The Universal Declaration of Human Rights*, p. 67.

55. See extensive list *ibid.*, pp. 67–96.

56. Quincy Wright, "National Courts and Human Rights—The Fujii Case," *American Journal of International Law* (January 1951), pp. 70, 71.

INDEX

International Court of Justice (*Cont.*)

United Nations Educational, Scientific, and Cultural Organization, 200*n*3

—cases, 227*n*10; UN Administrative Tribunal, awards of compensation, 31, 34-35, 52, 56, 201*n*18, 202*n*20; Corfu Channel, 78, 198*n*16, 209*n*18

—Statute: Art. *36*, 124; Art. *38*, 2, 6, 170, 200*n*3, 227*n*10

International Labor Organization (ILO): constitution, 10, 11, 147; Administrative Tribunal, ICJ advisory opinion, 200*n*3

International law, 152-53; resolutions as source of, 2-6; codification and development of, 3, 124; functions of ICJ in development of, 38-40

International Law Commission: establishment, 53; Rights and Duties of States, Draft Declaration on, 169, 173, 190; arbitration procedure, 173; code of offenses against peace and security of mankind (GA Resol. 177 [I]), 191; Statute, 201*n*18, 218*n*12; Diplomatic Intercourse and Immunities, Draft on, 226*n*10

International Monetary Fund, 63-64, 125

Iran, 72

Israel: admission to UN, 201*n*13

Italian peace treaty, 139, 141-42

Jessup, Philip C.: quoted, 172

Johnson, D. H. N., 169

Kellogg-Briand Pact (Pact of Paris), 182-83, 185, 188

Kelsen, Hans, 38, 77; quoted, 76, 77, 80

Klaested, Judge Helge, 154

Korea, 110, 111, 142, 213-14*n*49, 214*n*51; insignia for UN troops (GA Resol. 483 [V]), 36; UN Korean Reconstruction Agency, 51, 53; SC resolutions on, 78-79, 80-81, 90-91, 213-14*n*49; as a collective defense action, 86, 210-11*n*25; GA resolutions on, 89-90, 91, 93-94, 100, 102-3, 116; armistice, 103, 212-13*n*44, 213*n*45

Koretsky, Judge Vladimir M.: quoted, 43-44

Kunz, Josef L., 221*n*33; quoted, 211*n*26, 230*n*44

Lacharrière, René de, 86, 87, 210*n*25

Lachs, Manfred, 163, 227*n*10

Laos, 56, 205*n*58

Lauterpacht, Hersch, 124-25, 176, 194; quoted, 122, 152

Law, international, *see* International law

Law, Theory General of, 118-22

League of Nations, 3, 184-85; Administrative Tribunal, 22; mandatory resolutions, 26; transfer of assets to UN (GA Resol. 79 [I]), 36-37, 38, 161; Covenant, 55, 77, 130, 181, 187, 189, 190, 229-30*n*37; South-West Africa, 128, 219-22*n*19; precedent of binding recommendations, 139-40, 151; "executive-agreement" resolutions, 151, 155-56; abolition of force and peaceful settlement of international disputes, 181-82; Japanese occupation of Manchuria, 188-89; *see also* Permanent Court of International Justice

Locarno treaties, 181

Luna García, António de, 223*n*3

Peace and security (*Cont.*)
applications, 88-100; response of
member states, 100-3; *see also*
Collective security

Peace-keeping operations, 88-89,
203*n*30, 214-15*n*52; Special Committee on, 48; *see also* Congo;
United Nations Emergency
Force

Permanent Court of International
Justice, 140-41, 152, 155-56,
210*n*21

Personnel of the United Nations:
reparation for injuries suffered
in service of UN, ICJ advisory
opinion, 6, 33; awards of compensation by UN Administrative
Tribunal, 31, 34-35; Staff Regulations (GA Resol. 590 [VI]),
50-52; UN Joint Staff Pension
Fund, establishment (GA Resol.
680 [II]), 204*n*49; *see also* Privileges and immunities

Portugal, 116, 126-27

Privileges and immunities: of ICJ
personnel, 37; of UN and
Geneva headquarters (GA Resol.
98 [I]), 37; draft on, 226*n*10; on
high seas, drafts, 226*n*10

Puerto Rico, 217*n*5

Purposes and principles of the
United Nations: action *re* violations of, 13; external resolutions
toward fulfillment of objectives,
18

Resolutions: general concept, 1-2;
as source of international law,
2-6; legal effects of, 4-5, 15-16,
19, 20-21; as recommendations,
6-13, 64, 71, 128-38, 154-55; binding force of, 7, 9, 18, 19-21, 121,
127-49, 150, 198*n*13; "Uniting for
Peace" Resolution (GA Resol.

337 [V]), 11, 20, 21, 57, 81-103
(for analysis *see under* Peace and
security); sanctions in, 11-12, 48,
77-78; nonrecommendatory, 14-
20; mandatory nature of, 15-16,
17, 20-21; internal, 17-18, 22-69,
200*n*29; external (action), 18,
200*n*29; determination of existence of facts or concrete legal
situations, 18-19, 117-38; binding
force resting on non-Charter instruments, 19, 127-48; on structure and operation of UN, 22-69;
mandatory (decisions), 24-25, 27;
as proposals, 28, 62; as expression of a wish, 28-29; validity
resting on doctrine of implied
powers of UN, 34-38, 48-49, 131-
34; on financing of UN, 40-48;
creation of subsidiary organs, 52-
53, 55-60, 130-31; institutional,
53-55; of international conferences under UN, 60-62; nonmandatory, 62-63; directed to
independent bodies, 62-64; imperative, 64-65, 67, 121; between
hierarchically linked organs, 64-
67; as directives, 65-67, 121;
"services" by members of UN,
68-69; maintenance of international peace and security, 70-116;
determining existence of facts or
concrete legal situations, 126-38;
as expression of will of majority,
131-33; coercive application, 134-
38; expressing agreement among
members of an organ, 150-64;
"executive-agreement," 151-60,
in UN, 160-64; declarations and
other pronouncements, 165-96
(*see also* Declarations)
—specific, *see under* General Assembly; Security Council; subjects